A History of

Doughty's Hospital

Norwich, 1687–2009

*Figure 1. Portrait of William Doughty, 1687, artist unknown
(copyright Norwich Castle Museum and Art Gallery)*

A History of
Doughty's Hospital
Norwich, 1687–2009

Nigel Goose and Leanne Moden

University of Hertfordshire Press

First published in Great Britain in 2010 by
University of Hertfordshire Press
College Lane
Hatfield
Hertfordshire
AL10 9AB

British Library Cataloguing in Publication Data
A catalogue record for this book is available from the
British Library

ISBN 978-1-905313-93-8

Design by Arthouse Publishing Solutions Ltd.
Printed in Great Britain by Hobbs the Printers Ltd.

This book is dedicated to all residents, staff and trustees of Doughty's Hospital, past and present

The research for this book was facilitated by a
Knowledge Partners East of England award, and by a
Harry Watson Bursary administered by Norwich Heart

Contents

Figures

Plates

Tables

Abbreviations

ACC	Accession
BPP	British Parliamentary Papers
DOHI	Doughty's Oral History Interview
fo.	Folio
MF	Microfilm
NCC	Norwich Consolidated Charities
N/CCH	Norwich Consolidated Charities (NRO reference)
NCR	Norwich City Records
N/MC	Norwich Municipal Charities
NML	Norwich Millennium Library
NNH	Norfolk and Norwich Hospital
NRO	Norfolk Record Office
N/TC	Norwich Town Clerk's [Dept.]
TNA	The National Archives

Preface

The instigator of the project to write a history of Doughty's Hospital in Norwich was Lady Joyce Hopwood, at the time of writing Chair of the Trustees for Doughty's Hospital, who – unable to find a local historian willing and able to take on the task – was advised to make contact with the University of Hertfordshire, where I have been leading a project on the history of the English almshouse. Almost simultaneously the university's research office issued details of knowledge partnership funding available from the East of England Development Agency, known as KEEP3, which would provide funds towards the employment of a research assistant for a period of up to six months, plus small additional sums for travel and equipment, as long as the partner institution could provide matching funding. Leanne Moden, a recent graduate of the university, was now living within striking distance of Norwich, having produced a first class final year dissertation on the subject of leisure in nineteenth-century Norwich under my supervision. A chain of fortunate coincidences thus brought together the team that was to be instrumental in securing funding, coordinating the project and finally researching and writing the present book.

This project has been a joy to be part of, and all of those involved have been a pleasure to work with throughout. Joyce Hopwood, representing the trustees, has been helpful, cheerful and an enduring source of support – moral and practical – from start to finish. Leanne Moden has proved herself to be an industrious, capable and self-motivated researcher, besides providing valuable drafts of sections of this book. The residents and staff of Doughty's, past and present, have willingly given their time to provide us with oral testimony, and the staff at the Norfolk Record Office have given their full support and guidance throughout. Valuable commentary upon drafts of the book was received from Joyce Hopwood, Philip Blanchflower and David Walker, and we are grateful to each of them. Finally, we wish to acknowledge the support of the Harry Watson bursary, which provided a small additional grant to facilitate the conduct of the interviews that enriched the sections of the book dealing with the modern history of the hospital. Mr Watson is featured in colour Plate 15.

The intention of this book is to place the history of Doughty's Hospital into its broader historical context, besides providing a history of the institution itself. Hence there are substantial sections dealing with the history of social welfare, both state-sponsored and philanthropic, as well as information on the economic development of the City of Norwich, alongside more particular chapters charting the development of Doughty's. Those readers who have no interest in this broader context can select the chapters they wish to read accordingly, though we hope that most will realise that a full understanding of the development of the institution is only achievable with the wider history left in. It is this context, after all, that elevates local history above the parochial, and hence we hope that this history of Doughty's Hospital will make a contribution to the history of social welfare in England more generally across the past four centuries, as well as charting the development of Doughty's Hospital itself.

Nigel Goose
November 2009

PART I

The historical foundations of social welfare

CHAPTER 1
The origins of the almshouse in medieval England

Almshouses have existed, in various forms, for over a thousand years. They originated as places that provided care for the sick poor, and were usually attached to monasteries. The monastic life had come first to southern England when St Augustine reintroduced Christianity into the country in the year 597. The next fifty years saw the flowering of monasteries of a variety of different forms, the Rule of St Benedict being introduced in the seventh century, with houses large and small becoming established in Northumbria, Mercia, Wessex and Kent. Virtually all of these, with the possible exception of St Augustine's in Canterbury, were swept away within one hundred years of the invasion of the Norsemen, which began in 787. Monastic life in England was thus virtually extinct at the start of the tenth century. It was the work of Dunstan at Glastonbury, soon supported by Ethelwold and Oswald, that breathed new life into the monastic movement from the later tenth century, drawing upon continental influences alongside indigenous traditions to establish a new Rule, and planting the seed that produced both centres of distinction in learning and the arts, and reservoirs of intellectual attainment that could be drawn upon by successful rulers to man the Episcopal Sees of the nation. It was in this period that some of the great abbeys came into existence, such as St Albans, Evesham, Ely, Malmsebury, Peterborough and Westminster. Neither the Danish invasion of 1006, nor the subsequent Norman Conquest, proved to be nearly as disruptive as the earlier incursions, and by 1066 there were some thirty-five male religious houses in England and nine large nunneries. All operated under the Rule of St Benedict, and thus largely followed the practices current in the great abbeys of the European continent. The Norman Conquest confirmed the European influence, and led to both the expansion of existing houses, and the foundation of many more.[1]

---

1 D. Knowles and R.N. Hadcock, *Medieval religious houses. England and Wales* (Longman: London, 1971, first published 1953), pp. 8–15.

English monasteries were, of course, not only a component of international Christianity, but of European Catholicism, and were thus subject to the edicts of the wider Church. While England was suffering the depredations of the Danish invasions in the late eighth and early ninth centuries, the Synod of Aix held in 816 was busy establishing the social and moral duties of the monastic houses, to be performed alongside their educational functions. The Synod was a meeting of Catholic officials which stated that the Church had an obligation to provide care and alms for both the poor and the sick.[2] These alms, in the form of food or money, were often distributed at the gates of the monasteries but gradually the practice of providing board and lodging for travellers became more common, while aged and sick monks were also cared for on-site in a 'farmery', the origins of the modern word 'infirmary'. During the twelfth and thirteenth centuries these two practices often merged, as monasteries began to minister also to lay people who were sick or feeble, though this usually took place in separate establishments administered by the monks and lay brethren.[3] These lodgings were commonly known as 'hospitals', although they are far removed from modern medical hospitals. The label 'hospital' came from the word 'hospitality', and simply meant a place that provided care and lodgings for those in need, as well as rest for travellers.[4] While some historians have argued that they pre-date the Norman Conquest, hard evidence to support such claims is difficult to find, and the earliest clear records of hospitals as free-standing institutions occur in the 1070s. It was probably in 1077 that Lanfranc, Archbishop of Canterbury, established the very first of these, in a 'decent and ample house of stone' outside the walls of the City of Canterbury, with separate quarters for men and women suffering from infirmity.[5]

During the course of the medieval period, many different types of hospital were established, their form and function varying according to the local incidence of disease, proximity to large towns or to sites of pilgrimage, as well as according to the aspirations of founders and patrons.[6] In the eleventh century, lazar houses – named after the international hospital order of St Lazarus of Jerusalem – began to appear as places to care for those with leprosy. The first English

---

2   B. Bailey, *Almshouses* (Robert Hale: London, 1988), p. 15.

3   B. Howson, *Houses of noble poverty: a history of the English almshouse* (Bellevue Books: Sunbury-on-Thames, 1993), pp. 17–18.

4   H. Caffrey, *Almshouses in the West Riding of Yorkshire 1600–1900* (Heritage: King's Lynn, 2006), p. 2; W.H. Godfrey, *The English almshouse with some account of its predecessor the medieval hospital* (Faber and Faber: London, 1955), p. 15.

5   N. Orme and M. Webster, *The English hospital 1070–1570* (Yale University Press: New Haven and London, 1995), pp. 19–22.

6   S. Sweetinburgh, *The role of the hospital in medieval England. Gift-giving and the spiritual economy* (Four Courts Press: Dublin, 2004), p. 19; Bailey, *Almshouses*, p. 16.

evidence of leprosy (technically, Hansen's Disease) occurs in the fourth century, but it was only sporadic until a new epidemic reached Europe from China in the eleventh century. Leprosy was incurable, could result in hideous facial and bodily decay, and was often linked in the contemporary mind with lustfulness and heresy – a remarkably potent combination of adverse attributes. In 1175 the English Church Council of Westminster ordered that 'lepers should not live among the healthy', while four years later the Third Lateran Council at Rome endorsed this decision on behalf of the whole of the western Church. The result was that lepers were generally ostracised, in both town and countryside.[7] The following ordinance from Berwick-on-Tweed encapsulates the hostility frequently shown towards them, as well as indicating the provision for their welfare that was made:

> No leper shall come within the gates of the borough and if one gets in by chance, the serjeant shall put him out at once. If one willfully forces his way in, his clothes shall be taken off him and burnt and he shall be turned out naked. For we have already taken care that a proper place for lepers shall be kept outside the town and that alms shall be there given to them.[8]

Lazar houses were indeed often sited just outside the gates of towns to isolate lepers from the rest of the community, but were also situated on main thoroughfares, or close to town bridges or gates, to facilitate the collection of alms. One scholar has documented as many as 299 such houses founded before 1250, and about a dozen later foundations, figures that must be regarded as minima as some leper colonies were informal and may never have been recorded.[9] Their geographical incidence varied considerably, often in ways that defy simple explanation. Why, for example, were there more leper houses than ordinary hospitals in Nottinghamshire, while in neighbouring Leicestershire the reverse was true?[10] And while the siting of lazar houses on the outskirts of large towns was common, why were there as many as six near both York and Norwich?[11] The separation of lepers from non-lepers may also have been less complete than was laid down in national or local ordinances, the very repetition of those ordinances

---

7   Orme and Webster, *English hospital*, pp. 23–7.
8   Cited in *Ibid.*, p. 27.
9   This is from the work of Max Satchell, 'The emergence of leper-houses in medieval England, 1100–1250', D. Phil. thesis, Oxford University, 1998, cited in Sweetinburgh, *Role of the hospital*, pp. 22–3.
10 Sweetinburgh, *Role of the hospital*, p. 23.
11 *Ibid.*, p. 28, n. 45; C. Rawcliffe, *The hospitals of medieval Norwich* (Centre of East Anglian Studies: Norwich, 1995), pp. 163–4.

perhaps being indicative of the difficulties of enforcement. Even within the houses themselves, lepers and non-lepers could quite frequently be found living side by side, so much so that by the fourteenth century many leper houses were changing into hospitals for the poor and infirm more generally.[12] This trend, of course, was enhanced by the decline of leprosy in England from the fourteenth century, until it was no longer a major concern by the early sixteenth century.[13]

Hospitals for the sick poor more generally were founded alongside leper houses, and these in turn can be broadly distinguished from the later almshouses which catered more specifically for the elderly, local poor. Although medieval hospitals had begun as an extension of monasteries, it was not long before wealthy men and women began endowing hospitals or almshouses of their own. Royalty led the way: the hospital of St Leonard's in York was endowed by King Athelstan in 986 and dedicated to St Peter, only to be re-founded by King Stephen in 1145. Stephen's wife Matilda founded St Catherine By The Tower in London in 1148 and this hospital continued to receive royal patronage, with Henry VIII founding the Guild of Barbara on the site and sparing the hospital from dissolution after his split from Rome in 1539.[14] Hospitals were also founded by the landowning gentry, petty knights and baronets, the clergy, merchants, Lord Mayors and aldermen, and other private philanthropists. For example, St Cross Hospital at Winchester was founded by the Bishop of Winchester, Henry de Bois, in 1136.[15] There was a degree of self-interest in establishing a hospital, both for the clergy and for wealthy members of the laity, for the Catholic Church stressed the importance of good works – deeds such as giving money to the poor and the needy – which would assure the benefactor a place in heaven.[16] Bedehouses were founded upon this principle. They were almshouses, established by a single person, whose inmates were expected to pray for the soul of their founder, further ensuring the safety of the soul of the benefactor.[17]

It was from the early thirteenth century that lay foundations became more common, until they were soon the largest group among this array of institutions, and this coincided with the shift from lazar houses to non-leper hospitals. East Anglia, Yorkshire and Gloucestershire were the most active areas for lay foundations, followed by Northumberland and Durham, Shropshire, Kent and Wiltshire, and towns were the

12 Orme and Webster, *English hospital*, pp. 28–9; C. Rawcliffe, *Leprosy in medieval England* (Boydell Press: Woodbridge, 2006), ch. 6.
13 Rawcliffe, *Leprosy*, ch. 7; Orme and Webster, *English hospital*, p. 31.
14 Howson, *Houses of noble poverty*, p. 28.
15 Godfrey, *English almshouse*, p. 17.
16 Bailey, *Almshouses*, p. 27.
17 *Ibid.*, p. 16.

most favoured locations.[18] Some of these catered mainly for the poor and impotent, who formed the most important category of inmate, others for the sick and some for travellers – but most were multi-functional institutions which provided relief for all of these categories of the needy. Occasionally they would discriminate against particular classes of person, and occasionally they would discriminate in favour of particular groups, but selectivity was not at its height until the later middle ages. This phase of hospital foundation appears to have run out of steam by the mid-thirteenth century, as far as we are able to tell from the available records, and some may have been lost completely, or were amalgamated, as a result of the dramatic mortality during the Black Death of 1348–9, when perhaps one-third of the population of the country succumbed to plague.[19] A new phase of foundations has been detected from the very late fourteenth century, however, and it was now that the almshouse – as an institution specifically dedicated to the local, often elderly, poor – started to make its appearance. There was a particular rash of new foundations in Yorkshire, where they were often described as 'maisons dieu', and there is clear evidence that they appeared in many urban centres elsewhere too, although establishment of their precise chronological and geographical incidence must wait on further research.[20]

The late fourteenth and early fifteenth centuries were a period of economic buoyancy, produced by the establishment of a more viable balance between population and resources as a by-product of the ravages of epidemic disease, but further population decline and scarcity of hard currency by the mid-fifteenth century produced renewed and severe economic depression.[21] It was only after this depression had run its course that almshouse foundation picked up once again, and it was now that the almshouse fully evolved into its modern form – as a residence for the elderly poor of a particular locality. From the late fifteenth century English parishes started to play a fuller role in the relief of the poor, and parish fraternities increasingly accumulated stocks of land or animals, gave doles to the poor and sometimes (especially in market towns) established almshouses too. Just why these developments took place at this time is unclear, but it has recently been argued that there may have been a demographic imperative behind this growth in foundations. Research on the demography of late medieval monasteries

---

18   Sweetinburgh, *Role of the hospital*, pp. 31–2.
19   For an excellent and readable account see P. Ziegler, *The Black Death* (Penguin edition: Harmondsworth, 1970, first published 1969).
20   Sweetinburgh, *Role of the hospital*, pp. 24–34.
21   J. Hatcher, 'The great slump of the mid-fifteenth century', in R.H. Britnell and J. Hatcher (eds), *Progress and problems in medieval England: essays in honour of Edward Miller* (Cambridge University Press: Cambridge, 1996), pp. 237–72.

has revealed a dramatic deterioration in life expectancy in the last third of the fifteenth century, and if this can be generalised to the population at large it suggests that the capacity of families to deliver care to their members was probably at rock bottom, with charitable or semi-public provision in the form of almshouses and parish houses stepping in to fill the gap. So while tenancy arrangements had long made provision for elderly ex-tenants, the late fifteenth century saw an increase in the setting up of maintenance contracts with non-kin, often endorsed in manorial courts, as well as the growth of charitable provision.[22]

Professor Marjorie McIntosh has counted the number of almshouse foundations between 1400 and 1600, and her figures reveal an upsurge of new endowments after 1465 in the eight southern or Midland counties of Berkshire, Cambridgeshire, Essex, Hertfordshire, Leicestershire, Middlesex, Nottinghamshire and Suffolk, which might reflect the growing wealth of this broad region identified from analysis of the lay subsidy returns.[23] Across the rest of the country, however, the trend was remarkably flat. Furthermore, the granting of relief, whether inside or outside of an almshouse, became increasingly discriminating, favouring the respectable, local poor and excluding the shiftless, the mendicant and the migrant, and controlling 'misbehaviour' as never before.[24] The positive side of these developments was an increasing sense of place, a greater appreciation of community, involving inclusion as well as exclusion, which was in turn reflected in increasing amounts of cash being left in deathbed bequests – to the parish in general, and for the purpose of almshouse foundation in particular. So, late medieval England witnessed an accumulating stock of almshouses, while after *circa* 1450 the almshouse emerged in its modern form (and was increasingly referred to as an almshouse rather than a hospital) specifically intended to provide accommodation for local, elderly people who had fallen into poverty on account of their age or ailing health. Lay provision of poor relief had gradually assumed greater importance, leper houses were decreasingly needed and often converted to other charitable uses, while monastic hospitals continued to function alongside the growing

22 R. Smith, 'Situating the almshouse within demographic and familial changes, 1400–1600', lecture delivered to *The Almshouse Conference*, University of Hertfordshire, St Albans Campus, 22 September 2007.

23 R. Schofield, 'The geographical distribution of wealth in England, 1334–1649', *Economic History Review*, 18 (1965), pp. 483–510; J. Sheail, 'The distribution of taxable population and wealth in England during the early sixteenth century', *Transactions of the Institute of British Geographers*, 5 (1972), pp. 111–26. The lay subsidies were a particularly comprehensive early sixteenth-century tax assessment.

24 M. McIntosh, 'Local responses to the poor in late medieval and Tudor England', *Continuity and Change*, 3 (1988), pp. 217–25. See also her *Autonomy and community. The Royal Manor of Havering, 1200–1500* (Cambridge University Press: Cambridge, 1986), especially pp. 240–63, and *Controlling misbehaviour in England, 1370–1600* (Cambridge University Press: Cambridge, 1998).

number of lay institutions, and continued to provide sizeable sums to relieve the poor.

Various attempts have been made to count the number of hospitals and almshouses founded in medieval England. Our most reliable information is that on leper houses, and we have seen that there were approximately 310 of these, largely founded before 1250, their number declining from the fourteenth century onwards.[25] Sheila Sweetinburgh suggests that there was perhaps a similar number of non-leper hospitals founded in the medieval period, and possibly 225 almshouses proper, this latter figure being the most approximate of all and providing a bare minimum number.[26] Brian Bailey estimates a total of 700 charitable institutions by the end of the fourteenth century, variously described as lazar houses, hospitals, maisons dieu, infirmaries, bedehouses, refuges and almshouses, while a frequently quoted figure for the early sixteenth century, before the dissolution of the monasteries, is 800 establishments of all kinds.[27] Nicholas Orme and Margaret Webster, in a suitably cautious re-examination of existing evidence, have suggested a total of 585 institutions by the period 1501–30.[28] Finally, there is the ongoing research of Marjorie McIntosh, who has identified a total of 1,005 hospitals or almshouses *operating at some point* between 1350 and 1599, their number rising to a peak in the 1520s, and suggesting that the estimates of Orme and Webster are probably not too wide of the mark.[29]

---

25 See above, Satchell, 'Emergence of leper-houses', p. 5.

26 Sweetinburgh, *Role of the hospital*, pp. 22–3.

27 Bailey, *Almshouses*, p. 53; B. Howson, *Almshouses. A social and architectural history* (The History Press: Chalford, 2008), p. 27. Neither of these authors explain how they arrived at their figures.

28 Orme and Webster, *English hospital*, Table 1, p. 11.

29 We are most grateful to Marjorie McIntosh for allowing us to cite her unpublished estimates, which were presented at a conference entitled *English almshouses revisited*, held at the University of Hertfordshire's St Albans Campus, 7 March 2009. It must be emphasised that these are preliminary figures, which will be published in due course in a book on assistance to the poor in England 1350–1600, where a detailed description of the methodology used to generate these numbers will be provided.

CHAPTER 2
Early modern philanthropy and poor relief

While the precise number of hospitals and almshouses in existence by the early sixteenth century will not be known until further research has been completed, we can be sure of two things: that they numbered several hundred, probably in the region of 600, and that this number was dramatically reduced as a result of the Dissolution of the monasteries and chantries during the reign of Henry VIII.[30] Henry was seeking to annul his first marriage in order to marry Ann Boleyn in the hope of producing a male heir. This was at a time when Protestant arguments against Roman Catholicism were gathering pace and Henry used this to make his case for a break with Rome. In 1534 the Act of Supremacy was passed, which made Henry VIII the Supreme Head of a new Church of England and put him in control of Church funds and taxation. Philosophical concepts of the power of the King over the Church may have played a part in Henry's decision to suppress the monasteries, but so did his designs on their wealth. The monasteries, or some of them at least, were rich, and much of that wealth found its way directly or indirectly to the royal treasury. Some of the monastery buildings were sold to wealthy gentry for use as country estates, some were taken over by town corporations, others became sources of cheap building materials for local inhabitants. Beginning with those institutions worth less than £20 per annum and proceeding to the wealthier establishments, the monasteries and their associated charitable institutions were swept away in 1536 and 1539, while in 1545 and 1547 the Crown also confiscated the property of chantries, some hospitals and some parish religious fraternities.[31] A number of ecclesiastical hospitals managed to survive the Dissolution when municipalities or individuals bought them from the Crown or paid a fine for their retention. Other monastic hospitals used a legal device called a 'feoffment of use', under

---

30 McIntosh, 'Local responses to the poor', p. 228; R.M. Clay, *English medieval hospitals* (Methuen: London, 1909), Appendix B, pp. 277–337.
31 For an accessible but authoritative modern account of the break with Rome, see J. Guy, *Tudor England* (Oxford University Press: Oxford, 1988), ch. 5, pp. 116–53.

which the legal title of a building was transferred from the Church to a sympathetic purchaser, who leased the property back to a corporate body such as a town council for charitable purposes.[32] Nevertheless, between 1536 and 1549, McIntosh has estimated, some 260 hospitals and endowed almshouses were closed, representing almost half of the existing institutions. While the old historical orthodoxy emphasised the failings of the pre-Reformation monastic system of welfare, recent research has significantly modified this view, to re-emphasise the gaping hole in welfare provision that the Dissolution produced.[33] Into that breach stepped new private donors, and the Tudor state.

The contribution of the state is encapsulated in the establishment of the Elizabethan or 'Old' Poor Law, which represents the construction of the first ever national framework for welfare policy. Legislation to deal with sturdy beggars and vagabonds in the early sixteenth century was supplemented by concern for the impotent poor from 1547, first in the form of edicts to collect funds for poor relief during church services and later, in 1572, through provision for compulsory regular tax collections and the appointment of overseers of the poor. The codifying statute of 1598 and 1601 brought previous legislation together, created a clearer administrative hierarchy and gave greater powers of enforcement. The system was based upon the parish, and centred upon the levying of a property-based poor rate, the provision of work to the 'deserving' poor, the apprenticing of children and punishment of the vagrant. The deserving poor were defined as the 'lame ympotent olde blynde and such other amonge them being poore and not able to work'.[34] Local churchwardens and overseers of the poor (two or four per parish) were to be responsible to two Justices of the Peace, who were to receive their accounts and to play a supervisory role, while local officers were given the power to distrain the goods of those refusing to pay.[35]

How thoroughly the laws were applied and enforced remains controversial. Large towns were in the vanguard, about that there can be no doubt. Rural parishes followed more slowly, and many may not have started to levy a regular poor rate and distribute the proceeds to the parish poor until the second half of the seventeenth century. By

---

32 Howson, *Houses of noble poverty*, p. 83.

33 N.S. Rushton, 'Monastic charitable provision in Tudor England: quantifying and qualifying poor relief in the early sixteenth century', *Continuity and Change*, 16 (2001), pp. 9–44; N.S. Rushton and W. Sigle-Rushton, 'Monastic poor relief in sixteenth-century England', *Journal of Interdisciplinary History*, 32 (2001), pp. 193–216.

34 Quoted in S. Hindle, *On the parish? The micro-politics of poor relief in rural England c. 1550–1750* (Oxford University Press: Oxford, 2004), p. 227.

35 The best account of poverty and poor relief in this period is still P. Slack, *Poverty and policy in Tudor and Stuart England* (Longman: London, 1988). Hindle, *On the parish?* provides some updating and slight modifications, though is wholly rural in its focus. A useful short summary covering a longer time period is P. Slack, *The English poor law 1531–1782* (Macmillan: Basingstoke, 1990).

1700, however, the practice was 'well nigh universal', the number of taxpayers had increased and the amounts being paid in weekly relief to the poor had risen substantially too.[36] So whereas (in rural areas at least) state-sponsored poor relief could only have performed a supplementary function in maintaining the poor even as late as the mid-seventeenth century, forming just one part of their 'economy of makeshifts' (to use the common parlance of modern historians of welfare) by the end of that century it formed a central plank in the survival strategies of the poor. Indeed, Paul Slack has gone so far as to describe the English system of poor relief as 'unique' by the end of the seventeenth century, and to suggest that, 'it is not a total anachronism to call that institution, as it had developed by 1700, a welfare state'.[37]

The second response to the problem of the poor in Tudor England, initially triggered by the loss of resources for their support due to the Dissolution, and later exacerbated by the long-term growth of population, was private philanthropy. Quantification of this contribution is, however, extremely difficult. Casual almsgiving, in the street or at the farm or manor gate, is usually wholly impossible to measure, as it leaves no mark at all in the historical record. More formal charitable giving, usually in the last will and testament of the donor, is easier to trace. Sums were often left in a will to be distributed to the poor, either as a one-off payment or on a regular basis through the establishment of an endowment. It was this type of charity that formed the basis of W.K. Jordan's monumental study, *Philanthropy in England 1480–1660*, published in 1959, which was based upon charitable bequests left in many thousands of wills plus identifiable lifetime endowments discovered in ten English counties in the period 1480–1660, and this study must remain the starting point for any student of charitable giving in this period.[38] From this research Jordan concluded that the period witnessed a profound shift in charitable giving away from religious and towards secular ends, accompanied by an enormous outpouring of generosity. A total of £525,595 was left for charitable uses in these ten counties in the period 1481–1540 (approximately £87,600 per decade), while in the years 1601–40 the total reached £1,437,490 (approximately £359,370 per decade), representing more

---

36 Slack, *Poverty and policy*, pp. 173–87. Hindle suggests an earlier date for the general spread of rating and regular relief distributions, with perhaps a turning point in the 1630s: *On the parish?*, p. 251.

37 Slack, *Poverty and policy*, p. 206.

38 W.K. Jordan, *Philanthropy in England 1480–1660. A study of the changing pattern of English social aspirations* (Russell Sage Foundation: New York, 1959). He also published a number of follow-up studies, most notably *The charities of London 1480–1660; The aspirations and achievements of the urban society* (Russell Sage Foundation: New York, 1960); and *The charities of rural England. The aspirations and achievements of the rural society* (George Allen and Unwin: London, 1961). The latter volume includes a chapter on Norfolk.

than a fourfold increase.[39] Furthermore, well over one-third (36.4 per cent) of the total was dedicated to the relief of the poor.[40] Throughout his work Jordan waxed lyrical about the transformation he believed he had identified, and his enthusiasm is admirably demonstrated in the following extract:

> ... in the course of these years the curse of poverty had been chastened, humane care had been arranged for the derelict, and the area of opportunity for aspiring youth had been enormously enlarged. A quiet but veritable revolution had occurred during which private donors, men who held in view a vision of the future, had repaired the damage society had sustained from the slow ruin of the Middle Ages ... It was a revolution too in which men's aspirations for their own generation and those to come had undergone an almost complete metamorphosis, as the essentially religious interests of the later Middle Ages yielded to social aspirations which were most aggressively secular ...[41]

Unfortunately the power of Jordan's prose exceeded his historical and statistical insight, for he failed to take account in his calculations of either inflation or the growth of population, both of which were substantial in this period. On the other hand, it has also been pointed out that much charitable giving of this kind is cumulative, because endowments are not immediately used up but last as long as the trustees or other managers ensure the funds remain intact, and hence they accrete over time. Indeed, Jordan calculated that as much as 82 per cent of the total sum given for charitable uses in the period 1480–1660 took the form of capital, and would hence produce a long-term return.[42] So when Jordan's figures are reworked to take account of this, as well as of inflation, the results suggest that there was a fourfold increase in the sum available for poor relief in the 1650s compared with the 1540s, and a twofold increase in per capita terms.[43]

Almshouse endowment undoubtedly formed part of this. The latest figures produced by McIntosh show that after the mass closure of the 1530s and 1540s numbers started to recover once again to a peak in the late sixteenth century, with 479 institutions continuing in operation at

39 Jordan, *Philanthropy in England*, p. 246.
40 *Ibid.*, p. 250.
41 *Ibid.*, p. 240.
42 *Ibid.*, p. 24.
43 W.G. Bittle and R.T. Lane, 'Inflation and philanthropy in England: a reassessment of W.K. Jordan's data', *Economic History Review*, 29 (1976), pp. 203–10; J.F. Hadwin, 'Deflating philanthropy', *Economic History Review*, 31 (1978), pp. 105–17.

the very end of that century – a number, however, that still remains below the total achieved in the 1520s. McIntosh's research extends only to the end of the sixteenth century, but Jordan's continues to 1660. In his ten counties he calculated that 13.45 per cent of the total charitable and social relief given in 1480–1660 was spent on founding almshouses, ranging from a meagre 2.04 per cent in Lancashire to an impressive 25.24 per cent in Somerset. In total he found that 309 permanently endowed almshouses had been established within his sample counties, and a further 71 without a stock for maintenance.[44] Even if we disregard those which lacked an endowment as unlikely to have survived for long, approximately 10 per cent of English parishes benefited from almshouse accommodation by 1660, and larger towns were particularly well served.

---

44 Jordan, *Philanthropy in England*, pp. 27, 261–2.

CHAPTER 3
Medieval and early modern Norwich

Medieval: 1000–1500

Norwich had been one of England's leading provincial centres since at least the eleventh century. While all towns throughout the medieval and early modern periods were dwarfed by London, according to the Domesday Book of 1086 Norwich was already either the third or the fourth largest provincial town, exceeded only by York and Lincoln, and possibly also by Bristol. Population estimates based upon Domesday are hazardous, however, and no such estimate will be offered here.[45] Nevertheless, Norwich appears to have shared in the general urban expansion that occurred between 1000 AD and the fourteenth century, the subsidy return of 1334 suggesting it now stood in either fourth or fifth place among provincial towns in terms of taxable wealth, while the Poll Tax of 1377 indicates a population of about 7,500, and a rank order of fourth behind York, Bristol and Coventry.[46] Despite the general economic decline of the later middle ages, which afflicted some towns particularly severely, Norwich more than held its own in relative terms, and by the time the national tax assessments known as the exchequer lay subsidies were compiled in 1524–5 it had overhauled all of its rivals to stand at the top of the provincial urban hierarchy in terms of both population and taxable wealth.[47] Conversion of the lay subsidy returns to population totals is controversial, and various estimates suggest Norwich's population may

---

45 Estimates as high as 8,000 have been made from the Domesday Book, but such figures are difficult to square with more reliable estimates from later sources: C. Rawcliffe, 'Introduction', in C. Rawcliffe and R. Wilson (eds), *Medieval Norwich* (Hambledon Press: London and New York, 2004), p. xxxiv.

46 Some scholars suggest that the population of Norwich may have reached 25,000 by 1333, but even allowing for the dramatic mortality caused by the Black Death of 1348–9 and subsequent epidemics such a figure seems unlikely in view of the more reliable data contained in the Poll Tax: E. Rutledge, 'Immigration and population growth in early fourteenth-century Norwich', *Urban history yearbook 1988* (Leicester University Press: Leicester, 1988), pp. 15–30. A pre-plague population in the region of 12,000 is more likely.

47 D.M. Palliser (ed.), *The Cambridge urban history of Britain, vol. I: 600–1540* (Cambridge University Press: Cambridge, 2000), pp. 124, 752–67.

by now have been as large as 11,000, or as small as 7,000, but it was certainly a leading – and probably *the* leading – provincial town at this date, and far and away the dominant urban force in East Anglia.[48]

Norwich benefited from its religious endowments, which attracted custom to the city, as well as from its situation amid a wealthy agricultural region. Its occupational structure indicates a variegated economy by the early fourteenth century, a well-developed mercantile sector and important lines in fish, wool and cloth.[49] Thereafter it emerged as an important centre for both broadcloth and worsted production, and as the principal outlet in the region for distribution of worsted cloth, operating in tandem with the nearby port of Great Yarmouth.[50] The case that has been made for late medieval prosperity in Norwich, however – reflected in the development of the town's religious houses and glass painting – is not entirely convincing.[51] The city had lost the demographic vitality of the early middle ages, the geographical horizons of trade conducted through Yarmouth had narrowed considerably, and there is no doubting the 'profound recession' of the mid-fifteenth century, which mirrored the national experience.[52] Medieval urban historians have long been faced with the apparent paradox of a lively building industry amid general economic stagnation, and the situation may have been thus in Norwich, even if it had managed to avoid the outright decline experienced by some other urban centres, which included local rivals Great Yarmouth and King's Lynn. In the case of Norwich, however, we can certainly talk in terms of at least relative prosperity by the start of the sixteenth century, which is clearly reflected in its elevation to the top of the provincial urban hierarchy.

Norwich has a long history of charitable institutions which began in the medieval period with the construction of the Cathedral Priory. The seat of the See of East Anglia moved to Norwich in 1096, although the

---

48 Controversy arises because of different views on how the number of taxpayers should be manipulated to produce a population total. For the higher figure see J. Pound, 'Government to 1660', in C. Rawcliffe and R. Wilson (eds), *Norwich since 1550* (Hambledon Press: London and New York, 2004), p. 35. More common estimates are in the region of 9,000: A. Dyer, *Decline and growth in English towns 1400–1600* (Macmillan: Basingstoke, 1991), p. 72, gives 9,250; P. Slack, 'Great and good towns 1540–1700', in P. Clark (ed.), *The Cambridge urban history of Britain, vol. II: 1540–1840* (Cambridge University Press: Cambridge, 2000), p. 352, gives 9,000; J.F. Pound had suggested a lower figure of 8,500 in his *Tudor and Stuart Norwich* (Phillimore: Chichester, 1988), p. 28. For the lower estimate of c. 7,000 apply to the 1,423 taxpayers in Norwich the procedure suggested in N. Goose and A. Hinde, 'Estimating local population sizes at fixed points in time: part II – specific sources', *Local Population Studies*, 78 (2007), pp. 74–88.

49 E. Rutledge, 'Economic life', in Rawcliffe and Wilson (eds), *Medieval Norwich*, ch. 7.

50 P. Dunn, 'Trade', in Rawcliffe and Wilson (eds), *Medieval Norwich*, ch. 9.

51 C. Harper-Bill and C. Rawcliffe, 'The religious houses', and D. King, 'Glass-painting', in Rawcliffe and Wilson (eds), *Medieval Norwich*, chs 4 and 5 respectively; J. Finch, 'The churches', in *ibid.*, pp. 60–2.

52 Dunn, 'Trade', p. 220; Hatcher, 'The great slump'.

cathedral, built in stages, was not fully completed until 1148, which is not surprising in view of its vast scale.[53] The priory was constructed for the habitation of sixty Benedictine monks but records show that up to 250 people ate meals in the priory each day. In line with Catholic doctrine the monks of the priory also distributed alms to the poor at the gates of the cathedral.[54] The first hospital built for the relief of the sick was the Hospital of St Paul which was established in the early twelfth century and provided care for 'the sick, infirm and child-bearing poor' of Norwich, temporary beds for travellers, as well as permanent accommodation for aged and poor monks.[55] Several hospitals, in fact, sprang up in and around the city during the twelfth century.[56] There were also six leper houses in and around the town: St Mary Magdalen (Sprowston), St Stephen's, St Giles' Gate, St Benedict's, St Augustine's Gate and Magdalen Street, a number matched only by the City of York.[57]

The Great Hospital of St Giles was founded in 1249, adjacent to the Cathedral Close, by Bishop Walter de Suffield. It was originally established to provide care for decrepit chaplains of the diocese of Norwich but was also able to provide board for seven poor scholars, thirty beds for the infirm poor, extra accommodation for elderly or sick clergy, and meals for a further thirteen poor men.[58] Hildebrand's Hospital (also known as Ivy Hall) was established in King Street in about 1200 to care for poor travellers, and is one of the very few city hospitals founded by a layman, the eponymous Hildebrand le Mercer, one of the city's merchants.[59] Later almshouses founded in the city include God's House, St Margaret (1292), St Saviour (1305), God's House, St Giles (1306), Danyell's Almshouses (1418, but probably transitory) and Garzoun's Almshouses (early fourteenth century).[60] Many of Norwich's religious foundations were, however, rocked by the ravages of the Black Death of 1348–9, and here as elsewhere in England provision for the poor suffered in consequence.[61] Almost across the board in the fifteenth century the city's institutions for the relief of the poor and the sick either collapsed or curtailed their activities. As elsewhere in England, charitable giving in general appears to have become more discriminating as the century wore on. Various – sometimes generous

---

53 J. Campbell, 'Norwich before 1300', in Rawcliffe and Wilson (eds), *Medieval Norwich*, p. 41.

54 F. Meeres, *A history of Norwich* (Phillimore: Chichester, 1998), p. 24.

55 C. Rawcliffe, 'Sickness and health', in Rawcliffe and Wilson (eds), *Medieval Norwich*, Appendix to chapter 13, p. 325. After the Black Death it became an almshouse for respectable women.

56 Harper-Bill and Rawcliffe, 'The religious houses', p. 73; Rawcliffe, *Hospitals of medieval Norwich*, p. 164.

57 Rawcliffe, *Hospitals of medieval Norwich*, pp. 163–4.

58 *Ibid.*, ch. 3 and p. 165. See also C. B. Jewson, *History of the Great Hospital Norwich* (The Great Hospital: Norwich, 1966).

59 Rawcliffe, *Hospitals of medieval Norwich*, pp. 143, 164–5.

60 *Ibid.*, pp. 165–6. There is tentative evidence for two more.

61 *Ibid.*, p. 153.

– bequests for doles of money or bread can indeed be identified, but the same Norwich merchant class that was so ready to expand and adorn the city's churches proved singularly parsimonious when it came to the relief of its poor, while at the end of the middle ages hospital provision for sick paupers was 'very limited indeed'.[62] Norwich does not, therefore, appear to have participated in the upsurge of almshouse foundations in the late fifteenth century that has been identified by McIntosh in a number of other southern and Midland counties.[63]

Early modern: 1500–1700

While charitable giving may have been in decline in Norwich long before the Reformation, the Dissolution of the monasteries in the 1530s made itself felt here as elsewhere. The Great Hospital was taken into the king's hands in 1535, at which time it stood in danger of dissolution because, although primarily a charitable institution, it also employed priests to say masses for the souls of its benefactors. It may have been the value to the Crown of the loyalty of the city that saved it, and after a petition from the freemen of Norwich the hospital was re-established by Edward VI in 1547 and granted to the mayor, sheriffs and citizens.[64] The hospital was to house forty poor people and employ four women to attend to them, as well as a range of other officers ranging from a chaplain to a cook.[65] Despite complaints from the chaplain in 1550 about the curmudgeonly inmates, the difficulties he had in persuading them to attend church and in keeping them from brawling with each other, the Great Hospital survived its mid-century difficulties and was soon attracting new endowments. In 1558, for example, Thomas Codde, beer-brewer and a former mayor, left property to the hospital for the relief of the poor; in 1568 the silversmith Peter Peterson presented it with a silver chalice; while Thomas Parker, also a former mayor, granted forty shillings to buy sheets for the poor, as well as two pence per head to each poor inmate. In 1570 it received a further substantial endowment of land from Elizabeth I, confiscated from a conspirator against her, George Redman, grocer, of Cringleford in Norfolk.[66] Reinforced by further endowments in the seventeenth century, the hospital negotiated the Civil War and Interregnum unscathed.[67]

---

62 *Ibid.*, pp. 153–5 (the quote is on p. 153); Rawcliffe, 'Sickness and health', pp. 314–15; Finch, 'The churches', pp. 62–72.

63 McIntosh, 'Local responses', p. 221.

64 Jewson, *History of the Great Hospital*, pp. 21–2; J. Hooper, *Norwich charities, short sketches of their origin and history* (Norfolk News Company: Norwich, 1898), pp. 1–41.

65 Jewson, *History of the Great Hospital*, pp. 23–4.

66 *Ibid.*, pp. 25–6.

67 *Ibid.*, pp. 29–32.

Norwich had emerged as an important textile town in the fourteenth century, and worsted weaving stood at the top of the city's leading trades in 1525. A temporary eclipse towards the mid-sixteenth century was compensated by its development as a centre of consumption, and it proved increasingly attractive to the country gentry, many of whom kept houses there.[68] This new-found source of wealth was compounded from 1565 by the arrival of thousands of Dutch and Walloon religious refugees who brought new skills and techniques in worsted production and reinvigorated the textile industry in the city.[69] At their peak this immigrant community reached almost 6,000, and they still numbered almost 3,000 at the end of the sixteenth century, constituting approximately one-quarter of the town's total population.[70] Introduction of the lighter, cheaper and more colourful cloths known collectively as the 'new draperies' was their key contribution, with the result that the textile industry employed an estimated 28 per cent of workers in the city by the period 1600–25, rising to over 50 per cent by the beginning of the eighteenth century.[71] But this was by no means the only trade in the city. Leather-working was also important and Norwich had a large agricultural community as a result of its rural location.[72] It was also a regional capital, operating as a centre of social life for its region, and as such many of its citizens were engaged in the service industries, shopkeeping and trading.[73] The vibrant economy of the city between the sixteenth century and the end of the seventeenth century was accompanied by a growth of population, a total of about 12,000 at the end of the sixteenth century rising to 30,000 by 1700, at which date – although dwarfed by London – it remained at the very top of the provincial urban hierarchy.[74]

Wealth and poverty grew side by side in early modern Norwich. Although trade in the city was increasing, Norwich – like other substantial towns – also experienced large-scale poverty in this period. In 1570 Norwich Corporation conducted a census of the poor in order to estimate the scale of the problem. Some 28 per cent of the

68 J. Pound, 'The social and trade structure of Norwich 1525–75', *Past and Present*, 34 (1966), pp. 49–69.

69 Pound, 'Government to 1660', pp. 36–45.

70 N. Goose, 'Immigrants in Tudor and early Stuart England', in N. Goose and L. Luu (eds), *Immigrants in Tudor and early Stuart England* (Sussex Academic Press: Brighton, 2005), pp. 18–19.

71 Pound, *Tudor and Stuart Norwich*, p. 51; P. Corfield, 'A provincial capital in the late seventeenth century: the case of Norwich', in P. Clark and P. Slack (eds), *Crisis and order in English towns 1500–1700* (Routledge and Kegan Paul: London, 1972), pp. 275–6.

72 Meeres, *History of Norwich*, p. 37.

73 Pound, 'Government to 1660', p. 46; Corfield, 'Provincial capital', pp. 287–95.

74 Corfield, 'Provincial capital', p. 263; P. Corfield, 'Economic growth and change in seventeenth-century English towns', in C. Phythian-Adams *et al.*, *The traditional community under stress* (Open University Press: Milton Keynes, 1977), p. 37.

city's English population – a total of 2,359 people – were recorded as unable to sustain themselves, and this figure did not include any poor Dutch immigrants in the city. It has been calculated that 20 per cent of the men and 25 per cent of the women recorded on the census were over sixty years old. The elderly poor thus made up a significant group in Norwich, as indeed they did elsewhere. The poor rate was doubled in order to provide for the destitute but was insufficient on its own, and many people relied on a mixed economy of welfare, utilising the poor rates, endowed charities, help from relations and begging in order to maintain themselves.[75] By 1671, the Hearth Tax records show that only 7 per cent of citizens lived in houses with more than six hearths, while almost 60 per cent of the citizens of Norwich were exempt from the Hearth Tax on the grounds of poverty.[76]

In terms of the range of regulations and provisions for the discipline and care of the poor Norwich mirrored those found in many other provincial towns. Apart from continuing to raise both regular and emergency poor rates, the Corporation enacted the various regulations on plague, food supply and prices included in the Books of Orders issued by the Crown, while in 1571 it opened a new Bridewell, a 'house of correction' with an emphasis on work and religion, in an effort to render the 'idle poor' more responsible and god-fearing.[77] Towards the end of the seventeenth century it shared in the increasing level of poor relief payments that was a general feature of these years. In 1659–60 an estimated 30 per cent of households in the city contributed towards the poor rate, paying an average of 4.2 pence each.[78] Twenty years later the proportion chargeable had fallen a little, to 26 per cent, but now each household was paying 7.3 pence.[79] The result was a significant hike in individual poor relief payments. Whereas the average pension in 1578–9 stood at 5.3 pence per week, by 1659–60 it was 8.3 pence, and by 1679–80 11.2 pence. Furthermore, the proportion of families receiving relief had risen across this century from 5.1 per cent to 7 per cent.[80] In 1712 the Norwich Workhouse Act founded two new workhouses in the city, at St Andrew's Hall and in Bridge Street, and an elected court of guardians assumed control over the institutions, which had special powers to impose a tax to set the idle poor to work.[81]

With its control over the Great Hospital, management of the Bridewell and eventually also control over the lazar houses – which

---

75   Pound, 'Government to 1660', pp. 50–1.
76   Pound, *Tudor and Stuart Norwich*, pp. 42–3.
77   P. Griffiths, 'Inhabitants', in Rawcliffe and Wilson (eds), *Norwich since 1550*, p. 75.
78   These sums are expressed in pre-decimal pence, of which there were 240 to a pound.
79   Slack, *Poverty and policy*, Table 9, p. 178.
80   *Ibid.*, Table 8, p. 177.
81   M. Knights, 'Politics, 1660–1835', in Rawcliffe and Wilson (eds), *Norwich since 1550*, p. 185.

fulfilled a variety of functions in the pageant of relief once leprosy had disappeared – the City Corporation played a key role in the life of many institutions that had originated in the realm of religious and private philanthropy. It was also to play a management role in the Boys' and Girls' Hospitals, founded by Thomas Anguish and Robert Baron respectively, in 1621 and 1650.[82] Thomas Anguish, a former mayor of Norwich, specified in his will that ten years after his death in 1617 his property in Fishergate should be given to the Corporation to house and educate poor children. In 1620 Anguish's sons gave the property to the Corporation and ten boys and two girls were admitted. The boys and girls continued to live and be taught together until 1649 when Robert Baron endowed a separate girls' hospital which would provide poor girls aged 7–15 with training in spinning, knitting and dressing wool.[83] Anguish's will amply demonstrates both the severity of the city's social problems as well as the feeling that could be shown by its prosperous elite towards their poorer neighbours, for he writes of his 'compassion and great pitty' for poor children born in the city, 'and specially such as for want lye in the streets … whereby many of them fall into great and grievous diseases and lameness, as that they are fitting for no profession ever after'.[84]

Other notable bequests include the donation in 1619 of £1,395 for good works by Henry Fawcett, a woollen merchant and alderman of the city, while in 1614 Thomas Pye established a small almshouse of six tenements for the relief of six poor people over the age of fifty.[85] The Great Hospital continued to be the centrepiece of the care of the elderly poor in the city, housing fifty-four residents at the start of the seventeenth century, rising to ninety-five by 1665–6.[86] Cooke's Hospital, a clutch of ten cottages for elderly women over sixty years old, was built in 1700 by Robert and Thomas Cooke, both of whom had been aldermen in the city.[87] But numerous smaller bequests were made too, and there is no doubt that Norwich shared in the increase in charitable giving that has been identified by Jordan in the later sixteenth and early seventeenth centuries from his sample of English counties.[88] Indeed, the figures he provides for Norfolk indicate a total of 2,714

---

82 Griffiths, 'Inhabitants', pp. 75–87; Pound, 'Government to 1660', p. 53.
83 BPP 1834 Vol. XXI, *Commissioners of inquiry into charities in England and Wales: twenty-seventh report*, p. 546; Hooper, *Norwich charities*, pp. 60–79; Norfolk Record Office (NRO) NCR 16A Mayor's court book 1595–1603 fo. 399r; P. Griffiths, 'Masterless young people in Norwich 1560–1645', in P. Griffiths, A. Fox and S. Hindle (eds), *The experience of authority in early modern England* (Macmillan: Basingstoke, 1996), pp. 146–86.
84 Quoted in Pound, 'Government to 1660', p. 53.
85 W. White, *White's Norfolk directory* (reprinted by Redwood Press: Liverpool, 1969, first published 1845), p. 136; Pound, 'Government to 1660', p. 53.
86 NRO, NCR 24A Great Hospital Accounts 1601–9, 1665–6, 25F.
87 White, *White's Norfolk directory*, p. 136.
88 *Ibid.*; Jordan, *Philanthropy*, chapter VII.

donors during 1480–1660, who between them contributed £177,884, of which over 43 per cent was devoted to the relief of the poor and social rehabilitation. Of this total, fully £53,018 can be attributed to the City of Norwich itself.[89] The growth of philanthropy thus stood side by side with the development of formal, state-sponsored instruments for the relief of the poor, these twin responses to the poverty problem in the city – both public and private – often being administered by the town's Corporation.

Across England as a whole in the mid-seventeenth century it has been estimated that the income from private charity and that from the poor rates were roughly equivalent; by the end of that century the extension of the formal relief system probably meant that taxation was by now providing three times as much as private charity.[90] A detailed study of the town of Colchester similarly shows that by 1700 taxation imposed by the Colchester Assembly, which took a variety of forms over and above the regular poor rate, formed the senior partner, while the number of testators leaving bequests to the poor fell significantly in the late seventeenth century.[91] Substantial donors did not, however, disappear: in Colchester John Winnocke, baymaker, established six almshouses in the parish of St Giles in 1679 supported by an endowment of £41 per annum issuing from lands he held in the parish of St Peters, and made further bequests in his will five years later.[92] Nationally, high-profile hospitals were built and endowed by royalty and nobility in the late seventeenth century. Charles II commissioned the Royal Hospital at Chelsea for the relief of retired soldiers in 1682 and William and Mary gave money towards the building of a Royal Hospital at Greenwich for the provision of aged seamen in 1694.[93]

Norwich too found a major benefactor, for it was in March 1677 that William Doughty, a merchant living in East Dereham in Norfolk, petitioned Norwich's Mayoral Court, requesting that he be allowed to take up residence in the city and be freed from all rents and charges that usually accompanied that privilege. To these terms the court conceded, on condition that Doughty should use his wealth to benefit the poor of Norwich.[94] This he did, leaving £6,000 for the endowment of an almshouse in the city in his will dated 25 April 1687.[95]

89   Jordan, *Philanthropy*, pp. 241–51.
90   Slack, *Poverty and policy*, p. 171.
91   N. Goose, 'The rise and decline of philanthropy in early modern Colchester: the unacceptable face of mercantilism?', *Social History*, 31 (2006), pp. 469–87.
92   *Report of the commissioners for inquiring concerning charities, 32nd report part I*, 536–7; TNA, PROB 11, Cann 50, PCC will of John Winnocke, baymaker, of St Peters, drawn 1684, proved 1685.
93   Howson, *Houses of noble poverty*, pp. 109–10.
94   NRO, Case 16a/24, MF 629/2 Mayors Court Books 1666–77, 25 March 1677.
95   NRO, Case 20f/14, William Doughty's Will, 25 April 1687.

PART II

Doughty's Hospital, 1687–1833

CHAPTER 4
The bequest of William Doughty

L ittle is known about William Doughty's background, although the will of his father, also called William Doughty, gentleman, of East Dereham in Norfolk, survives in the records of the Prerogative Court of Canterbury.[1] This will, written in 1650, has much in common with that of the later benefactor of the same name, including an understated religious preamble which refers to his belief in 'the resurrection and to be saved through the only merritts of Jesus Christ', as well as a somewhat puritanical insistence that there should be no mourning clothes supplied to his children or to any others at his funeral, unless they should choose to pay the cost themselves, 'nor any other vanity or vain expense'. His charitable bequests were more modest than those of his son, amounting to three shillings each to twenty of the poorest families in the street where he lived, and one shilling apiece to 150 poor families residing elsewhere in East Dereham. To his wife Dorothy he left only that which had been agreed when he married her, when he claimed to 'have had a hard bargain', plus a few household items 'if she shall deal fairly'. While he gave freehold and copyhold lands in a number of Norfolk parishes as well as property in the town of King's Lynn and £300 in cash to his son Thomas, he was insistent that his property in East Dereham should go to his son William. Thomas was required to give up any claim in that regard and was ordered not to cause trouble, 'for I do deal better with him than he hath any cause to expect'. If his son William were to die without an heir, that property was to go to his daughter Elizabeth, the wife of Alexander Fraiser, doctor of physic, and in turn if they lacked heirs to his daughter Lydia, widow, late the wife of William Corbett, gentleman. It is this network of relatives that links this will with certainty to that of our own William Doughty.

Various parcels of land in the parishes of Walpole and Terrington were left by William Doughty senior to his son Robert and his daughter

---

1   TNA, PROB 11/214, PCC will of William Doughty of East Dereham, gent. The PCC was reserved for testators holding property in more than one diocese, and thus generally catered for the wealthy.

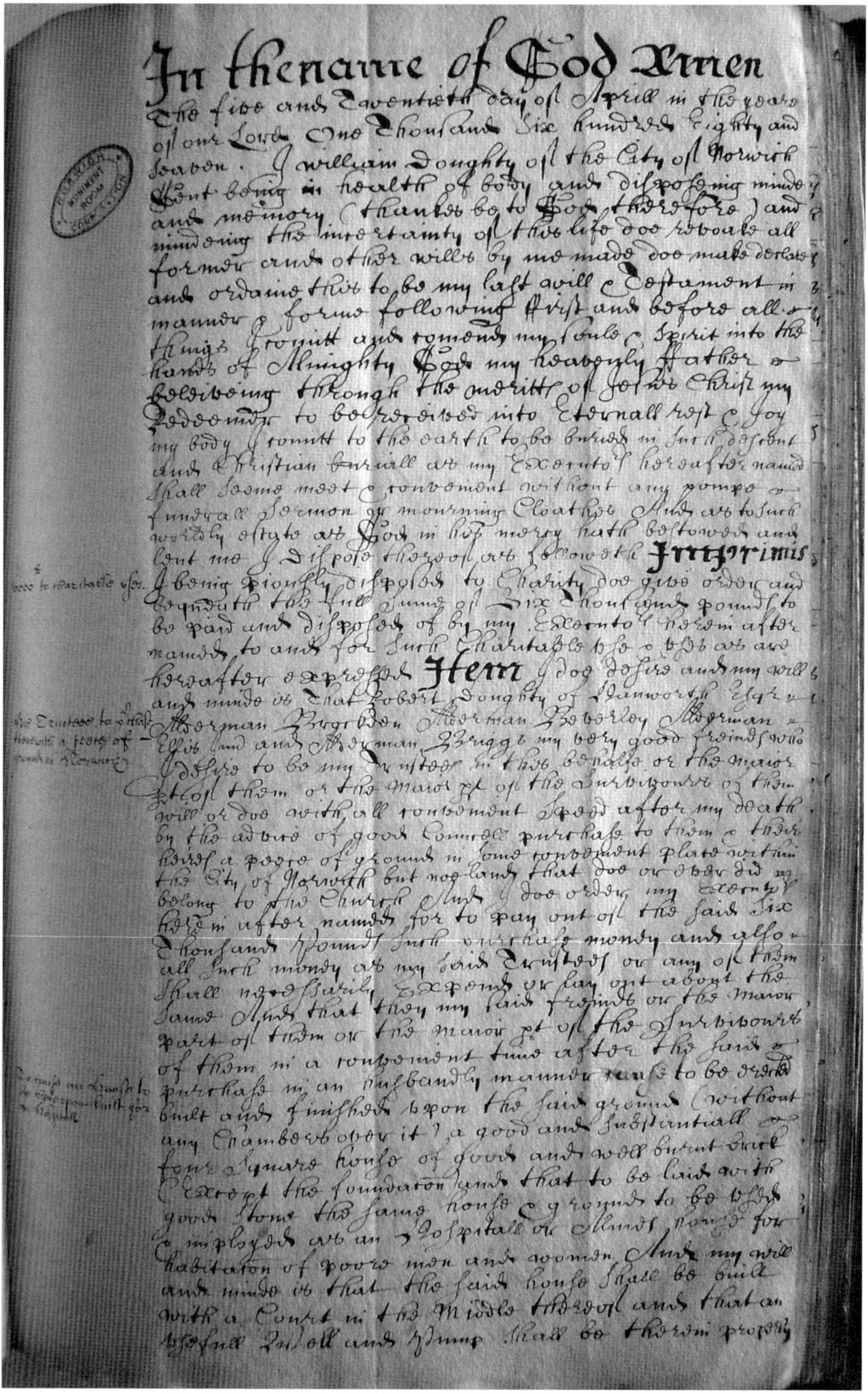

In the name of God Amen
The five and Twentieth day of Aprill in the yeare of our Lord One Thousand Six hundred Eighty and seaven. I William Doughty of the City of Norwich Gent being in health of body and disposing minde and memory (thankes be to God therefore) and mindeing the uncertainty of this life doe revoake all former and other wills by me made doe make declare and ordaine this to be my last will & Testament in manner & forme following First and before all things I commit and commend my soule & Spirit into the hands of Almighty God my heavenly Father beleiveing through the meritts of Jesus Christ my Redeemer to be received into Eternall rest & Joy my body I committ to the earth to be buried in such decent and Christian buriall as my Executor hereafter named shall seeme meet & convenient without any pompe or funerall Sermon or mourning Cloathes And as to such worldly estate as God in his mercy hath bestowed and lent me I dispose thereof as followeth Inprimis

£6000 to charitable uses

I being piously disposed to Charity doe give order and bequeath the full summe of Six Thousand pounds to be paid and disposed of by my Executor herein after named to and for such Charitable uses & ends as are hereafter expressed Item I doe desire and my will and minde is that Robert Doughty of Hanworth Esqr

The Trustees to purchase therewith a peece of ground in Norwich

Alderman [illegible] Alderman Beverley Alderman [illegible] and Alderman Briggs my very good friends who I desire to be my Trustees in this behalfe or the maior part of them or the maior pt of the survivours of them will or doe with all convenient speed after my death by the advice of good Councell purchase to them & their heires a peece of ground in some convenient place within the City of Norwich but noe lands that doe or ever did belong to the Church And I doe order my Executor herein after named for to pay out of the said Six Thousand pounds such purchase money and also all such money as my said Trustees or any of them shall necessarily expend or lay out about the same And that they my said friends or the maior part of them or the maior pt of the survivours of them in a convenient time after the said

To purchase an house to be there upon built for an Hospitall

purchase in an husbandly manner cause to be erected built and finished upon the said ground (without any Chambers over it) a good and substantiall four square house of good and well burnt brick (except the foundation and that to be laid with good stone the same house & ground to be used & imployed as an Hospitall or Almes house for habitation of poore men and women And my will and minde is that the said house shall be built with a Court in the middle thereof and that an usefull well and pump shall be therein properly

Figure 2. The first page of William Doughty's will, 1687

Elizabeth, besides further bequests of cash and debts owed. The Manor of Martley Hall and other parcels of land lying in the parish of Easton in Suffolk he assigned to his daughter and son-in-law Elizabeth and Alexander Fraiser, on condition that they pay £30 per annum to his daughter Lydia for the rest of her life, while further legacies in cash and lands were left to the widowed Lydia. The proceeds of the parsonage of Bawburgh in Norfolk with its various lands, woods and appurtenances were to be dedicated for two years to the payment of his debts, and then to proceed to his son William, if he should die to son Robert, and if he should die to son Thomas, revealing a pecking order of trust and affection that is underlined by the naming of son William, daughter Lydia and servant Christopher Johnson as executors of the will. William, the father of the William Doughty who founded the hospital that bears his name, had thus been a wealthy man, a member of the landed gentry of Norfolk, who took considerable pains to ensure that all of his children (both male and female) were adequately catered for when he died, but who also had clear ideas about the relative merits of his offspring, and appears to have been well aware of the potential for false dealing among them.

As to William Doughty junior, his will is revealing too.[2] His religious preamble is similar to that of his father, if a little more fulsome: 'I commit and commend my soul and spirit into the hands of Almighty God my heavenly father believing through the merits of Jesus Christ my redeemer to be received into eternal rest and joy'. He too insisted on a modest funeral, 'without any pomp or funeral sermon or mourning clothes' and costing no more than £40, and this, allied to his substantial charitable bequests and attitudes to hard work, have led some historians to characterise him as a Puritan.[3] However, unlike many founders of almshouses, William Doughty did not impose any religious restrictions or requirements on the inmates of Doughty's Hospital, which suggests he was a devout man of solid Protestant, but by no means evangelical, religious beliefs.

There is no mention of a wife or children in his will and this, coupled with his large charitable gifts, suggests that he was a bachelor or a childless widower. However, he was not without kin, and in accordance with his father's will he conveyed all his freehold and copyhold land in East Dereham to his nephew Alexander Fraiser, esquire, which he had surrendered to the use of his will in the Court of Common Pleas in 1653.[4] He left the same nephew £1,000, and his

---

2   NRO, Case 20f/14, William Doughty's Will, 25 April 1687.
3   C. Jewson, *Doughty's Hospital* (Norwich, 1979), pp. 1–2.
4   By law copyhold land could not be conveyed by will, so had to be surrendered in advance to the 'use' of the holder's will to ensure that it was passed on to the desired legatee.

niece Elizabeth Fraiser, now Widow Bromley, a further £1,000. But these legacies were on condition that the recipients give up all claims to the Manor of Martley Hall and all other lands held in Easton or elsewhere in Suffolk, and drop all legal actions entered upon against him in this regard as executor of his father's will 'from the beginning of the world to the day of my death'. It appears that in 1653 Doughty had paid £850 to his sister and brother-in-law Elizabeth and Alexander Fraiser, and a further £300 to his sister Lydia Corbett alias Thurlowe, to cancel their claims to Martley Hall and other lands in Suffolk, but had left the name of Alexander Fraiser out of the agreement because he was currently 'beyond sea with King Charles the Second', and he had been advised to omit his name to avoid the danger of sequestration. The consequences are best expressed in Doughty's own words: 'My kindred well requites me in bringing me into suits for those my kindnesses to them. Therefore I have good reason and just cause to bind all and every of them by law … as fully and firmly as the law can … for if I had not trusted to their fair words they had not deceived me'. Perhaps it was this family discord that persuaded William Doughty to dedicate so much of his estate to charity.

Apart from a number of other small bequests to a variety of kinsmen and women, two other issues are mentioned that suggest that William was not blessed with the most reliable or trustworthy of relatives. His executors – John Barneham, hosier, and William Barneham, John's son, both of Norwich – are enjoined in the will to revive his suit in the Court of Chancery relating to lands held in Walpole and West Walton, mortgaged by Robert Doughty, merchant, deceased, to Robert Doughty of Aylesham, gent, also deceased, who in turn mortgaged the same to William for £400 to redeem the equity, a sum that appears to have been outstanding. An even more troublesome relative was his kinsman and namesake William Doughty, who may have been his nephew, the son of his brother Thomas, or his cousin.[5] This William Doughty 'laid in Wood Street Counter and the King's Bench for debt from one thousand six hundred eighty and two to one thousand six hundred eighty and three and was put into Norwich prison about the month of August which was in the year of our Lord one thousand six hundred eighty and four and remained in Norwich prison for debt until one thousand six hundred eighty and seven'. He was to be allowed just £10 per annum, to be paid to him quarterly for his maintenance, his executors to demand a receipt before three credible witnesses, and no part of that legacy was to be assigned to any

---

5   The contemporary use of the term 'cousin' to denote any but immediate kin is potentially confusing, and it seems more likely that the William Doughty in question was a nephew.

of his creditors. William again turns his attention to his impecunious namesake towards the end of his will, again enjoining his executors to pay no money to his cousin William nor to his creditors except by a decree in Chancery and by a Statute of Bankruptcy taken out against him, because his executors 'can never know all Mr Doughty's creditors. Some are broke some are dead some gone beyond sea some abscond themselves and some conceal themselves and [their] debts'.

Doughty is at pains to justify his legacies, carefully listing the payments he had made in accordance with his father's will, as well as those made to his sisters and brother-in-law subsequently, while also noting that the remainder of his father's personal estate had been 'spent in suits with my unkind relatives … so I have given unto my kinsmen and kinswomen more than they could or can expect'. Furthermore, 'my personal estate hath been gotten and increased by God's blessing my own judgement and my voyages into Spain Italy France and Holland and other places', and hence what he had accumulated 'by God's blessing and my own industry' he was determined, 'being piously disposed to charity', to apply 'to what uses intents and purposes I shall please and do think meet and convenient'. He had, of course, been the primary heir to a wealthy member of the Norfolk landed class, and the fact that he claims to have increased his wealth largely on the back of overseas trade sheds an interesting light upon the close relationship between the landed and mercantile classes in late seventeenth-century Norfolk. But if his will sounds just a little self-congratulatory in view of his privileged start in life, we should perhaps remember the contrasting fate of his namesake, be thankful that he had invested his talents so wisely, and that the fruits of his labour were to redound so handsomely to the benefit of the poor of the City of Norwich.

Before we turn to the endowment of Doughty's almshouse, we should note that he also made a range of other charitable bequests. A loan fund of £600 was entrusted to the Corporation, £250 of which was to be lent interest free for five years to ten worsted weavers living in the city, £250 to shopkeepers or tradesmen on the same terms, and £100 to five poor bargemen, lightermen or keelmen engaged in the carriage of goods between Norwich and Yarmouth. A further £20 was left as a one-off payment to be divided between the poor of the four great wards of the city, and a further £3 each to every little ward.[6] The twelve poorest families who lived closest to the house he inhabited in Norwich were to receive 10 shillings apiece (an echo of his father's will), while the poor of the parish within which he died were to receive

---

6   Larger towns were commonly divided into geographical units called wards as well as into parishes.

£3, and every bearer of his body at his funeral a ring worth 10 shillings. The residue of his estate – if any there be after his legacies had been duly paid and the expenses of his executors and supervisor defrayed – he left towards the building of additional housing on the piece of land purchased for the purposes of erecting the almshouse that bears his name, or towards the purchase of additional land nearby if the original plot were of insufficient size. Each inmate of this second almshouse, if it should be built, was to receive 2 shillings weekly, a chauldron of coals annually, and a purple gown every two years, the master of the first almshouse also to have oversight of the second. There is no evidence that any surplus ever became available in addition to the original bequest of £6,000, and no record of any tenements being constructed beyond the original thirty-two, but this particular specification ensured that when Doughty's Hospital possessed the means to expand, it could legally do so.

With regard to the construction and administration of the endowed almshouse the instructions in Doughty's will were very specific.[7] Six hundred pounds of the endowment was to be used to purchase land 'in some convenient place' in Norwich on a site that had never been owned by the Church. It was here that the hospital was to be constructed. The structure itself was to be a substantial four square house of thirty-two tenements, eight on each side of the square, thus conforming to one of the traditional forms of almshouse construction, that of the courtyard.[8] In the middle of this courtyard was to be a well and pump, besides a 'house of office' for use by the inmates. The front of the building was to be made from freestone with a gate 'so narrow that a cart could not pass through it', most probably a means to ensure the seclusion, tranquility and privacy of the inmates.[9] At the entrance a dwelling for the master of the hospital was to be erected. The foundations were to be made from well-burnt brick or stone and the structure was to consist of a single storey with 'no chambers above it'. The will also specified that the building should have a large cellar for the laying in of coals, and that there should be enough room on the land for a walled garden for the residents.

Doughty instructed that the remaining £5,400 of his endowment be used to purchase property in Norfolk with a combined annual rent of at least £250, though again this was to include no land that

---

7   In his will Doughty used the terms 'almshouse' and 'hospital' interchangeably, sometimes referring to it as an 'almshouse or hospital', showing that no distinction remained by this period.

8   Numerous books focus upon almshouse architecture. See, for example, Godfrey, *English almshouse*; A. Hallett, *Almshouses* (Shire Publications: Princes Risborough, 2004), pp. 23–36; Caffrey, *Almshouses*, pp. 21–48; Howson, *Almshouses*, pp. 77–108.

9   Caffrey, *Almshouses*, p. 35.

belonged, or ever had belonged, to the Church and – very sensibly – no land that was liable to flooding or subject to taxes to provide sea defences. It was the income from these rents that would fund the maintenance of the hospital and its residents. From these proceeds his trustees were first to deduct the charges of repairing the almshouse, and defray all their charges and expenses in executing the trust. The sum remaining was dedicated to the management and maintenance of the hospital and its residents.

With regard to the residents of the hospital, Doughty specified that the institution should accommodate twenty-four poor, aged men and eight poor, aged women, these to be elected by his trustees, and replaced when they died. Each of these residents was to have an allowance of 2 shillings paid to them every Saturday morning, in order to buy food.[10] They would also be provided annually with a chauldron of coal each, and a gown or coat of purple cloth on their election to the almshouse and every two years thereafter. None were to be placed in the hospital 'but such as shall be upwards of three score years of age and not younger'. The rules of the institution were that each resident must dwell constantly in the hospital, and wear their coat or gown, on pain of ejection. Also on pain of removal from the almshouse, none were to 'misbehave themselves by cursing swearing drunkenness keeping bad hours or wilfully neglecting or refusing to observe such orders for the decent governing of the said Hospital as shall from time to time be made by my said Trustees …'. A stone plaque, engraved around the time the hospital was being built and now on display in the stairwell at Doughty's, similarly enjoins the residents to 'live peaceably and … as becomes Christians, neither cursing, swearing, keeping bad hours nor being drunk'. Finally, Doughty specified that the institution should be run by a 'discreet and sober single man', who would dwell constantly in the hospital and see to the governing of its residents. This master was to report any disorders or misdemeanours of the residents to the trustees and, if the trustees found him to be neglecting his duties, they had the power to replace him. His wage was 4 shillings a week, and his duties included distribution of the weekly allowance, delivering the coal to each resident and keeping order among the inmates.

William Doughty named five executors in his will, his 'very good friends', who were given the responsibility of carrying out his wishes. They were his kinsman Robert Doughty, and four Norwich aldermen – William Barnham, Michael Beverley, Augustine Briggs and Mr Ellis Junior. Doughty's will stated that six years after his own death, and having built the almshouse, the executors were to convey the hospital,

---

10   Two shillings in pre–decimal currency equals 10 new pence.

its lands and property, to the Corporation of Norwich for them to administer. Doughty died on 29 March 1688 and on 23 June Alderman Barnham brought the will to the Mayoral Court where the clerk recorded the particulars.[11]

---

11   C. Jewson, *Doughty's Hospital* (Norwich, 1979) p. 6; NRO, Case 16a/25, MF 629/3
      23 June 1688.

CHAPTER 5

In and out of the fire: the achievement of financial stability

Doughty's Hospital was erected on land purchased in the parish of St Saviour in Norwich with part of the £600 bequeathed for that purpose, the remainder of that sum being used to build the almshouse.[12] The precise date of completion is not recorded. Although Doughty had been very clear in his will about the procedure for the establishment and early governing of the hospital, the transition from governance by the original trustees to the Corporation of Norwich was not straightforward. Whether it took the executors longer to establish the almshouse than Doughty had expected, or whether they were reluctant to relinquish control, is unclear. In either case, the change in administration was by no means a smooth one. By 1694, six years after Doughty's death, the executors were still dealing with his estate, and in June of that year Norwich Corporation ordered that they pass on to them the accounts of the hospital, as the will had instructed.[13] The trustees refused, and by December 1694 the Corporation was consulting its legal counsel to determine who had the right to appoint residents to the hospital.[14] It was not until April 1698, some ten years after the death of their friend, that the executors of Doughty's will were finally ready to surrender control of the almshouse.[15] However, the debate over who held control over appointments continued, and in October 1698 the Mayor's Court declared that if any of the original trustees sought to elect an almsperson without the express permission of the court, they would be sued by the Corporation.[16] These threats

---

12 NRO, N/TC 63/2: *Commissioners of inquiry into charities in England and Wales: twenty-seventh report*, BPP 1834, Vol. XXI (225), p. 556.
13 NRO, Case 16a/25, MF 629/4, 6 June 1694.
14 *Ibid.*, 22 December 1694.
15 *Ibid.*, 23 April 1698.
16 *Ibid.*, 12 October 1698.

seem to have worked and from that date all admissions to the hospital were recorded in the Mayoral Court books.[17]

In anticipation of receiving control of Doughty's Hospital, Norwich Corporation obtained letters patent from the Crown which granted them the right to purchase lands and tenements, not exceeding a yearly value of £1,000, in support of Doughty's Hospital.[18] The licence, granted on 21 February 1698, allowed the Corporation to obtain lands at Wolterton, Erpingham, Colby, Wickmer, Ingworth and Blickling. Two manors at Hellington and Calthorpe and a messuage in Burston were also purchased to secure finance for the institution.[19] Additionally, the hospital was the recipient of an endowment from the Reverend Samuel Chapman, who left £200 to Doughty's Hospital in his will in 1700.[20] Other charities in Norwich at this time raised revenue in similar ways. For example, in 1700 the Town Close Estate Charity was benefiting from rents paid on property held in Norwich. These rents were used to benefit poor freemen in the city and the money was used to fund pensions and gifts for infirm or incapacitated freemen, or the widows of freemen.[21]

The first master of Doughty's Hospital, a man named William Sydner, died in 1701 and in his stead a Mr William Doughty was unanimously elected.[22] Although it is not expressly stated, one might speculate that this William Doughty was the debtor nephew (or possibly cousin) of the founder of the hospital.[23] Perhaps it was foolish for the trustees to have elected him as master, for the finances of the hospital soon began to suffer.[24] In October 1702, the Mayoral Court allowed the master to sell timber from the Calthorpe estate in order to raise money to buy clothes for the poor of the hospital.[25] Two years later the situation was considerably worse. In March 1704, after several years of poor finances, the trustees decided that there were to be no more appointments to Doughty's Hospital until further notice.[26] The appointment of Alderman Robert Bene as treasurer and the death of William Doughty the master, both in 1704, went some way towards

---

17 The first entry is the death of Mr Edward Hargroves, an inmate at the hospital: NRO, Case 16a/25, MF 629/4, 7 December 1698.

18 White, *White's Norfolk directory*, p. 135.

19 NRO, N/TC 63/2: *Commissioners of inquiry into charities in England and Wales: twenty-seventh report*, BPP 1834, Vol. XXI (225), p. 556. 'Messuage' was a term used to denote a dwelling house and its surrounding property, including outbuildings.

20 NRO, N/TC 63/2, p. 557; C. Mackie, *Norfolk annals. A chronological record of remakable events in the nineteenth century*, 2 vols (Norwich Chronicle Office: Norwich, 1901), Vol. 1, p. 361.

21 Hooper, *Norwich charities*, pp. 118–23.

22 NRO, Case 16a/26, MF 630/1, 31 May 1701.

23 NRO, Case 20f/14, William Doughty's Will, 25 April 1687.

24 NRO, Case 16a/26, MF 630/1, 31 October 1702.

25 *Ibid.*, 31 October 1702.

26 *Ibid.*, 29 March 1704.

rectifying the situation, but the financial problems continued, and were not helped by some dubious dealings.[27] In 1707 it emerged that one of the original executors of Doughty's estate, Robert Doughty, had used his position to admit his son, and on his son's death his daughter, to copyhold lands at Calthorpe without paying the requisite fines to the hospital. In January 1707, the Mayoral Court ordered that in consequence Robert Doughty should pay a fine of £10 to the Corporation but by December of the same year the matter was still unresolved.[28]

In April 1708 the Corporation established a special Hospital Committee to manage the expenditure and estates of the four main hospitals in Norwich. As well as Doughty's, the committee also dealt with the finances of the Great Hospital and the Girls' and Boys' Hospitals.[29] The Hospital Committee minute books detail the expenditure of the four hospitals and any leases and rents on property belonging to them. However, the Mayor's Court continued to deal with the admission of inmates to Doughty's Hospital, as well as the appointment of masters.[30] The financial situation remained poor, however, with the consequence that the hospital was compelled to let some of its tenements on a commercial basis. In March 1707 Ann Daldy and John King were each granted the use of a room at Doughty's and in July 1709 Robert Murrill was also given permission to lodge there. In 1711 Marther Money was given lodging at Doughty's and in 1712 the courts decreed that Mary Croft should continue to rent a room at the institution until further order.[31] That order came in January 1713 when the financial situation had improved and all lodgers were served with notice to vacate the property. It is unclear how many of the cottages were commercially let during this period, but on 13 June 1713 twenty-four poor, elderly men and women were placed in the hospital. This may suggest that twenty-four of the thirty-two tenements had been rented out, or that some cottages were rented while others were left empty. Either way, the introduction of the twenty-four new almspeople ensured that the institution was exclusively charitable once more.[32]

It was the additional monetary endowments that Doughty's Hospital received during the eighteenth century that enabled the institution to achieve financial stability. For example, in 1733 the £200 left to Doughty's Hospital by the Reverend Samuel Chapman

---

27   *Ibid.*, 27 September 1704.
28   *Ibid.*, 17 January 1707.
29   NRO, N/MC 2/3 Hospital Committee minutes, April 1708–April 1720.
30   NRO, Case 16a/27, MF 630/2, 9 February 1717.
31   NRO, Case 16a/26, MF 630/1, 29 March 1704; 19 March 1707; NRO, Case 16a/27, MF 630/2, 7 February 1712.
32   NRO, Case 16a/27, MF 630/2, 14 January 1713; 13 June 1713.

was used, together with £600 from the Great Hospital, to enable the two institutions jointly to purchase property and land at Cringleford. Doughty's then received one-third of all subsequent rent on the property, with the remaining two-thirds being used for the benefit of the Great Hospital.[33]

The men (and they were invariably men) who left gifts and endowments to Doughty's Hospital would often stipulate the conditions under which the money was to be paid. Some, as we shall see, wanted to pay for the maintenance of specific residents, but others had different intentions that did not fit with the ethos of the original foundation. In 1725 Jeremiah Revans, vicar of East Tuddenham, a small village to the west of Norwich, left a bequest to Doughty's Hospital, specifying in his will that £4 annually from the rent charges on his property in Foulsham should be paid to the Bishop of Norwich in order that clergymen might be employed to care for the souls of the residents. Nothing appears to have ever been received in respect of this bequest, however.[34] We must remember that despite the power of the established Church, and the existence of such an extensive diocese centred upon Norwich Cathedral itself, the city was a locus of nonconformist activity.[35] William Doughty was himself reputed to be from a nonconformist background, and in his will had specified that his almshouse ought to be built on land that had 'never been occupied by the Church', while he made no injunctions regarding the religion or worshipping habits of its residents.[36] Perhaps as a result of the lack of religious specification from its founder, no provision of clergy for Doughty's Hospital was ever made, and residents were able to practise any Christian religion they chose.

By the 1740s, the annual income of Doughty's Hospital was greater than the expenditure of the institution and it was in a much stronger financial position. The famous historian of Norfolk, Francis Blomefield, writing in 1745, recorded its finances for 1742. The income from rents and interests was £278 9s. 2d., and the expenditure was £229 4s. 8d., leaving approximately £49 in the hands of the treasurer at the end of the financial year. Of that expenditure, £179 18s. 0d. went on the salary of the master and the nurse, as well as the weekly payments to the almspeople. Four pounds each was paid for the annual employment of Mr Thomas Johnson, who was listed as 'apothecary to the hospital', and of Mr Edward Molden, the bailiff. The purchase and transportation

---

33 White, *White's Norfolk directory*, p. 136.
34 NRO, N/TC 63/2: *Commissioners of inquiry into charities in England and Wales: twenty-seventh report*, BPP 1834, Vol. XXI (225), p. 560.
35 R. Wilson, 'Introduction', in Rawcliffe and Wilson (eds), *Norwich Since 1550*, p. xxiv.
36 See above, pp. 27, 30–1.

of thirty-two chauldrons of coals for the hospital from a Mr Thomas Cappwin cost £40 11s. 8d. The engrossing or transcribing of the accounts cost £10, and 'emptying the muckbing' a further £5 per annum.[37]

Endowments to Doughty's Hospital continued to be received throughout the eighteenth century, and these helped to keep the institution in a good financial position. The larger endowments were recorded in the Charity Commissioners' Report of 1834. These gifts included £200 granted to the hospital by Jehosaphat Postle in a deed dated 24 February 1764. Mr Postle considered the weekly stipend of the almspeople of two shillings to be too little on which to live comfortably, particularly 'on account of their great age and increasing infirmities', and asked that his endowment be used to add 6d. per week to the allowances of four poor men and three poor women – those who had lived there the longest (the master excluded).[38] Reciting Postle's gift, John, the Earl of Buckinghamshire, and Thomas Harvey, by deed of gift dated 26 July 1765, each gave £100, also to provide an additional 6d. per week to four men and three women who had been resident at Doughty's the longest, excepting only the master and those who were in receipt of Postle's gift.[39] In his will dated 28 November 1789, Charles Maltby, a former medical officer at Doughty's, left £105 to the institution, a sum which amounted to more than his wage for the twenty-one years that he served as surgeon to Doughty's Hospital.[40]

A complex bequest was initiated by Thomas Vere, in a codicil to his will dated 19 February 1766, wherein he bequeathed £200 to the Corporation to be invested by them in 3 per cent bank annuities, the dividends to be applied to the maintenance of one poor old man in Doughty's Hospital, this legacy to be paid within one year of the death of his son and daughter. Sixteen years later, in 1782, Mr Vere junior transferred to the trustees £642 11s. 6d. in 3 per cent stock (reduced annuities), in respect of this and a similar legacy to the Girls' Hospital, the proceeds to be paid to him and his wife for their joint lives. In 1796, Mr and Mrs Vere both being dead, the stock was transferred to the Corporation. In 1807 £199 was paid to the Girls' Hospital, and the whole dividend of the remaining account was returned to Doughty's.[41]

37 F. Blomefield, *Essay towards a topographical history of the county of Norfolk* (Norwich, 1745), Vol. IV, p. 449.

38 NRO, N/TC 63/2: *Commissioners of inquiry into charities in England and Wales: twenty-seventh report*, BPP 1834, Vol. XXI (225), p. 557.

39 *Ibid*.

40 NRO, Case 16a/31, MF 631, 16 August 1746; 24 December 1767; NRO, N/TC 63/2: *Commissioners of inquiry into charities in England and Wales: twenty-seventh report*, BPP 1834, Vol. XXI (225), p. 558.

41 NRO, N/TC 63/2: *Commissioners of inquiry into charities in England and Wales: twenty-seventh report*, BPP 1834, Vol. XXI (225), p. 557.

Other endowments included bequests in the wills of William Pagan, who gave £100 to the hospital in 1769, William Lindoe, who gave £100 in 1771, and Cary Haywood, who gave £10 in 1785. These sums were all invested in stock, or put out at interest, by the Corporation.[42]

The eighteenth century witnessed an enormous rise in the amount of money devoted to formal, state-sponsored poor relief, total national poor law expenditure increasing by a factor of ten and per capita expenditure by a factor of six. Allowing for inflation reduces these increases considerably, though expenditure per head of the population expressed in terms of the price of wheat still quadrupled between 1696 and 1802–3.[43] But the same century also witnessed a renewed growth of charitable giving, and a change in its form. Now the new 'associational' charities raised funds by subscription, communally celebrating both the giver and the gift, and providing a more powerful mechanism to fund substantial projects. Religion, humanitarianism and perhaps also social aspiration fuelled these endeavours, with further impetus coming from the evangelical revival of the late eighteenth and early nineteenth centuries, as well as from the challenges to social relations in England precipitated by the Napoleonic Wars (1793–1815).[44] This renewed philanthropic impulse might explain the rise in endowments to Doughty's Hospital during this period, just as it inspired endowments to a wide range of other charitable institutions elsewhere.

Of course charitable endowments presuppose the wealth to fund them, and Norwich's fortunes were chequered during the eighteenth century. At the start of the eighteenth century it was a city of nearly 30,000 souls, and the second city of the kingdom.[45] Sustained by immigration from East Anglia, particularly from Norfolk and east Suffolk, it continued to grow until the mid-1780s when it reached a total of 40,000 inhabitants. Norwich continued to exhibit the range of economic functions that typified towns of this standing, as a focus for the produce of a fertile agricultural hinterland, and as a regional, county and ecclesiastical centre. But its continued growth, much slower than in the preceding century, was still underpinned by its famous textile industry, which had adapted further in the late seventeenth century to cater for a market that was high-cost, fashion-sensitive and focused upon both local and distant markets.[46] The

42   *Ibid.*, p. 558.
43   Slack, *English poor law*, Table 1, p. 30.
44   D. Owen, *English philanthropy 1660–1960* (Harvard University Press: Cambridge, MA, 1964), ch. II; H. Cunningham and J. Innes (eds), *Charity, philanthropy and reform from the 1690s to 1850* (Macmillan Press: Basingstoke, 1998), chs 3 and 9.
45   P. Corfield, 'From second city to regional capital', in Rawcliffe and Wilson (eds), *Norwich since 1550*, p. 142.
46   *Ibid.*, pp. 144–8; A. Armstrong, 'Population, 1700–1950', in Rawcliffe and Wilson (eds), *Norwich since 1550*, Table 10.1, p. 245.

output of the industry may have doubled during the course of the eighteenth century, and the third quarter of that century marked its zenith. Thereafter, competition from the West Riding of Yorkshire, over-reliance upon Irish yarn imports, failure to innovate and the headlong rise of the cotton industry, all conspired to produce a long and protracted decline, a decline exacerbated by the decision of the Norwich master weavers to enter directly into the export trade, for which they were ill-equipped.[47] These difficulties were highlighted by Frederic Eden in 1797, who also noted the 'great number of paupers' in the town's two workhouses – one 'old' and one 'new'.[48] Indeed, by 1802 the two workhouses accommodated 1,300 paupers, whilst a further 3,700 were in receipt of outdoor relief.[49]

By 1801 the town's population had declined a little, the 1801 census revealing approximately 38,500 inhabitants. Still a leading town, the tenth largest in England and Wales, it was starting to experience relative eclipse as the industrial towns and cities of the Midlands and the north expanded apace. Increasingly it was sustained by its role as regional capital, as the commercial, administrative, social and financial focus of a wealthy region, and as a cultural intermediary with northern Europe too.[50] Though no longer at the cutting edge of industrial growth and innovation, it remained, in the words of Angela Dain, 'an enlightened and polite society', capable and determined to engage in philanthropy, inspired by both concern with social stability and by practical humanitarianism.[51]

Voluntary hospitals embodied the humanitarian spirit of enlightened thinking and were funded through donations and subscriptions. The Bethel Asylum, the earliest purpose-built asylum in the country, was founded in Norwich in 1713 by Mary Chapman, the wife of Reverend Samuel Chapman, the Rector of Thorpe. Her inspiration was the appalling treatment meted out to her relatives when they had suffered mental incapacity.[52] Mrs Chapman's asylum was dedicated to the care of 'poor lunaticks', defined as those 'afflicted with lunacy or madness (not such as are fools or idiots from their birth)'.[53] The aim of the asylum was to provide care for the mentally ill in the hope of curing bouts of illness, rather than simply housing incurable cases. Mary Chapman died in

47   R. Wilson, 'The textile industry', in Rawcliffe and Wilson (eds), *Norwich since 1550*, pp. 230–7.
48   F.M. Eden, *The state of the poor*, 3 vols (Thoemmes Press edition: Bristol, 2001; first published J. Davis: London, 1797).
49   S. Cherry, 'Medical care since 1750', in Rawcliffe and Wilson (eds), *Norwich since 1550*, p. 274.
50   Armstrong, 'Population', Table 10.1, p. 245; Corfield, 'Second city', pp. 156–63.
51   A. Dain, 'An enlightened and polite society', in Rawcliffe and Wilson (eds), *Norwich since 1550*, pp. 193–218.
52   *Ibid.*, p. 213
53   White, *White's Norfolk directory*, p. 131.

1717, leaving all her estates for the benefit of the hospital.[54] The hospital was able to accommodate up to forty patients, most of whom were private cases who paid four shillings per week for their care. However, there was room for up to ten charitable cases, which were often funded by money from the parish or the Corporation.[55] By the early 1770s accommodation was planned by the governors for thirty-three women and twenty-two men.[56] Records for 800 of the 1,300 patients of the institution between 1760 and 1880 suggest that approximately one-third were pronounced cured or relieved, but that the average residence of those who died in the hospital during the early half of the nineteenth century was fourteen years.[57] Whatever the success rate, the institution provided far more humane care of those suffering from mental weakness or instability than had previously been available.

By the late eighteenth century it was increasingly clear that a medical hospital was needed in Norwich. The Bishop of Norwich, Thomas Hayter, wrote to local surgeon Benjamin Gooch in 1758 with the idea for a city and county hospital, but Hayter was translated to London in 1761 and the plans for the institution fell through. It was not until William Fellowes, a local man, arranged a subscription for the construction of a city hospital in 1770 that plans for the institution began to take shape.[58] The Norfolk and Norwich Hospital was funded and built by subscription and admitted its first inpatients in November 1772.[59] The hospital again reflected the enlightened thinking of the age and there were no religious or political restrictions on patients. However, hospital stay was conditional on securing a subscriber who was able to nominate the patient to the institution and pay for their care. In emergency cases this rule was overlooked, but patients with incurable illnesses, or infectious illness, were turned away, as were those with mental problems. This was because the hospital was keen to maintain a high rate of 'cured' patients, as positive results ensured financial support.[60] The opening of the Norfolk and Norwich Hospital gave Doughty's the opportunity to remove almspeople with chronic or sudden illnesses and have them cared for in a more appropriate environment.[61]

The residents of Norwich engaged in more short-term, practical assistance too. During years of high food prices, such as 1720, 1756–7, 1766 and 1772, as well as during the French Wars (1793–1815), soup

54 *Ibid.*
55 Meeres, *History of Norwich*, p. 110; M. Winston, 'The bethel at Norwich: an eighteenth-century hospital for lunatics', *Medical History*, Vol. 38 (1994), pp. 27–51.
56 Dain, 'Enlightened and polite society', p. 213.
57 *Ibid.*
58 Hooper, *Norwich charities*, pp. 137–47.
59 Meeres, *History of Norwich*, p. 110.
60 Cherry, 'Medical care since 1750', pp. 274–5.
61 *Ibid.*

kitchens were set up, while flour and meal supplies were subsidised to keep prices down. Specific assistance to poor weavers in the town, victims of the long-term decline of the city's textile trade, was given on occasion through the organisation of 'crepe balls', the proceeds being used to help the unemployed, while in 1790 'the opulent inhabitants of Norwich' established the Benevolent Association for the Relief of Decayed Tradesmen, their Widows and Orphans.[62]

By the 1780s, shrewd investments in property and shares had ensured that Doughty's Hospital was financially secure, so much so that the treasurer of the institution was able to give £500 to Norwich Corporation in the form of a loan in 1785.[63] From 1789 the Hospital Committee recorded a list of approved workmen to be used for the coming year by the four hospitals they administered, perhaps reflecting a tightening of control over the maintenance of these institutions. The list was extensive, and included bricklayers, carpenters, plumbers, tailors, drapers, whitesmiths, coal merchants, bakers, shoemakers, hosiers and coopers.[64] By 1791 Doughty's was wealthy enough to consider expansion for the first time and six new cottages were erected in the courtyard, with four more old men and two more old women able to enter the almshouse in October of that year.[65] The financial situation was dramatically augmented in 1810, when Thomas Cooke of Pentonville, Middlesex, a man quite unfairly known as 'Cooke the Miser', left £6,600 to Doughty's Hospital in 3 per cent consolidated annuities. Cooke specified that the money should be used to augment the allowances of the almspeople, but his will made it clear that the master was not to benefit from the endowment. Despite the words of Cooke's will, the trustees decided to use the funds to increase the master's weekly wage to 10s., as well as increasing each resident's stipend to 5s. 6d. per week. They justified this by arguing that, according to the will of William Doughty, the master was meant to receive double the residents' stipend, even though this increase was against the express wishes of the donor.[66] By the early nineteenth century, therefore, Doughty's Hospital had shaken off the difficulties of its early years, had modestly expanded the number of its residents, had increased their stipends, and was in good financial shape, the balance of funds in hand for the three years 1829/30, 1830/31 and 1831/2 never falling below £1,000.[67]

---

62 Dain, 'Enlightened and polite society', p. 213.

63 NRO, Case 16a/35, MF 632, 5 March 1785.

64 NRO, N/MC 2/6, 3 June 1789.

65 NRO, Case 16a/36, MF 632, 8 October 1791.

66 NRO, N/TC 63/2: *Commissioners of inquiry into charities in England and Wales: twenty-seventh report*, BPP 1834, Vol. XXI (225), pp. 557–8; Hooper, *Norwich charities,* p. 48.

67 *Ibid.*, p. 559.

CHAPTER 6
Managing the institution

At Doughty's Hospital it was the job of the master to ensure that the rules, as set out in William Doughty's will, were followed.[68] As with all institutions housing a large number of people, there were sometimes disagreements. The first recorded instance of discord and misbehaviour among the inmates occurred in April 1700 when William Sidney Meister, a resident of the hospital, complained about the misconduct of three of his fellow almspeople.[69] The matter was brought to the Mayor's Court in May 1700 and Thomas Thurloe and Edward Hilton were both dismissed from the hospital. Although the relevant minute book does not record the precise nature of the 'several misdoings' of which the men were accused, it does mention that Mr Thurloe used 'opprobrious words' towards the mayor, which doubtless did not help his defence.[70] A third man, Daniel Wright, was also brought before the Mayor's Court, but he apologised humbly and promised to amend his conduct, and consequently was allowed to remain at the hospital.[71]

Doughty had made no provision in his will for any nursing facilities at the almshouse, and the trustees had left the sole care of the residents in the hands of the master. Because of their age, some inmates were prone to illness and when this occurred it was the responsibility of their family to care for them. For example, on 2 June 1725 an almsman named Mr Pleasant was permitted to leave the hospital and go to one of his children's homes in order that they should 'take care of him'.[72] In March 1727 the Mayor's Court recorded that there was a deficiency of care at the hospital and that 'the poor people there [were] not clothed and [were] unwell'.[73] It was resolved that the next vacancy should be reserved for a nurse and in January 1728 Katherine Day, a nurse from St Clement's Parish, was placed in the room on a wage of 4s. per week.[74]

---

68 See above, p. 31.
69 NRO, Case 16a/26, MF 630/1, 24 April 1700.
70 *Ibid.*, 4 May 1700.
71 *Ibid.*
72 NRO, Case 16a/28, MF 630/3, 2 June 1725.
73 *Ibid.*, 8 March 1727.
74 *Ibid.*, 27 January 1728.

The trustees continued to allocate one room of the hospital to a nurse, but in the 1730s, fifty years after its original conception, Doughty's was still without a qualified surgeon. This was unusual because the three other hospitals in Norwich, the Great Hospital and the Girls' and Boys' Hospitals, all had a surgeon dedicated to the relief of their sick. The Norwich Corporation Hospital Committee employed Mr Johnson, for 'surgery and physick' at the other three hospitals and in 1737 Johnson agreed to extend his practice and provide care for the inmates of Doughty's as well. His salary was £30 per annum, of which Doughty's was liable for £4.[75] This system was a success and on 1 August 1746 when Charles Maltby was elected as medical officer he was still responsible for the four hospitals at a wage of £30.

Other changes occurred in the eighteenth century that were clearly in contradiction to both the letter and the spirit of Doughty's will. In 1745 Francis Blomefield noted that the master, Nathaniel Palmer, was not a single man, 'contrary to the express will of the donor', but was married and lived with his wife in the hospital.[76] There is no mention in the Mayoral Court books of any discipline taken against Palmer as a result of this indiscretion. He held the post of master for a total of fifteen years and died in 1757, and from this it must be concluded that the trustees were aware of his marital status and chose either to embrace it, or just to ignore it.[77] By the nineteenth century masters were commonly married, and lived undisturbed in the hospital with their wives.[78] It was not only the masters, however, who flouted the specifications of William Doughty's will. In 1777 the Mayor's Court ordered that the master of the hospital should refuse to give the allowance of money and coals to those appointees who did not reside in the hospital, indicating that some beneficiaries failed to comply with the injunction to 'dwell constantly within the almshouse'.[79] It was also ordered that the master keep a book of all absences. This was designed to help prevent abuses, and to enable the trustees to discharge any inmates who failed to comply with the rules.[80]

As a hospital for the elderly in Norwich, Doughty's admitted its share of local celebrities. Blyth Hancock, a schoolmaster and mathematician, was admitted to the hospital in 1791. Hancock had

75 N/MC 2/5, Hospital Committee minute books, 2 December 1737.
76 Hooper, *Norwich charities*, p. 50.
77 NRO, Case 16a/30, MF 631/2, 9 April 1742; NRO, Case 16a/31, MF 6313, 1757.
78 1841 census: HO107/791, book 1, civil parish: St Saviour, County: Norfolk, Enumeration District: Doughty's Hospital, fo. 41, p. 2; 1851 census: HO107/1813, fo. 92, pp. 15–17; 1861 census: RG9/1212, fo. 90, pp. 27–8, RG9/1211, fo. 14, p. 23; 1871 census: RG10/1809, fo. 86, pp. 23–5; 1881 census: RG11/1939, fo. 83, pp. 27–9; 1891 census: RG12/1520, fo. 116, pp. 18–19; 1901 census: RG13/1836, fo. 51, p. 2.
79 NRO, Case 20f/14, William Doughty's Will, 25 April 1687.
80 NRO, Case 16a/34, MF 632/1, 24 December 1777.

already published two books of calculations and had earned free admission to the United Friars Society, a fraternity in Norwich which promoted science and learning. In 1788 the society had decided to admit promising candidates who might be able to further scientific and literary knowledge but whose circumstances would not allow them to pay a subscription. Hancock benefited from this new policy, and it was during his time with the society that he met Alderman John Harvey, a hospital trustee, and the man responsible for Hancock's admission to the institution. Hancock continued to write papers from Doughty's until his death there in June 1796.[81]

Another local celebrity was admitted in January 1835.[82] Elizabeth Bentley was a local poet who had published several volumes of her work. Bentley was baptised in 1767 at All Saints Church in Norwich, and in 1785 she discovered an 'inclination for verse'.[83] Her poems won the support of the United Friars Society who secured 1,500 subscribers for her first publication, *Genuine Poetical Compositions on Various Subjects*, in 1791.[84] She published a second volume of poems in 1821 and was a frequent contributor to the *Norfolk Chronicle*. Her third anthology, *Miscellaneous Poems being the Genuine Compositions of Elizabeth Bentley of Norwich*, was published in 1835, just after her admission to Doughty's Hospital.[85] She continued to write until her death there in April 1839.[86]

By 1833 Doughty's Hospital was a well-established almshouse with thirty-eight tenements. It was one of the largest almshouses in Norwich, second only to the Great Hospital in size. Along with the Boys' and Girls' Hospitals and the Great Hospital, Doughty's was run by Norwich Corporation who appointed almspeople and managed the finances of the institution. However, in 1833 a Royal Commission was established to inspect the operations of city authorities throughout the country, and this led to widespread reforms. In Norwich, the 1835 Municipal Corporations Act removed the administration of philanthropic institutions from the local Corporation and placed it in the hands of independently selected trustees, who were answerable to a panel of Charity Commissioners in London. The regulation of charity by the state had begun.[87]

---

81 Jewson, *Doughty's Hospital*, p. 10.
82 NRO, Case 16a/46, MF 634/4, Mayors Court Books, 10 January 1835.
83 D. Landry, 'Bentley, Elizabeth (bapt. 1767, d. 1839)', *Oxford dictionary of national biography* (Oxford University Press, Oxford, 2004).
84 Jewson, *Doughty's Hospital*, p. 12.
85 *Eastern Daily Press*, Saturday 13 June 2009.
86 Landry, 'Bentley, Elizabeth'.
87 *A digest of the evidence taken before two of His Majesty's Municipal Corporation Commissioners at the Guildhall in the City of Norwich on Monday 25th day of November 1833 and twenty one following days with an appendix* (Norwich, 1834); The Charitable Trusts Act, 1855 (18 and 19 Victoria cap. 124); Bailey, *Almshouses*, p. 165; Howson, *Houses of noble poverty*, p. 141.

PART III

The age of Victorian philanthropy, 1833–1908

CHAPTER 7
Social welfare in nineteenth-century England

It is a truism that the nineteenth century witnessed profound changes in England – in politics, in economy, in society and in culture – many of which were a continuation of developments set in motion in the later part of the eighteenth century. At the very heart of these changes was the Industrial Revolution, the first such revolution to occur in human history.[1] From the final third of the eighteenth century the nation witnessed unprecedented rates of industrial growth, with cotton textiles, coal and iron forming the leading sectors, but a growth that had widespread ramifications right across the industrial sector, stimulating the spread of traditional production too in a wide range of crafts and trades. It also involved a revolution in technology and in organisation, underpinned, in certain sectors at least, by the development of new machinery – most notably in the textile industry with its flying shuttles, spinning jennies, water frames, mules and power looms – the harnessing of new forms of power (especially steam power), and the rise of large-scale centralised production in the form of factories, iron works and mines.

Traditional industries expanded too alongside these more clearly revolutionary developments, particularly in the early stages of industrialisation, and hence the number of hand-loom weavers grew at the same time as the technology was being developed to eventually replace them, and this was true of a wide range of crafts and cottage industries, from shoemaking to straw plaiting. Indeed, even as late as the 1830s the retail and handicraft trades remained the leading source of employment in the country as a whole, and this is even more clearly the case if one excludes the counties of Lancashire and the West Riding

---

1   There is a huge literature. One of the best single-volume introductions is F. Crouzet, *The Victorian economy* (Methuen and Co.: London, 1982). For a more up-to-date study see R. Floud and P. Johnson (eds), *The Cambridge economic history of modern Britain. Vol. 1: industrialisation, 1700–1860* (Cambridge University Press: Cambridge, 2004).

of Yorkshire where industrial production was so heavily concentrated.[2] Furthermore, horse, wind- and water-mills provided more power in England in the early nineteenth century than did steam engines, which were heavily concentrated in the cotton industry.[3] Nevertheless, there is no doubting the profound impact of this long and complex process of industrial growth, the result of which was the gradual replacement of the 'advanced organic economy' of the late pre-industrial period by the 'energy-based mineral economy' of mature industrial England.[4] By the mid-nineteenth-century England was 'the workshop of the world', and its world dominance was amply reflected in the numerous inventions and innovations displayed at the Great Exhibition held at Crystal Palace in 1851.[5]

Alongside this industrial advance came transformations in other sectors of the economy such as agriculture, commerce, transport and finance. The early nineteenth century also saw England achieve the highest rate of population growth that had ever been seen (and was ever to be seen again), as well as a rate of urbanisation that tipped the urban–rural balance – just – in favour of towns by the time the 1851 census was taken. Fifty years later over three-quarters of the population of England and Wales lived in town rather than countryside.[6]

All of this had profound implications for the distribution of wealth and income, and for how this was divided up between the different social groups. Many merchants and traders, of course, waxed rich, and a more clearly articulated middle class emerged in towns and cities up and down the country, whose wealth and influence at least began to challenge that of the traditional landed ruling classes, and whose political rights were firmly asserted through the passage of the Great Reform Act in 1832. As for the other end of the social scale, there has been a long and tortuous academic debate about whether (or when) the benefits of industrialisation began to filter down to the working classes, a debate that has been hampered by an undue emphasis on the importance of indices of male real wages – as opposed to the more significant measure of the family wage – as well as by the difficulties involved in trying to weigh in the balance both quantitative and

---

2   E.A. Wrigley, 'Men on the land and men in the countryside: employment in agriculture in early nineteenth-century England', in L. Bonfield, R. Smith and K. Wrightson (eds), *The world we have gained. Histories of population and social structure* (Oxford University Press: Oxford, 1986), pp. 295–304.

3   A.E. Musson, 'Industrial motive power in the United Kingdom, 1800–70', *Economic History Review*, Vol. 29 (1976), pp. 415–39.

4   The terms are E.A. Wrigley's, taken from his stimulating study, *Continuity, chance and change. The character of the Industrial Revolution in England* (Cambridge University Press: Cambridge, 1988).

5   J.D. Chambers, *The workshop of the world. British economic history 1820–1880* (Oxford University Press: Oxford, 1961).

6   Crouzet, *Victorian economy*, Table 20, p. 90.

qualitative factors such as standards of health, living conditions and more amorphous aspects of the 'quality of life'. To cut a long story short, it is not until the mid-nineteenth century that there is clear evidence of general improvement.

Before then the fortunes of workers in different sectors, different industries and different parts of the country were diverse. We have already seen that in the late eighteenth century, as the Norwich textile industry increasingly faced competition from the West Riding of Yorkshire and failed to adopt new methods of production, its long decline had begun, producing more precarious employment and downward pressure on wages. The archetypal victims of the Industrial Revolution were, however, the hand-loom weavers in the cotton industry in the north, for these had multiplied in considerable numbers in the years 1780–1820 due to an imbalance in spinning and weaving technology in the industry, only to be replaced in their turn by machine production, which rapidly reduced the piece rates they could command and brought them into a state of immiseration, of which there is such ample testimony by the 1830s.[7]

Another (very large) group experiencing difficulties by the early nineteenth century was the agricultural labour force of the arable counties of south and east England.[8] Rural population growth in the second half of the eighteenth century, partly due to declining mortality but mainly the product of rising fertility, had increased their number and the average size of their families. Alongside this growth of the rural population, enclosure of the open fields may have led to some withdrawal of access to common rights that had previously been customarily enjoyed, while the decline of hand spinning also had serious implications for female employment and hence for family incomes. Southern agricultural labourers' real wages (that is, wages compared with prices) were probably already falling by the end of the eighteenth century and this, allied to the seasonality of agricultural employment and the loss of other sources of income, was already causing distress, which is reflected in the rising tide of poor relief payments that were necessary by the end of that century.[9] Some relief was produced by the abnormal condition of the French Wars, but with the end of war in 1815 the situation in many agricultural counties – especially on the heavier clay soils – became dire, as wartime overproduction and a spate of good harvests sent prices plummeting, and hence threatened

---

7   D. Bythell, *The sweated trades. Outwork in nineteenth-century Britain* (Batsford: London, 1978), pp. 36–48.

8   A. Armstrong, *Farmworkers in England and Wales. A social and economic history 1770–1980* (Batsford: London, 1988), pp. 30–43.

9   Slack, *English poor law*, pp. 29–34.

employment at a time when the rural population was still rising and returning troops reinforced the numbers in the countryside. Albeit with local and regional variations, rural distress reached new depths, the pressure on the poor rate intensified, and social relationships in the countryside were strained to breaking point.[10]

The New Poor Law

These difficulties provide the context for the introduction of the new system of poor relief, shaped by the Royal Commission on the Poor Laws which was convened in 1832 and enshrined in the Poor Law Amendment Act of 1834. Despite increasing provision for relief in the workhouse in the eighteenth century, outdoor relief – payment to families or individuals in their own homes for them to spend as they pleased – remained by far the dominant form of relief at the end of that century, with only 8 per cent of the one million recorded paupers in 1802–3 residing in workhouses. As the burden of the poor rate upon farmers and landowners grew further in the early nineteenth century, the cries for a complete reform of the system grew ever louder. These cries were reinforced by new ideas in political economy, which taught that the market was paramount, and free private initiative and vigorous competition would result in improvement to the general welfare of all. State intervention, therefore, was to be minimised. At the same time the influential Reverend Thomas Malthus argued that the poor laws encouraged excessive breeding and early marriage by providing support to labourers with large families, and thus undermined the prudential restraint that he saw as a necessary check to population growth. Malthus would have done away with the system of poor relief altogether, but this would have been anathema to another contemporary intellectual current – that of utilitarianism. Utilitarianism was a system of moral philosophy developed by Jeremy Bentham, which advocated pursuit of the 'greatest happiness of the greatest number', and recognised that the state had a role in the achievement of this through the development of appropriate social policies. Edwin Chadwick, a follower of Bentham, was one of the key figures behind the development of the New Poor Law, and drafted the Report of 1834 upon which it was based.[11]

Under the New Poor Law only the indigent were to be given outdoor relief: those who were sick, old, orphaned and so forth were therefore to be granted relief on the old terms. The independent able-bodied poor, however – and this meant essentially able-bodied men

---

10 Armstrong, *Farmworkers*, pp. 61–78.
11 A. Kidd, *State, society and the poor in nineteenth-century England* (Macmillan: Basingstoke, 1999), pp. 13–24; D. Englander, *Poverty and poor law reform in 19th century Britain, 1834–1914* (Longman: London, 1998), pp. 3–13.

– were to be discouraged from dependency and hence 'pauperism' at all costs. Under no circumstances were they to be granted outdoor relief, but were only to be relieved in the workhouse, where conditions were to be harsh and regimented, and hence only the truly indigent would wish to enter them. This was the principle of 'less eligibility': the situation of the able-bodied pauper was to be rendered less eligible than that of the poorest independent labourer. And it was underpinned by the notion that poverty, to quote from the report, arose from 'fraud, indolence or improvidence': it was a voluntary, and therefore eminently reversible, condition.

To achieve these ends, the Poor Law Amendment Act of 1834 required the establishment of unions of parishes, each of which was to build its own large workhouse. Local control was to be in the hands of Boards of Guardians, elected on a restricted property franchise, and these were in turn responsible to a three-man Poor Law Commission. The system was to be a national one, uniform and centralised. It required the redeployment of resources on a large scale to build the necessary workhouses, and represented the culmination of a period of over thirty years in which basic notions of poverty were redefined, to emphasise once again the culpability of the poor, unless they were by some means disabled. It signalled the withdrawal of paternalism, and its key aim was to reduce dependency in general, and the burden of the poor rate in particular. In this respect it was very successful. From a national total of £8.6 million in 1831–2, by the mid-1840s poor relief expenditure had fallen to around £5 million, and stabilised at between £5 million and £6 million for the next twenty years. This was achieved despite the fact that the national population of Great Britain grew from about 16 million in 1831, to 26 million in 1871, indicating a significant per capita decline in poor law expenditure in the 30–40 years following the introduction of the New Poor Law.[12]

Victorian philanthropy

The New Poor Law represents the harsh face of nineteenth–century social welfare, even if its impact was often moderated in practice, either through formal policy or through the difficulties of local implementation, while its effects were also moderated by rising working-class living standards in the second half of the nineteenth century. But one of its central tenets – the need to render the poor more self-reliant – also formed a thread running through private philanthropy. The ideology of self-help, which laid the blame for poverty squarely on the shoulders of the poor, underpinned both the New Poor Law and the rise of

12 Kidd, *State, society and the poor*, pp. 24–44; Englander, *Poverty and poor law reform*, pp. 13–19.

philanthropy, and its roots lay in the evangelical revival which began in the late eighteenth century. Evangelical religion, alongside its bedfellow Christian economics, stressed that salvation, either religious or material, could only result from individual effort – via one's personal relationship with God in the case of religion, or through one's own personal efforts in the material realm. To the evangelical Christian the two were inseparable, for bringing the poor to salvation was both a religious and a moral quest at one and the same time. Charitable effort, therefore, as long as it was well-directed, constructive and discriminating, would produce social amelioration. The very same charitable effort, of course, would also increase the store of virtue of the philanthropist, and thus charity was as much about saving the souls of the rich as it was about redeeming the physical and spiritual condition of the poor.[13]

This, at least, was the underlying philosophy of many of the formal charitable organisations of the nineteenth century, ranging from the graphically named Bath Society for the Suppression of Common Vagrants and Impostors, Relief of Occasional Distress, and Encouragement of Industry, founded in 1805, or the better known and more powerful Society for Organising Charitable Relief and Repressing Mendicity (the COS) founded in 1869. But there was another face to the evangelical movement too, for if on the one hand it promoted self-help, it could also play a leading role in the crusade that led to the abolition of slavery.[14] Furthermore, it is difficult to deny the place of humanitarianism in the enormous panoply of Victorian philanthropy, a humanitarianism that spawned the regulation of child and female labour, the amelioration of working conditions in factories, mines and workshops and the enormous expansion of medical charities – the greatest absorber of nineteenth-century relief funds – that spawned 385 general hospitals, and a host of more specialised institutions, by 1891. Motives may often have been mixed, but they were various too, ranging from the desire to evangelise the poor, to impose social control and to ensure both personal salvation and self-aggrandisement at one end of the spectrum, to the selfless desire for improvement, the exercise of social responsibility and the expression of compassion and sympathy for those less fortunate at the other.[15] The growing visibility of poverty in expanding urban centres, which, as we will see, included Norwich, was another factor that contributed to the mix. Regardless of its intellectual or moral roots, the Victorian

---

13 Kidd, *State, society and the poor*, pp. 70–4.
14 Owen, *English philanthropy*, pp. 124–5.
15 A valuable summary of the various theories that have been deployed to explain philanthropy can be found in M. Gorsky, *Patterns of philanthropy. Charity and society in nineteenth-century Bristol* (The Boydell Press: Woodbridge, 1999), pp. 1–12.

era, according to one historian, was the 'age of charitable societies'.[16] As a Victorian statesman, Charles Greville, was to write, 'We are just now overrun with philanthropy, and God knows where it will stop, or whither it will lead us'.[17] For 'if the first half of the nineteenth century saw philanthropy ascendant, the second half witnessed its triumph'.[18] As the social surveys of the later nineteenth century were to show so graphically, the Victorians may have been wrong to prioritise private philanthropy over state aid as the solution to society's ills, but they had a most impressive stab at proving the point nonetheless.

---

16   F.K. Prochaska, *Philanthropy and the hospitals of London: The King's Fund 1897–1990* (Clarendon Press: Oxford, 1992), p. 1.
17   Quoted in Owen, *English philanthropy*, p. 89.
18   F.K. Prochaska, *The voluntary impulse. Philanthropy in modern Britain* (Faber and Faber: London, 1988), p. 41.

CHAPTER 8
Philanthropy in Victorian Norwich

The late eighteenth-century stagnation of Norwich's population continued into the early nineteenth century, the census of 1811 recording just under 39,000 inhabitants. Thereafter rapid growth was resumed, to produce a total of over 62,000 by 1831 which, after a short pause, then climbed more steadily, to 88,000 in 1881 and 112,000 by the turn of the century.[19] Norwich remained roughly double the size of Great Yarmouth, its nearest urban rival in the county, throughout the nineteenth century, while the stagnation of King's Lynn after 1851 left the town trailing in Norwich's wake.[20]

The textile industry which, as we have seen, had thrived in Norwich during the seventeenth and eighteenth centuries, had started to falter towards the end of the eighteenth century and to decline in the nineteenth. The problems of competition from the West Riding of Yorkshire and failure to innovate were compounded by the dislocation of European markets during the French Wars (1793–1815), which did incalculable damage. Temporary recovery thereafter was followed by a protracted recession from 1825 to 1837, by which time the weavers of Norwich were succumbing to the fate that had already befallen hand-loom weavers in other parts of the country. By the time Norwich was able to introduce steam power to textile production in the city, with the aid of the railways in the 1840s and 1850s, it was too late to revive the declining industry. The wages of many hand-loom weavers were driven down in order to cut costs in the 1830s and 1840s, as a result of which expenditure on poor relief rose from £21,822 in 1825 to £30,318 by 1845.[21]

---

19 Armstrong, 'Population', Table 10.1. p. 245; *idem, The population of Victorian and Edwardian Norfolk* (University of East Anglia: Norwich, 2000), Table 1.2, p. 7. In the first of these publications Armstrong applies small correction factors to census totals to allow for probable under-registration.

20 Armstrong, *Population of Victorian and Edwardian Norfolk*, Table 1.2, p. 7.

21 Wilson, 'The textile industry', pp. 230–41; C. Clark, 'Work and employment', in Rawcliffe and Wilson (eds), *Norwich since 1550*, pp. 385–8; M.F. Lloyd Prichard, 'The decline of Norwich', *Economic History Review*, Vol. 3 (1950–1), p. 371.

The decline of the textile industry in Norwich was, however, compensated by the growth of other industries, such as boot and shoemaking, printing, iron-founding, starch and mustard production and brewing.[22] Shoemaking was the most important of these in providing alternative employment to textiles, with 2,753 male and 2,285 female employees recorded as working in the trade in the census of 1851, numbers that were already beginning to rival those in the textile industry: a decade later, shoemaking had pulled significantly ahead, while the textile industry continued its headlong fall.[23] Notable too were the various food and drink trades, a particular feature of which in the second half of the century was the manufacture of mustard. Colman's Carrow Works opened in 1852, and 2,300 workers were employed there by the end of the century.[24] It was these new industries, coupled with the growth of the city's commercial and service sectors, that led to such brisk expansion, to produce an overall population increase of 77 per cent in the first half of the century and a further increase of 64 per cent in the second.[25] By now, of course, Norwich had fallen far behind the great industrial and commercial towns of the Midlands and the north, such as Birmingham with its 437,000 inhabitants in 1881, or Manchester with 462,000 and Liverpool with 627,000, and did not even rank among the top twenty-five towns and cities in the country.[26] It remained a city of considerable wealth and vitality nevertheless, with a well-developed middle class quite willing and able to play their part in the great enterprise that constituted Victorian philanthropy.

One of the more notable philanthropists was Caroline Colman, wife of Jeremiah Colman who owned the eponymous mustard manufacturing business and also represented Norwich as its Liberal member of parliament. Caroline Colman epitomised the blend of religious inspiration, paternalism and desire to effect moral improvement upon the working classes that runs through so much Victorian philanthropy, and her activities can be compared with the Cadbury's chocolate company at Birmingham, in terms of both intent and in the range of initiatives she introduced.[27] Hence she initiated various schools – technical classes for men, and sewing and cooking classes for women – clearly reflecting a stark gender stereotyping that was also apparent at Cadbury's, while her Sunday School brought children

---

22 J.K. Edwards, 'The industrial development of the city 1800–1900', in C. Barringer, *Norwich in the nineteenth century* (Gliddon Books: Norwich, 1984), p. 152; Clark, 'Work and employment'.

23 Clark, 'Work and employment', Tables 16.1 and 16.2, pp. 390–1.

24 *Ibid.*; Rawcliffe and Wilson (eds), *Norwich since 1550*, plate 57, between pages 450 and 451.

25 Calculated from Armstrong, *Population of Victorian and Edwardian Norfolk*, Table 1.2, p. 7.

26 G. Best, *Mid-Victorian Britain 1851–75* (revised edition, Granada Publishing Ltd: St Albans, 1973), p. 29.

27 For Cadbury's see S.O. Rose, *Limited livelihoods. Gender and class in nineteenth-century England* (University of California Press: Berkeley and Los Angeles, 2002), pp. 37–45.

into the fold at an early age as well as generating funds that were used for a variety of other charitable purposes, including support of the local hospital. She also hired sick nurses and visitors for the employees at the Carrow Works, distributed hampers at Christmas, established a home for girls, a lending library, a milk scheme for children, a medical club, mothers' meetings, a clothing club with 900 members and a sick benefit society which provided relief in times of ill health for 500. Her aim was to 'raise the moral as well as the commercial standing of the firm', and hence – like the model villages built for their workforce by Titus Salt at Saltaire or Lord Leverhulme at Port Sunlight – her activities might be described in terms of 'enlightened self-interest'. The complaint of Caroline Colman that, despite all of the above initiatives, a household to run and six children to raise, she just did not have enough time to spend on her charitable activities might suggest that, in her case, enlightenment came a clear first and self-interest a poor second. Indeed, many of her charities survived to provide long-term benefits to individuals and charities in Norwich, including Doughty's itself, which benefited from a £1,000 gift from the Colman House Trust in September 1955.[28]

Charities for the relief of medical complaints received much wider support in the nineteenth century than hitherto and, because of further advances in medical care and techniques, specialist infirmaries were established for the relief of particular illnesses. In Norwich Thomas Tawell established a home for the indigent blind in Magdalen Street in 1805, and the institution was both a school for blind children and a home for the elderly blind.[29] The Norwich Eye Infirmary opened on Pottergate in 1822 and offered to treat those who were unable to pay for care, providing they had a subscriber to nominate them.[30] The infirmary was founded by Lewis Evans and Robert Hull, local physicians, and Thomas Martineau, a Norwich surgeon. A subscription of one guinea a year entitled the subscriber to recommend one in-patient and seven out-patients, while half a guinea entitled the subscriber to nominate four out-patients.[31] Norwich also gained a specialist children's infirmary in 1854 as a result of several fund-raising concerts given by the Swedish singer Jenny Lind. The hospital was named the Jenny Lind Infirmary in her honour and started with just twelve beds at a house in Pottergate. In the first six months the hospital admitted 30 in-patients and 113 out-patients and by the 1860s was treating 500 sick children annually.[32]

---

28 Prochaska, *Philanthropy*, pp. 372–3; L.E. Stuart, *In memoriam Caroline Colman* (Norwich, 1896); Owen, *English philanthropy*, pp. 381–3; and see below, Part IV, p. 131.
29 Cherry, 'Medical care', p. 273.
30 *Ibid.*, p. 279.
31 Hooper, *Norwich charities*, p. 171.
32 Cherry, 'Medical care', p. 279.

Like the Norfolk and Norwich Hospital, the Jenny Lind Infirmary was funded by subscription.[33]

The Jenny Lind Infirmary was not the only charity in Norwich to raise funds through concerts and performances. The Norfolk and Norwich Hospital, which was originally built by subscription in 1771, was the recipient of the money raised by the first Norfolk and Norwich Triennial Music Festival in 1824. In the first year the festival generated £2,399 4s. 10d., and between 1824 and 1864 over £6,000 was raised for the institution. By 1843, the Norfolk and Norwich Hospital had catered for 1,555 patients, 758 of whom were in-patients.[34] The hospital was enlarged in 1883 at a cost of £57,112. This was paid for by donations and subscriptions and it received a good deal of patronage from wealthy benefactors, such as the Earl of Leicester who gave £15,000 towards the extensions.[35]

The nineteenth century also saw the establishment of numerous smaller visiting charities, which usually involved groups of ladies who attended the poor and the sick and offered them relief in their own homes.[36] In Norwich, the Society for the Relief of the Sick Poor was established in 1816 and a committee of ladies took turns to visit the poor and provide them with relief in the form of money or food. Funding for this project was raised by subscription and also through the sale of 'fancy items' by the women.[37] The Norwich Magdalen was established in 1827, its aim to '[afford] asylum to females who, having deviated from the path of virtue, may be desirous of being restored to their station in society, by religious instruction and the formation of moral and industrious habits'.[38] Rather than focusing on past indiscretions, as did some of its counterparts elsewhere in the country, the charity sought to reform wayward women through study and prepare them for useful work in domestic service.[39]

The two homes for poor children, Thomas Anguish's Boys' Hospital and the Girls' Hospital endowed by Robert Baron, continued to provide relief for poor and orphaned children in Norwich in the nineteenth century. The Girls' Hospital became more like a boarding school in the 1800s, and after 1802 the girls were maintained by friends and family at a cost of £8 per year. That said, the number of girls the hospital was able to accommodate increased: whereas there were twenty-four

33   Hooper, *Norwich charities*, p. 165.
34   White, *White's Norfolk directory*, p. 131. It was originally built on three acres of land leased to it by the Great Hospital for £6 per annum: Jewson, *History of the Great Hospital*, p. 35.
35   Hooper, *Norwich charities*, p. 145.
36   Kidd, *State, society and the poor*, p. 84.
37   White, *White's Norfolk directory*, p. 132.
38   *Ibid.*
39   Hooper, *Norwich charities*, pp. 199, 202.

girls at the hospital in 1802, the charity looked after thirty-two by 1807 and by 1824 there were forty-four girls living at the school.[40] In September 1862 the Charity Commissioners sanctioned a scheme for the establishment of an industrial school for girls in place of the Girls' Hospital. Forty girls aged 9–11 entered the institution when it opened on Hospital Lane in Lakenham in 1864.[41] Anguish's Boys' Hospital was similarly popular in the nineteenth century and by 1835 there were sixty-one boys living on the premises, their uniform of a blue jacket and a red cap earning it the nickname 'Red Cap School'.[42]

For the almshouses of the city, the nineteenth century was a period of growth and expansion. After a period of difficulty during the Napoleonic Wars during which it raised money by selling the lead from its roofs, rising income from its Norwich properties allowed the Great Hospital to indulge in a considerable building programme. New wards were constructed in 1820, 1822 and 1829, while in 1826 twenty cottages were added, most of which were purpose built for occupation by married couples. In 1850 another new ward was built at a cost of £1,100. The extension of the hospital allowed the trustees to admit more residents and the 98 almspeople that the institution held in 1800 increased to 129 in 1823 and 166 in 1830, while by 1843 the hospital had 181 residents, 93 men and 88 women.[43] Still it expanded. In 1849 five more cottages were erected, another nine in 1860, a sick ward was added in 1889, and twelve more cottages were erected in 1906.[44] The Great Hospital was much larger than any other almshouse in Norwich, and while Doughty's Hospital had just one nurse and one master in the mid-nineteenth century, the Great Hospital was able to support a master and ten nurses.[45] This was probably a consequence of the enormous amount of property the Great Hospital owned, both in Norwich and in rural Norfolk. In the late nineteenth century the average annual rent of the lands belonging to the hospital was estimated at £7,500, and by the end of the century the number of residents housed there was over 200, with 202 almspeople living on the site in 1898.[46]

The total sum devoted to philanthropy in Victorian Norwich is impossible to estimate, simply because many of the voluntary, subscription or associated charities did not leave records. This is true even of the more formal charities of this kind, while it is more impossible still to quantify the monetary value of less formal

40   *Ibid.*, p. 67.
41   *Ibid.*, p. 69.
42   *Ibid.*, pp. 67–8.
43   White, *White's Norfolk directory*, p. 135; Jewson, *Great Hospital*, p. 36.
44   *Ibid.*, p. 40.
45   White, *White's Norfolk directory*, p. 135.
46   Cherry, 'Medical care', p. 272; Hooper, *Norwich charities*, p. 39.

activity, such as the numerous visits made by many small societies and individuals to the homes of the poor. But while the nineteenth century saw the continued growth of charities of this kind, it also witnessed the development and continued growth of endowed charities, whether that endowment was made by will or by deed of trust, and this is a feature of nineteenth-century philanthropy that is rarely given its due credit.[47] From 1861 the Charity Commission started to compile digests of endowed charities, continuing this work through to 1876, and publishing the results of this exercise for every county in England and Wales in House of Commons' reports between 1867 and 1876.[48] The survey for the county of Norfolk, conducted in 1862–4, revealed a total gross annual income from endowed charities of £50,487 13s. 11d., and expenditure per capita of the population of £0.12, placing it in joint sixth place among the fifty-four counties of England and Wales, and substantially above the county average for England and Wales of £0.07.[49] The total gross annual income for the City of Norwich from endowed charities was £20,047 7s. 9d., fully 40 per cent of the total for the county of Norfolk, and amounting to £0.23 per head of the population of the city as recorded in the 1861 census – almost double the per capita figure for the county as a whole.[50]

---

47 For an echo of this view and some evidence for the city of Bristol see Gorsky, *Patterns of philanthropy*, pp. 39–62.

48 The reports, too numerous to list here, can be found among the British Parliamentary Papers. A major project to analyse these documents and produce an historical geography of endowed charity is currently underway at the University of Hertfordshire.

49 These calculations are based on detailed analysis of all the published digests allied to the 1861 and 1871 censuses to establish population totals and thus per capita incomes. London is excluded, and the three Ridings of Yorkshire are counted independently. These numbers are calculated as percentages of a pound, and are thus equivalent of pence.

50 Calculations from *Endowed charities. Copies of the general digest of endowed charities for the counties and cities mentioned in the fourteenth report of the Charity Commissioners*, BPP 1867–8, Vol. LII, Pt. II (c.433). Fully £16,772 3s. 10d. of this total was managed by the Corporation.

CHAPTER 9

Doughty's Hospital and the rise of state regulation

The reform of municipal corporations

A Royal Commission was launched in 1833 to enquire into the running of city authorities throughout the country. In November 1833 two of His Majesty's Municipal Corporation Commissioners visited Norwich to inspect the operations of local government. The commissioners found that the responsibility for the appointment of inmates to the four main almshouses fell to the aldermen of the city through a process of rotational nomination, and concerns were raised that this process was being exploited by some aldermen for political gain.[51]

One witness who spoke to the Commissioners during their inspections was Mr John Francis, a prominent manufacturer in the city. He claimed that the Corporation engaged 'in every species of bribery and strife' and that its patronage was 'invariably exercised in favour of political adherents'.[52] When asked if he himself had ever engaged in bribery, Mr Francis admitted to 'buying a bunch of four [men] in the market for £8 at the late election of the Freeman's Sheriff', and also offering £5 to a man for his vote. These confessions added weight to Mr Francis' earlier statement that bribery was rife in the city.[53] Another witness, Mr A. Barnard, had testified that he knew several instances of aldermen exchanging places in the hospitals in return for votes, a process known as giving 'hospital notes'. Although he was reluctant to give the names of the aldermen in question, he did identify them as Whigs, which perhaps says more about his own political leanings than about the corruption of any one particular party.[54] Mr William Wilde, a Corporation clerk, also testified that hospital notes were often

---

51 *A digest of the evidence taken before two of His Majesty's Municipal Corporation Commissioners at the Guildhall in the City of Norwich on Monday 25th day of November 1833 and twenty one following days with an appendix* (Matchett and Co: Norwich, 1834), pp. 170–1.
52 *Ibid.*, p. 170.
53 *Ibid.*, p. 170.
54 *Ibid.*, p. 171.

written to freemen to ensure their vote, and that he had written notes on behalf of more than one alderman. He remembered a specific note given to a Mr Burrage promising 4s. per week until his aunt was able to be admitted to one of Norwich's hospitals.[55] The Commissioners also heard evidence from serving aldermen. Alderman Springfield argued that although hospital notes were legitimate as a means of negotiating almshouse appointments, they were also frequently given in exchange for votes.[56]

The Commissioners were keen to remove such practices, and in their summary report stated that the instances described were enough to 'illustrate the character of abuses' and prove that the 'object of the trust has been lost sight of'.[57] As a result of similar country-wide abuses, the Municipal Corporations Act was passed in 1835. This Act made all charities answerable to the Lord Chancellor, and the administration of Doughty's Hospital passed from the hands of the Corporation into those of an independent body of trustees, appointed by the Lord Chancellor, known as the General List trustees.[58]

As a result of fractious rivalries between the governing parties in Norwich, and the belief that the composition of one group of trustees might favour one or other political party, two separate administrative bodies were established to deal with charities in the city in 1837.[59] The Church List dealt with charities that had a religious background, like the Great Hospital, while all other charities, including Doughty's Hospital, were placed under the General List.[60] The Lord Chancellor appointed a body of fifteen trustees for each group, with seven representatives from the city council and eight co-opted trustees.[61] But hostile political factions were not the only reason why two separate administrative bodies were established: it was also a question of the sheer number of charities in the city. The General List was responsible for the administration of half of Norwich's charities and this responsibility extended to five almshouses, fifteen large loans charities and twenty-five smaller loans charities, which had all previously been administered by Norwich Corporation.[62]

---

55 *Ibid.*, p. 172.
56 *Ibid.*, p. 179.
57 *First report of the Commissioners appointed to inquire into the Municipal Corporations in England and Wales.* House of Commons papers; reports of commissioners (c.116). BPP 1835, Vol. XXIII.1, p. 48.
58 NRO, N/CCH/109, 16 February 1837.
59 Jewson, *Doughty's Hospital*, p. 13.
60 Meeres, *History of Norwich*, p. 169.
61 A.C. Kay and H.V. Toynbee, *The endowed and voluntary charities of Norwich: extract from appendix to volume XV of the report to the Royal Commission* (Norwich Charity Organisation: Norwich, 1909), p. 24.
62 NRO, ACC 2008 52, pp. 1–2.

The reform of endowed charities

The drive towards regulation of the nation's charitable trusts pre-dates the activities of the Municipal Corporation Commissioners. Indeed, the *Abstract of the returns of charitable donations for the benefit of poor persons 1786–88*, commonly known as the 'Gilbert Return', was of enough interest to be reprinted in 1810 and again in 1816, and although it was flawed in its coverage it did give some indication of the substantial annual income available for charitable uses, amounting annually to £258,710 19s. 3d. in England and Wales as a whole.[63] It also revealed the jungle that constituted the endowed charity sector, where some trusts were archaic, others socially harmful, some 'lost', and all lacking in proper administrative supervision. Redress of abuses could only be had through proceedings in Chancery, by way of application to the Attorney General, and this process was not only tortuous, but could also prove to be prohibitively expensive, on occasion devouring a charity's entire endowment. The Charitable Donation Registration Act of 1812, which required the listing of endowments, was all too often ignored, and the Charities Procedure Act, also of 1812, provided a 'summary remedy', but one that was interpreted according to the lights of the Court of Chancery itself. Into the fray stepped the utilitarians, led by Henry Brougham. Primarily interested in forwarding the cause of educational reform, he and his supporters persuaded parliament to authorise a commission of enquiry, which was at first restricted to educational charities only, but was extended in 1819 to include non-educational charities. Through the activities of this commission, between 1819 and 1840 nearly 30,000 endowed charities were enquired into, on a parish by parish basis, and the results published in successive reports in the British Parliamentary Papers, to produce a veritable 'Domesday Book' of endowed charity.[64]

The Charity Commissioners conducted a rigorous inspection of the affairs of Doughty's Hospital, which seems to have met with general approval, although it did not receive an entirely clean bill of health. They closely scrutinised the various indentures and deeds dating back to 1704 by which the trust had acquired property, and could find little to complain of. The fact that members of the Corporation were from time to time admitted as tenants to the trust's copyhold lands in Burston was noted, but without objection. The exchange in 1831 between the Corporation and the Earl of Orford of the Manor of Calthorpe for eight closes in Gissing was also recorded, but although it was remarked that 'the Corporation had at that time no authority

---

63 *Abstract of the returns of charitable donations for the benefit of poor persons 1786–88*, BPP 1816, Vol. XVI, A.1, p. iv.
64 Owen, *English philanthropy*, pp. 182–91.

to alienate the premises', the Commissioners added that this exchange 'does not seem to have been otherwise than beneficial to the charity', and hence they rested content. The fact that the enhancement of the master's salary out of the gift of Thomas Cooke was 'contrary to the express directions of the donor' is simply recorded, but again without further comment or criticism. The rental income from trust lands, plus interest, annuities and stocks, is fully described, and the Commissioners noted that the accounts for the three years 1829/30–1831/2 showed in each case a surplus of over £1,000 in the hands of the treasurer. The lands are reported to have been 'let at their full value', with the exception of the farm at Cringleford, one-third of which was held by Doughty's, and two-thirds by the Great Hospital.[65] In the section of the report relating to the Great Hospital, this is explained as a product of the fact that the Corporation nominated to the curacy of Cringleford, but instead of receiving a stipend the curate was allowed the rectorial tithes at a nominal rent. Although the Commissioners questioned to what extent the powers of the Corporation should allow them to increase the stipends of the various incumbents supported by the almshouse charities, in the great majority of instances (Cringleford included) they felt that the Corporation's discretion 'seems to have been well exercised up to the present time'.[66] The Commissioners also approved the manner in which the various articles of clothing allowed to the almspeople, as well as the annual allowance of coal, were only purchased after careful comparison of various tenders delivered by different tradesmen, a policy introduced, as we have seen, in 1789.[67]

There were, however, two issues that concerned the Commissioners, the first of which they found particularly objectionable. Colonel John Harvey, an alderman of Norwich, had served as treasurer for both Doughty's and the Great Hospital since 1821. His practice had been to receive the various rents of the two almshouse's properties from the surveyor, and pay them into his own private Norwich bank account. That bank paid interest on these sums at the rate of 2 or 2.5 per cent, and this profit accrued entirely to Colonel Harvey. The Commissioners calculated from the balances held in the last five years that this would have amounted to about £26 on average each year, and Harvey admitted that before the recent increase in the number of almspeople the balances were considerably larger. The judgement of the Commissioners reads as follows:

---

65   NRO, N/TC 63/2: *Commissioners of inquiry into charities in England and Wales: twenty-seventh report*, BPP 1834, Vol. XXI (225), p. 559.
66   *Ibid.*, p. 529.
67   *Ibid.*, p. 559; and see above, Part II, p. 41.

At the present time the amount of the interest cannot be considered more than sufficient to pay a clerk to keep the accounts, and the treasurer receives no other remuneration for his troubles, or the expense of a clerk. This appears, however, to be an objectionable mode of giving the treasurer any remuneration, particularly as the amount might be greatly increased by deferring the payment of the tradesmen's bills to the end of the year … It is also objectionable on the ground that the interest may be at periods more than a sufficient remuneration, (though at other times it may fall short) and that no person auditing the accounts can ascertain the amount.[68]

The Commissioners recommended that the Corporation give their attention to this issue, for in their opinion 'this system ought to be immediately abolished'.[69]

Another matter of concern to the Commissioners was the large balances Doughty's was holding, a considerable proportion of which, they felt, ought to be invested. No additional comforts were required by the almspeople, except perhaps for a larger allowance of coal, while the trust's income appeared perfectly sufficient to support the present establishment. Furthermore, in the longer term, the Commissioners suggested, thought should be given by the trustees to the possible expansion of the hospital to allow it to support a larger number of residents.

Both of these issues received further notice in a supplementary report, submitted with the Commissioners' report on the county of Norfolk, published in the following year.[70] On the issue of the balances held which were currently paid into the treasurer's private bank account, the Commissioners had recommended that a dedicated bank account should be opened into which these funds should be paid, and any interest accruing should be applied to the benefit of the charities themselves. The treasurer, instead of receiving interest on these balances, should be paid a stipend sufficient to pay any clerk or assistant that he needed to employ. The response of the trustees to this suggestion is recorded in the report, which simply notes: 'Not adopted by the Court of Assembly, being satisfied that the alteration would be injurious to the charities; the balances in hand being now so small, the banker's interest would be insufficient to pay the accountant'.[71] With regard to

---

68 *Ibid.*, p. 521.
69 *Ibid.*, p. 59.
70 *Commissioners of inquiry into charities in England and Wales: twenty-ninth report*, BPP 1835, Vol. XXI (216), pp. 880–2.
71 *Ibid.*, p. 880.

the excessive balances being held by Doughty's, the Commissioners had recommended the investment of an additional £280 in 3 per cent reduced annuities, to raise the total held in that stock to £1,700, drawing back from suggesting a larger sum in view of a barn and other buildings currently being erected at the trust's farm at Hillingdon. The response to this suggestion was equally negative: 'Resolved by the Court of Assembly, that, in consequence of new farm buildings being necessary, no part of the balance should at present be invested'.[72] While one might harbour suspicions that these two decisions were connected, there is one fact that is perfectly clear: the Brougham Commission lacked teeth, and the Corporation of Norwich knew it.

It was not until several years later that the trustees of Doughty's Hospital acted on the second of these proposals, and carried out some modest expansion of the number of units available to house almspeople. In 1843 two more rooms were added, specifically for women, to make a total of forty tenements.[73] Four years later, in 1847, another two tenements were added and occupied by women, to bring the total available to forty-two.[74] As will be discussed in more detail later, from the 1840s onwards the gender balance in the almshouse shifted away from that laid down by William Doughty, to include increasing numbers of female residents, until by the early twentieth century they came to form a clear majority of appointed almsfolk.[75]

It was also many years before the more general recommendations of the Brougham inquiry received serious parliamentary attention. The Commission had unearthed many irregularities in the course of its enquiries – some venal, some incompetent, some merely archaic. Its key recommendation was to establish a permanent board with supervisory powers over the nation's endowed charities, mainly administrative but armed too with some of the judicial functions of Chancery, and promising more expeditious and economical resolution of anomalies. It was a further thirteen years after the publication of the last part of the Commission's final report before the Charitable Trusts Act was passed in 1853.

In the meantime periodic scandals pointed up the need for greater supervision of charitable endowments. In one of the more famous cases, the Reverend Francis North (later Earl of Guildford), master of the St Cross Hospital in Winchester, was accused in 1843 by the *Hants Independent* of embezzling up to £10,000 of the charity's funds. Following an extended Chancery enquiry inaugurated in 1849, North

72 *Ibid.*
73 NRO, N/CCH 109: General List Minute Book, 1837–47, 3 October 1843.
74 *Ibid.*, 28 April 1847.
75 See below, pp. 88–90.

was eventually allowed to resign in 1855 under a cloud of scandal, but was required to repay a mere £4,000 out of an estimated income he had received from the charity during his forty-seven years as master of anything from £45,000 to £305,700. This high-profile case was one of the factors that inspired parliament finally to pass the Charitable Trusts Act in 1853, reinforced by the amending Act of 1855.[76]

The Charitable Trusts Act was a moderate piece of legislation, however, for although it established a permanent and paid Commission, its powers were mainly inquisitorial rather than executive. They could examine trusts' affairs, and trustees were obliged to submit annual accounts, but beyond that they possessed no real power to effect change, except by exposure. Provision was made for the voluntary transfer of a trust's funds to the Commission, at no cost, for the purposes of safe-keeping and investment, and in the long run this proved to be of great benefit. But the Commissioners lacked the authority even to appoint new trustees. Revision of the use of an endowment, even if it conformed to the doctrine of *cy-près* – which allowed for variation of a trust as long as it remained as close as possible to the testator's original intentions – still required recourse to Chancery, while more sweeping reorganisation required an Act of parliament. It was not until the passage of a further Charitable Trust Act in 1860 that the Commission gained any real authority, for this Act gave the Commissioners the powers that hitherto had only been held by the courts: to appoint and expel trustees, authorise financial transactions and to establish new schemes. This last power – clearly the most crucial – was, however, limited to charities with an annual income of £50 or less, and while this captured some 80 per cent of them, it left a large proportion of total charitable funds out of their immediate jurisdiction. For charities with an annual income of over £50, the making of a new scheme required the agreement of a majority of the trustees.[77]

During the 1870s and 1880s there was no real increase in the Commission's powers. But despite this, and although it was also badly under-staffed, during the 1870s it issued approximately 400 orders per year for the appointment of trustees or the establishment of schemes, and in order to ensure it had a comprehensive record of extant endowed charities set about compiling the county by county digest

---

76 P. Hopewell, *Saint Cross. England's oldest almshouse* (Phillimore: Chichester, 1995), pp. 102–16; Owen, *English philanthropy*, pp. 196, 202, 205; Bailey, *Almshouses*, pp. 162–5; Howson, *Houses of noble poverty*, p. 141. This scandal also provided Anthony Trollope with the theme for his novel *The Warden* which, through the fictional Hiram's Hospital, offered a more sensitive consideration of the implications of a charitable endowment that had grown beyond the objects of its charity.

77 Owen, *English philanthropy*, pp. 197–208.

that has been referred to above.[78] A temporary relaxation of the strict interpretation of *cy-près* in 1881 by the Master of the Rolls gave the Commission more leeway to revise the deployment of endowments, but this was revoked by a further decision from that same authority in 1910, and thereafter the Commissioners were much more wary in their interpretation of that elusive, but limiting, doctrine. In the meantime they also gave help and advice to local authorities on the democratisation of local charities, in which process they were aided by the reconstruction of local government by the Acts of 1888 and 1894 which established county councils and parish councils.[79]

It was on just such a matter that they were to intervene once again in the affairs of Doughty's Hospital in the 1880s. In 1870 fresh charges of corruption, similar to those of the 1830s, where levelled at the trustees of the General List, as a result of a parliamentary election in Norwich. During an inquiry into the corrupt practices that had taken place during the election, Mr Jacob Henry Tillett, a Liberal candidate, was accused of using his nomination to Doughty's Hospital to obtain a favourable vote. Although, in this instance, hospital notes had not been used to garner votes, and Tillett was found not guilty of the charges, the evidence he gave again revealed a system of nomination which remained open to abuse.[80] Candidates were selected for Doughty's Hospital by the trustees on a rotational basis of nomination. The system required a single trustee to assess the potential of an applicant, based on his testimonials and reputation – a system that was completely non-transparent and therefore susceptible to misuse. Tillett defended himself by arguing that he could not be guilty of corruption, as he had promised his turn to a man named Simon Watling, who was subsequently admitted to the hospital in September 1871.[81] The system, however, ensured that people with good contacts could apply for entry to Doughty's, and might be favoured over those who may have been in greater financial need.

A change in policy was not immediate. In July 1882 the trustees of the General List contacted the Charity Commissioners regarding the possible absorption of the funds of two loans charities – Luke Fisher's and Cocke's Charities. Doughty's Hospital hoped to use the funds of the two loans charities to ease the institution's financial problems.[82] In order to state their case, the trustees included details of the procedures for the nomination of residents, and the Charity Commissioners made

---

78   *Ibid.*, pp. 299–304; and see above, p. 59.
79   Owen, *English philanthropy*, pp. 299–329.
80   1870 [c13] [c14] *Report of the commissioners appointed to inquire into the existence of corrupt practices at the last election for members to serve in parliament for the City of Norwich*.
81   NRO, N/CCH 112, 27 September 1871.
82   See below, pp. 74–5.

it clear that they could not sanction the practice of the selection of residents by individual trustees in rotation.[83] In November 1884, under a new scheme set out by the Charity Commissioners, the trustees appointed an inquiry officer to provide an independent report upon the personal circumstances of each potential resident.[84] By May 1893, the election of inmates had become even more transparent. When vacancies occurred at the hospital, they were now advertised through the local newspapers and candidates were asked to apply in writing to the inquiry officer with sufficient testimonials and other evidence of their qualification for the appointment. The trustees were also asked to keep a record of all almspeople – their name, age, date of birth, and the date of their appointment – in a special residents' book.[85] As a result of this the trustees saw a list of potential candidates for each vacancy, then elected the person they felt was most deserving of the position.[86] Notwithstanding this democratisation, further intervention from the Charity Commission was soon again required to authorise deviation from the strict letter of the original endowment, to help the hospital cope with the financial difficulties it experienced in the later nineteenth century, as we will shortly see.

83   NRO, N/CCH 113, 31 July 1882.
84   *Ibid.*, 26 November 1884.
85   NRO, N/CCH 114, 17 May 1893.
86   *Ibid.*, 20 September 1893.

CHAPTER 10
Finance and refurbishment

The financial health of Doughty's Hospital was quite clear from the Brougham Commission's report of 1834, so much so that the Commissioners were concerned that in the short term the balance of funds should be invested, and in the longer term they envisaged the prospect of expansion of the hospital.[87] Rents received from lands held at Burston, Gissing, Hellington and Cringleford, plus the letting of the Hospital garden, totalled £520 in 1829/30, £590 in 1830/1 and £471 in 1831/2. Income from dividends in each of these three years was £290, and interest payments on money put out to loan was £65. The 'current' return of rents from land was given by the Commissioners as £642, while the other figures remained the same. Thus the hospital had an annual income, averaged across these four years, of approximately £911. Average annual expenditure shown in the three annual accounts between 1829/30 and 1831/2 stood at £978, but even in the last of these three years a surplus of £921 remained in the hands of the treasurer, and if the current return from rents of £642 was maintained, the hospital finances were in good shape.[88]

Returns from landed property could fluctuate, however, and tenants periodically had difficulty in paying their rents. Falling prices had hit many farmers hard in the immediate aftermath of the French Wars (1793–1815) and into the 1820s, and landlords had to respond by lowering rents, while farmers in their turn reduced agricultural wages and introduced innovations that increased productivity. Areas of light soil, which included Norfolk, were the first to turn the tide, and renewed prosperity was already evident in such regions by the early to mid- 1830s.[89] These general considerations did not mean, however, that individuals were immune to economic difficulty, and in March 1841 Mr Carter, a tenant of a farm at Gissing owned by the hospital, was unable to pay his rent on the property. In total, Carter owed £111 in

87   See above, pp. 62–5.
88   NRO, N/TC 63/2: *Commissioners of inquiry into charities in England and Wales: twenty-seventh report*, BPP 1834, Vol. XXI (225), pp. 58–60. These figures have been rounded to the nearest pound.
89   Crouzet, *Victorian economy*, pp. 156–9.

arrears. The debt was written off and the trustees required that Carter provide two good sureties for his payment of future rents or else he should quit the land in September.[90] Such difficulties must have been temporary rather than general, however, for otherwise the further expansion of the hospital's capacity, made in 1843 and 1847, which increased the total number of units from thirty-eight to forty-two, would hardly have been possible.[91]

Even during the so-called 'Golden Age' in English agriculture between 1850 and 1873, which witnessed an increase in rents across England by an average of 16 per cent, occasional years of difficulty could arise. The returns of Doughty's Hospital to the Charity Commissioners for the period between 1853 and 1857 show a gradual decline in income and no reduction in expenditure. In 1853 the receipts of the hospital totalled £1,160 2s. 5d., while expenditure was £1,117 5s. 6d., and the accounts thus showed a small surplus. However, in 1855 expenditure outweighed the income of the charity by £268, costs having risen suddenly to £1,354 18s. 1d., and despite some reduction in expenditure thereafter the accounts for 1856 and 1857 both showed a small deficit, of £24 and £87 respectively.[92]

Further details of the hospital's finances are available from the *Digest of endowed charities* compiled for Norfolk for the years 1862–4, which also provides comparison with the earlier returns of the Brougham inquiry.[93] The gross income of the charity now stood at £1,098 7s. 0d. compared with £980 3s. 0d. some thirty years earlier. Doughty's had done little more than to hold its own, and this at a time when the gross endowed charitable income in the county of Norfolk as a whole had leapt from £36,522 to £50,487.[94] While £1,158 of this increased county total was due to the discovery of charities that had been missed by the earlier inquiry, and a further £1,330 the result of new foundations, the great majority of the increase – £11,477 – was the result of improved income.[95] To compare closer to home, Doughty's investments had also performed worse than those of the Great Hospital, whose gross income had risen from £5,830 11s. 4d. to £7,088 9s. 11d. The Boys' Hospital saw a modest rise in income from £1,150 18s. 4d. to £1,379 16s. 11d., and the Girls' Hospital a more significant

90 NRO, N/CCH 109, 31 March 1841.

91 See above, p. 65.

92 *Return from charity trustees in England and Wales of gross annual amounts of receipts and expenditure, 1853–7*. 1859, session 1, House of Commons Papers; accounts and papers (ii) XX, 493.

93 *Endowed charities. Copies of the general digest of endowed charities for the counties and cities mentioned in the fourteenth report of the Charity Commissioners*, BPP 1867–8, Vol. LII Pt. II (c.433), County of Norfolk, p. 104.

94 *Ibid.*, p. 150.

95 *Explanatory memoranda and tabular summaries of the general digest*, BPP 1877, Vol. LXVI (15), Table III.

proportional increase from £536 9s. 0d. to £897 6s. 0d. Of the six Norwich almshouses only Pye's and Cooke's had performed worse, Pye's merely maintaining its tiny income of £6 16s. 9d., while Cooke's Hospital returned a small decline, down from £138 2s. 10d. in 1834 to £127 4s. 0d. in 1862–4. The return to Doughty's from houses and lands now stood at £745 9s. 6d., a sum higher than that returned in any year in the early 1830s, but the returns from investments and money out on interest had stagnated.[96] Financial stability had been achieved, but there appeared to be no danger of the trustees having to agonise – as did the master of Hiram's Hospital in Trollope's novel *The Warden* – over what should be done with the surplus funds.

This financial stability was, however, enough to encourage the trustees to seek to remodel the hospital in the 1860s. The accommodation was considered small and cramped and the trustees began to enquire into the possibility of altering the cottages in order to make them 'more comfortable' for residents.[97] In 1867 the trustees considered plans to improve the quality and comfort of the tenements. On 22 August 1867, the architect Mr Benest was called in to draw up some preliminary sketches.[98] Shortly after, on 3 January 1868, the trustees inspected the cottages at Doughty's, and arranged also to inspect the cottages at the Great Hospital in order to compare the space available in each.[99] The trustees had considered the idea of giving each resident two small rooms but on 24 January the master of the Great Hospital stood before the trustees of Doughty's Hospital and suggested that one large room instead of two smaller ones would be more suitable for residents. The trustees unanimously agreed to his proposal to convert two of each of the present tenements into one, so that each resident might have a larger living space.[100] It was also decided that a second storey of similar proportions should be added on top of the present one, a decision that contravened William Doughty's original express instruction that the almshouse should have 'no chambers above it'.[101]

In February 1868, Mr Benest, who had by now been appointed architect for the project, presented the trustees with two alternative sets of specifications. The trustees settled on plan two, which, as well as incorporating the enlargement of the rooms and the building of a second storey, also involved elongation of the east and west sides of the

96 *Ibid.*, Norfolk, p. 104. No details of actual expenditure are provided in these returns: it is simply assumed that expenditure matched income.
97 NRO, N/CCH 111, 24 January 1868.
98 *Ibid.*, 22 August 1867.
99 *Ibid.*, 3 January 1868.
100 *Ibid.*, 24 January 1868.
101 NRO, Case 20f/14, William Doughty's Will, 25 April 1687.

square, and the complete removal of the south side.[102] In June the tender of Mr James Webb for £1,303 12s. 0d. was accepted and work began on the alterations on 10 June 1868.[103]

The north side of the courtyard was the first to be converted and during this time, the residents – eight in all – were housed elsewhere. Three of them were moved into empty rooms in the hospital and the remaining five homeless residents were temporarily housed in a property in Colegate, formerly occupied by the master of the hospital and thought by the trustees to be suitable for such a purpose. The expense of removing furniture was borne by the trustees, and any residents displaced by the building works and compelled to find their own lodgings were to receive an extra 1s. 6d. per week allowance from the charity.[104] The project was completed on 23 March 1869 and, after an inspection by the trustees, residents were able to move back in on 6 April 1869.[105] The new rooms were allocated in order of seniority of admission and the women residents were housed in the eight tenements which made up the north wing and four cottages along the northern corner of the west wing.[106] The result was the creation of forty-four housing units in total, but now with considerably more internal space in each dwelling, and distributed over two floors rather than one.

The cost of the extensive conversion work was estimated at a little over £1,300 by the contractors and £1,100 of 3 per cent consolidated annuities was realised in order to meet the costs. However, by the time all the bills had been met in 1871 the total cost had risen to over £1,600.[107] In March 1870 the trustees agreed that the payment of all bills was to be deferred until July when there would be money to defray them. Furthermore, because the funds had 'run very close this year', any further vacancies at the hospital would be left unfilled for a period of three months.[108] The accounts were studied in September 1870 and it was found that the charity had overspent by £30 and would need to go overdrawn. As a result of this the trustees agreed only to offer clothing to the inmates once every two years instead of annually as had previously been the custom.[109] Originally Doughty's Hospital had provided a cloak of purple cloth to each inmate upon entry to the hospital and every two years after that. By 1841, however, the hospital was providing male inmates with a suit of clothes each

102 NRO, N/CCH 111, 21 February 1868.
103 *Ibid.*, 4 June 1868; 10 June 1868.
104 *Ibid.*, 10 June 1868.
105 *Ibid.*, 23 March 1869; 6 April 1869.
106 *Ibid.*, 23 April 1869.
107 Jewson, *Doughty's Hospital*, p. 15.
108 NRO, N/CCH 111, 25 March 1870.
109 *Ibid.*, 27 September 1870.

year, and thirty suits were produced that year by Brays at a cost of
26s. 6d. per suit.[110] William White, writing in 1845, listed the annual
clothing allowance for each inmate as follows: one pair of shoes, blue
clothing and linen for shirts and shifts.[111] The return to provision of
clothing on a biennial rather than an annual basis, therefore, effected a
significant saving to the trust.

Seven years later, by 1877, the financial situation had still not
improved and the trustees again ordered that no vacancies should
be filled until further notice.[112] Nominations were held sporadically
from 1877 to 1880, however, but on 18 March 1881 it was ordered
that nominations were to be completely withheld until further notice
because of 'unsatisfactory finances'.[113] The trustees would be unable to
appoint new residents from the City of Norwich for the next eight
years.[114]

Renewed agricultural depression hit the country in the early 1870s,
with a particularly adverse effect on grain prices, and over the next
twenty-five years the average price of wheat almost halved. The basic
cause was the opening up of the central plains of the United States,
the Canadian prairies, the Argentinian pampas and certain regions of
Australia, against which the British market was wholly unprotected by
customs barriers. Prices of most animal products held up better, falling
later and less dramatically. As in the depression which had followed the
French Wars, farmers on the lighter soils fared better than those farming
heavy clays, and this was particularly true of the barley growers of East
Anglia. Nevertheless, not only did farm profits fall substantially, but
rents followed too, declining by an average of one-quarter in England
between 1874/8 and 1894/8, while it became increasingly difficult to
attract and keep tenants.[115]

Doughty's Hospital did not escape the impact of this extended
agricultural depression. In 1881, three of the farms let by the trustees
were in arrears. Mr Carter at Gissing Farm had not paid £70 due to
the hospital, and Mr Goddard of Hellington and Mr Dixon of Burston
were both £100 in debt to the hospital. All three men were given more
time to pay their rents.[116] These debts were reported to the trustees
of Doughty's Hospital by the steward, who was responsible for the

110 NRO, N/CCH 109: Minute book for general charities 1837–1847, 23 December 1841.
111 White, *White's Norfolk directory*, p. 136.
112 NRO, N/CCH 112, 26 March 1877.
113 NRO, N/CCH 113, 18 March 1881.
114 NRO, N/CCH 114, 28 June 1889; 25 September 1889. They were only able to nominate
    residents exclusively from the parish of St John de Sepulchre under the scheme of Luke
    Fisher's and Cocke's Charities, which was finalised in 1884, which is discussed below: NRO,
    N/CCH 113, 26 November 1884.
115 Crouzet, *Victorian economy*, pp. 166–75.
116 NRO, N/CCH 113, 23 June 1881.

maintenance of both the hospital building and of the properties owned by the charity from which rents were collected. As such, the steward, one Mr Hornor, dealt directly with the tenants and relayed any problems to the trustees of Doughty's Hospital by way of report. By December 1882, there were eleven vacancies at Doughty's, but the trustees were reluctant to fill them because of the continuing problems in collecting rents from their tenants.[117] It was these difficulties, coupled with the cost of repairing and rebuilding farm buildings on both the Gissing and Hellington properties, that placed the hospital in urgent financial difficulty, and the trustees struggling to find an effective solution.[118]

The first idea proposed by the trustees in March 1881 to resolve the situation was to lower the expenditure of the hospital by filling up vacancies with residents who would live in the cottages without charge, but not receive a stipend or an allowance of coal.[119] This, however, was soon rejected in favour of a more permanent solution. In March 1882 the clerk wrote to the Charity Commissioners asking if the trustees might use the money from two small loan charities, Luke Fisher's and Cocke's, to augment the income of Doughty's Hospital. As these two charities were active in the parish of St John de Sepulchre, the trustees suggested that one tenement at Doughty's should be reserved for a deserving poor, aged man or woman from that parish, in return for a fixed annual sum of £24 from the loan charities.[120] The Charity Commissioners rejected this *ad hoc* proposal, insisting that the trustees follow the proper channels for the alteration of the scheme.[121]

What followed was a prolonged argument over the details of a new scheme, with neither side willing to compromise. The Charity Commissioners suggested that, rather than absorbing the funds of the two loan charities in order to recover their financial position, the trustees might save money by getting rid of their permanent medical officer, a move which would save them £20 each year.[122] The trustees would not submit to this suggestion, however, as they felt that the medical officer was an absolutely necessary expense. In September 1884, the matter remained unsettled and a committee of Royal Commissioners was called to look into the disagreement. Finally it was decided that the medical officer should remain in employment on an annual sum 'not exceeding £20'.[123] The Charity Commissioners also allowed the

---

117 *Ibid.*, 19 December 1882.
118 *Ibid.*
119 *Ibid.*, 8 March 1881.
120 NRO, N/CCH 113, 24 March 1882.
121 *Ibid.*, 30 August 1882.
122 *Ibid.*, 25 July 1883.
123 *Report from the Select Committee on Charitable Trust Acts; together with the proceedings of the committee, minutes of evidence and appendix 1884.* House of Commons papers, reports of committees, BPP 1884, Vol. IX (306).

trustees to use the income of Luke Fisher's and Cocke's Charities for the benefit of Doughty's Hospital. The trustees resolved to elect four residents, rather than just the one that was originally proposed, because the funds of the loans charities were more generous than they had first anticipated. In November 1884 four new residents were accepted from the parish of St John de Sepulchre and each was paid for by an annual sum of £24 from the two loan charities.[124]

Despite the new scheme, Doughty's Hospital still had empty cottages and no funds to fill them. It was not until June 1889 that Mr Hornor, the steward of the hospital, reported that Doughty's was in a better financial position and it was decided to appoint three aged men from the city.[125] Reuben Willis, aged 79, of Sussex Street, John Hardy, aged 71, of Lakenham, and Robert Crosby, aged 69, of Ninham's Court were appointed to the hospital in September of the same year.[126] After the scheme for the provision of accommodation with funds drawn upon Luke Fisher's and Cocke's Charities was finalised in 1884, other charitable institutions came forward wishing to pay a yearly sum in order to nominate men and women to the hospital. In 1892, the loan charity known as the Town Close Estate agreed to pay a yearly sum of £25 per person in return for the power to nominate six freemen to cottages at Doughty's Hospital.[127] In 1897, the trustees were approached by the representatives of two Friendly Societies – the Independent Order of Oddfellows Unity Manchester and the Independent Order of Oddfellows Norfolk and Norwich Unity – and it was agreed that six idle cottages at the hospital could be inhabited by qualified applicants, providing that each applicant was sponsored to the tune of at least 5s. a week by one or other of the societies. These residents would receive all the benefits of the hospital, aside from the 5s. 6d. allowance from the trustees. These schemes eventually allowed the hospital to fill more of its cottages and accommodate a wider range of applicants while simultaneously keeping costs low.[128]

After the financial difficulties of the 1870s and 1880s it was clear that Doughty's Hospital would be unable to expand for the foreseeable future. However, ten more cottages were added to the institution when Doughty's absorbed another almshouse in 1899. Cooke's Hospital had been built on Rose Lane in 1700 by aldermen Thomas and Robert Cooke and left to the Corporation in the will of Thomas Cooke (see Figure 3).[129] The cottages had been declared unsafe in 1883, however,

124 NRO, N/CCH 113, 26 November 1884.
125 NRO, N/CCH 114, 28 June 1889.
126 *Ibid.*, 25 September 1889.
127 *Ibid.*, 17 August 1892.
128 NRO, N/CCH 115, 14 July 1897.
129 White, *White's Norfolk directory*, p. 136.

Figure 3.   Cooke's Hospital, 2009

and the hospital was closed in 1887.[130] In June 1889 the trustees bought land from the Great Hospital in St Martin's Lane for £125 with a view to the erection of a new Cooke's Hospital on that site, and building was completed in August 1892.[131] However, the new hospital had no master and therefore no-one to exercise control and supervision over the residents there. In April 1899 the trustees asked Mr Inwood, the master of Doughty's, to also act as master to Cooke's, his salary to increase to £2 10s. per week, and the deal was agreed. From this point onwards, the two hospitals were run in tandem.[132]

As Doughty's regained its financial footing as a result of the help from the Town Close Estate Charity, Luke Fisher's and Cocke's Charities and the Friendly Societies, it was able to begin investing in the structure of the hospital once more. Large-scale refurbishments were out of the question but the trustees made small improvements and embraced new technologies as the twentieth century approached. In March 1893 a W.C. was placed inside the master's house and in February 1907 the clerk was instructed to arrange for the installation

130 NRO, N/CCH 113, 13 June 1883; NRO N/CCH 114, 27 July 1887.
131 NRO, N/CCH 114, 28 June 1889; 17 August 1892.
132 NRO, N/CCH 115, 19 April 1899.

of a telephone at the hospital, while making sure it was provided 'at minimum cost'.[133]

In May 1907, Mrs Florence Boardman and Mrs Lucy Henderson, two wives of trustees, reported upon the desirability of introducing gas cooking facilities. The ladies concluded that it was not desirable for residents to have gas stoves in their cottages, but that gas cookers and gas burners should be installed in the cottages of the two nurses and the laundrywoman. It was also suggested that the nurses be authorised occasionally to cook for residents and charge a halfpenny per joint of meat. It was recommended that only the nurses be allowed to cook for residents, leaving the laundrywoman free to fulfil her duties, apart from 'in an emergency', although it is difficult to determine when a roast dinner might constitute an emergency![134] Whether demand for cooked dinners outstripped supply is unclear, but in October 1913 the trustees began the gradual process of fitting gas cookers into residents' cottages. From this date until the early 1930s these new gas cookers were periodically fitted into rooms throughout the hospital.[135]

In June 1907 the question of installing electric lighting was raised. Mr Hornor, the steward, estimated the annual cost of lighting for the laundry and the residents' cottages would be around £27. It was resolved that it should be installed.[136] However, the operation of the system experienced a few teething problems. In February 1909 the clerk reported that the lights were turned off at night, and so, if an inmate needed a light after dark, they were obliged to light a lamp or candle, thus frustrating the object of installing the electric lighting in the first place.[137] Mr Hornor was instructed to make arrangements to ensure that Doughty's was able to have a supply of electricity during the night. The new electric lighting was not universally welcomed by the residents either. One elderly inmate, Mrs Dawson, resisted the installation of the lighting in her flat and apparently threatened the master with violence.[138] Her weekly allowance was removed and she soon agreed to have the lights fitted, apologising for her previous behaviour.[139] We will shortly see that Mrs Dawson was far from the first or the last troublesome inmate of Doughty's Hospital.

133 NRO N/CCH 114, 15 March 1893; NRO, N/CCH 116, 20 February 1907.
134 *Ibid.*, 15 May 1907.
135 NRO, N/CCH/119, 29 October 1913; NRO N/CCH 122, 8 June 1932.
136 NRO, N/CCH 116, 19 June 1907.
137 *Ibid.*, 17 February 1909.
138 *Ibid.*, 17 July 1907.
139 *Ibid.*, 16 October 1907.

CHAPTER 11
Of masters and men

Running Doughty's

At Doughty's Hospital the period of administrative upheaval between 1833 and 1837 did not seem to affect the day-to-day running of the institution. The role of the master of the hospital remained unchanged throughout and beyond this period but the argument over his family circumstances continued. William Doughty's will had specified that the master of his hospital should be a 'discreet and sober single man',[140] but according to the census returns from 1841 to 1901 every master was married and each lived with his wife, and sometimes with dependent children too, in the hospital.[141] In 1745 Francis Blomefield had expressed disgust that the master of the hospital should be married, as this contravened the wishes of William Doughty.[142] However, James Hooper, writing in 1898, argued against Blomefield's harsh criticism of a married master. Hooper reasoned that the world had changed since Doughty's original instructions and that married men were 'better suited' to this kind of work. He also suggested that a master's wife could play 'a useful part in the conduct of these establishments', presumably as a "calming female influence" over the management of the hospital.[143]

Robert Minns was appointed as master to the hospital in May 1838 in the place of Christmas Church.[144] According to census data from 1841, Minns was 62 years of age at the time of his appointment, and went on to hold the position for twenty-six years.[145] In 1864 the trustees sought to overhaul the management of the hospital, and re-

---

140 NRO, Case 20f/14, William Doughty's Will, 25 April 1687.
141 1841 census: HO107/791, book 1, civil parish: St Saviour, County: Norfolk, Enumeration District: Doughty's Hospital, folio 41, p. 2; 1851 census: HO107/1813, folio 92, pp.15–17; 1861 census: RG9/1212, folio 90, pp. 27–8, RG9/1211, folio 14, p. 23; 1871 census: RG10/1809, folio 86, pp. 23–5; 1881 census: RG11/1939, folio 83, pp. 27–9; 1891 census: RG12/1520, folio 116, pp. 18–19; 1901 census: RG13/1836, folio 51, p. 2.
142 NRO, Case 20f/14, William Doughty's Will, 25 April 1687.
143 Hooper, *Norwich charities*, p. 50.
144 NRO, N/CCH 109, 1 May 1838.
145 1841 census: HO107/791, book 1, civil parish: St Saviour, County: Norfolk, Enumeration District: Doughty's Hospital, folio 41, p. 2.

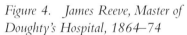

Figure 4.   James Reeve, Master of Doughty's Hospital, 1864–74

Figure 5.   Martha Galloway Reeve, wife of the master

evaluate the role of the master of Doughty's. They agreed that any master appointed should be fit enough to carry out his duties for a reasonable length of time, and that once he was no longer fit enough to continue working he should be kept on at the institution, to have a cottage and the same privileges as other inmates. This new ordinance was very likely the result of Robert Minns' increasing infirmity while continuing in his role as master. It was also decided that the master would receive 11s. per week and two chauldrons of coal annually, but that he was not to receive any other special privileges. His other duties were also rehearsed. The master was expected to maintain a standard of cleanliness in the cottages, visit each resident daily and report any instances of insobriety or immoral behaviour to the trustees. He was also expected to keep records of the inmates and report to the quarterly meetings of the trustees. His final task was to lock the gates of the hospital at 10pm every night.[146]

The repetition and refinement of many of the rules might suggest a slip in standards during Minns' time as master at the hospital, for there would be little need to restate these rules if they were being

146 NRO, N/CCH 111, 11 February 1864.

followed correctly. Minns had been a particularly long-serving master, and was still in post in 1861 at the ripe old age of 85.[147] However, it is equally possible that the trustees simply wanted to reaffirm the basic regulations of the hospital in preparation for the appointment of a new master. On 11 February 1864, James Reeve, shown with his wife in Figures 4 and 5, was appointed to the position.[148]

James Reeve experienced a tumultuous period as master of the hospital and clashed with both residents and members of staff over his conduct. In September 1872 the trustees received complaints from several residents that they were not receiving their proper allowances of coal.[149] In the same month the laundress complained that she was not being provided with the proper brushes to carry out her duties.[150] The trustees examined the complaints and Mr Reeve was informed that they now felt obliged to refine the system for the weighing of coals, and also recorded that they felt there had been 'great irregularities in his management of the hospital', which minute was read out in the master's presence.[151] The story of these controversies over the coal allowance is told more fully below.[152]

James Reeve was eventually exonerated of any irregularities with respect to the coal allowance, but these clashes may have taken their toll on his health, for he died in October 1874 leaving his wife Martha Galloway Reeve a widow at 70. The trustees now appointed William Kett Finch as master to the hospital, and Mrs Reeve applied to become a resident there, to be relieved upon the foundation. The trustees refused to offer her a place at the institution, however, but showed at least some pity by allowing her to have the use of a vacant cottage at the hospital until the following Christmas.[153]

Mr Finch is often mentioned in the minute books and these entries give an idea of the role of the master of Doughty's Hospital. For example, in September 1886 he was given the task of appointing a female nursing attendant and it is clear that he was also responsible for supervision of the nursing staff, for in 1892 he complained to the trustees that one of the nurses, Mrs Holman, had failed to obey his instructions.[154] The trustees spoke directly to Mrs Holman who promised to obey the orders of the master in future. This shows the hierarchy of authority at Doughty's Hospital, the master imposing the rules upon the nurses

---

147 1861 census: RG9/1212, folio 90, pp. 27–8.
148 NRO, N/CCH 111, 11 February 1864.
149 NRO, N/CCH 112, 11 September 1872.
150 *Ibid.*, 11 September 1872.
151 *Ibid.*, 25 September 1872.
152 See below, pp. 94–5.
153 NRO, N/CCH 112, 26 October 1874.
154 NRO, N/CCH 113, 22 September 1886; NRO, N/CCH 114, 25 April 1892.

and residents, and the trustees able to intervene and enforce the rules on both the staff and the master. However, Finch experienced further problems while master of Doughty's Hospital, primarily with one particular member of the nursing staff. In June 1885 the clerk recorded that he had received a 'large number' of letters of complaint from nurse Ottaway regarding the master.[155] After a thorough investigation by the trustees, the details of which remain sadly unrecorded, Mrs Ottaway was asked to tender her resignation. Interestingly, three years earlier, it was Mr Finch who had recommended Mrs Ottaway for the position of nurse, suggesting that a once amiable relationship had turned sour.[156]

William Kett Finch died in February 1896, and applications were invited for his replacement. Benjamin Inwood, a trustee of the hospital, sought to resign his position in order that he might become master of Doughty's. His resignation was accepted and on 26 February Mr Inwood's and Mr Dann's applications for the position were both considered.[157] It was resolved unanimously that Benjamin Inwood take the appointment, on a salary of 12s. 6d. per week, plus the accustomed accommodation in the hospital and an allowance of coal.[158]

As well as a master to the hospital and various nursing and laundry staff, the trustees also employed a clerk and a steward. The clerk was responsible for all the paperwork at the institution and as such recorded the minutes of each meeting of the trustees. He also composed letters in the name of the trustees, such as those written during exchanges with the Charity Commissioners, and composed advertisements to be placed in the local papers.[159] For instance, in 1882 the clerk was instructed to advertise for a nurse in the local papers after the present nurse became unfit to discharge her duties.[160] In May 1893 the trustees agreed to advertise for candidates for the almshouse as a result of the Charity Commissioners' lack of enthusiasm for the old system of appointment by rotational nomination, and it was again the clerk who composed the advertisements.[161]

The steward to Doughty's Hospital was responsible for the maintenance of its buildings, and ensured that any repairs that were needed were reported to the trustees. Once the trustees had given their approval, the steward was then able to organise the repairs, by hiring contractors and buying necessary materials. For example, in May 1838 the steward, described simply as 'Mr Steward', was called to inspect the

155 NRO, N/CCH 113, 19 June 1885.
156 *Ibid.*, 29 November 1882.
157 NRO, N/CCH 115, 26 February 1896.
158 *Ibid.*
159 NRO, N/CCH 113, 15 May 1884.
160 *Ibid.*, 29 September 1882.
161 NRO, N/CCH 114, 17 May 1893.

chimneys at the hospital, which looked to be in a 'dangerous state'.[162] In March 1877 the steward reported that the laundry door was in need of repair and also that the west end of the gallery required attention. The trustees then ordered that these repairs be carried out.[163] The steward was also responsible for inspecting the buildings that Doughty's Hospital rented out to tenants and, with the trustees' approval, was able to repair buildings on the estates owned across Norfolk.[164] As a result of this, Mr Hornor, who was the steward for the hospital from the 1860s to the 1890s, was consulted when Doughty's finances were weakened by agricultural decline in the 1880s. There were eleven vacancies at the hospital in the winter of 1882, but the trustees were unable to fill them due to heavy outlays reported by the steward on both the Gissing and Hellington properties. On Hellington Farm, new bullock and turnip houses were required at a cost of £156 2s. 10d., while at Gissing Farm the new buildings needed, it was estimated, would cost £361.[165]

Turning to medical and nursing care, by 1833 the duties of the medical officer had become more restricted than formerly, and when Mr W. Griffin was appointed he was only responsible for the two hospitals reserved for the care of the elderly – the Great Hospital and Doughty's Hospital – rather than the four which had formerly been the remit of a single individual. A yearly salary was granted of £40, £10 of which was paid by the treasurer of Doughty's, no doubt a fair reflection of the relative size of the two institutions.[166] In March 1850 the salary for the surgeon increased again and Doughty's Hospital was now liable for £12 a year in return for the services of the medical attendant.[167]

Through the nineteenth century Doughty's Hospital continued to employ a nurse. The census data shows that in 1841 Maryann Thirkettle, the nurse of the hospital, was married to an inmate, perhaps suggesting an informal system of nursing was in operation.[168] However, in 1851 the current nurse, Harriet Stevenson, had no apparent family ties to any of the residents of the hospital, despite being listed as married.[169] This pattern continues in the 1871 census and seems to indicate that by now a more formal system of nursing had been put into practice.[170] The information in the General List minute books for this period

---

162 NRO, N/CCH 108, 1 May 1838.
163 NRO, N/CCH 112, 26 March 1877.
164 NRO, N/CCH 108, 3 August 1841; NRO, N/CCH 110, 18 June 1862.
165 NRO, N/CCH 113, 19 December 1882; 13 June 1883.
166 NRO, N/MC 2/8, 6 February 1833.
167 NRO, N/CCH 110, 27 March 1850.
168 1841 census: HO107/791, book 1, civil parish: St Saviour, County: Norfolk, Enumeration District: Doughty's Hospital, folio 41, p. 2.
169 1851 census: HO107/1813, folio 92, pp. 15–17.
170 1871 census: RG10/1809, folio 86, pp. 23–5.

shows that this was indeed the case, and in June 1871 the expectations and duties for a nurse at Doughty's Hospital were recorded for the first time. As well as attending to any inmates who were sick or infirm, she was required to wash the laundry of all forty-five residents and was instructed to find her own soap for this purpose. She was expected to wash three articles of clothing once a week, a flannel once a fortnight and two sheets and a pillow-case once every month, for each resident. Her duties also included cleaning all the passages and water closets of the hospital.[171] She was, therefore, not only a nurse, but also cleaner and laundrywoman for the institution and all its residents.

On 2 February 1876, a meeting of the trustees was called to hear the complaints laid against the nurse of the hospital. She was accused of leaving the hospital without the permission of the master, something that the trustees agreed she was not at liberty to do. She was also chastised for refusing to wash a flannel petticoat without charge and for the laundry being 'occasionally poorly done'.[172] The nurse was told that she should endeavour to complete the laundry to a more satisfactory standard and that she must obtain permission from the master before leaving the premises. It was recorded that the nurse intended to comply with these regulations, but it appears that it proved all too much for her, as she handed in her notice of resignation on 20 March.[173] After this resignation, the trustees finally acknowledged the need for a separate washerwoman and one was appointed on 30 March 1876.[174] The following April two new nurses were appointed at a weekly wage of 8s. each.[175] The additional staffing provided in 1876, which split the duties previously undertaken by a single nurse between two nurses and one laundrywoman, theoretically made the system more organised and better adapted to deal with the needs of the residents. However, despite the increase in staff, there were still problems at the hospital. Instances of insubordination, and the ill-health of members of staff, were frequently recorded in the trustees' minute books. In 1882, for example, Miss Tuck, the nurse at the hospital, was declared unfit to discharge her duties due to her failing health and was demoted to assistant nurse at a rate of 6s. per week for a twelve-month probationary period.[176] The clerk was instructed to advertise in the local newspapers for the post of nurse, at 8s. a week plus a house and coals. He was also instructed to impose an age limit of between 40 and 50 years old upon the applicants for the

---

171 NRO, N/CCH 111, 23 June 1871.
172 NRO, N/CCH 112, 2 February 1876.
173 *Ibid.*, 20 March 1876.
174 *Ibid.*, 30 March 1876.
175 *Ibid.*, 3 April 1876; 27 April 1876; 1881 census: RG11/1939, folio 83, pp. 27–9; NRO, N/CCH 111, 21 February 1868.
176 NRO, N/CCH 108, 29 September 1882.

position.[177] This age range was probably due to the fact that women under forty were more likely to have dependent children, while those over fifty might be physically less capable of carrying out their duties.

In May 1884, the master, William Kett Finch, complained that Mrs Howes, the laundress, had disregarded his authority by allowing a man to reside in her cottage with her. Mrs Howes was dismissed at once and was paid a week's wages in lieu of notice.[178] In September 1886, Miss Tuck's health finally incapacitated her and she was admitted to the hospital as a resident. The position of assistant nurse was advertised and now the clerk was instructed to recommend that only women 'aged no less than sixty years' should apply for the job.[179] Perhaps this was because the position of assistant nurse was less physically demanding than the role of nurse, or possibly the trustees now felt that employing an older woman might lessen the chance of a repeat of Mrs Howes' indiscretion.

The duties and responsibilities of nursing staff at Doughty's Hospital continued to be a contentious issue. After Mrs Morse resigned her position as nurse in September 1894, having only been appointed in February of the same year, the trustees decided to prepare a written code of conduct laying out the duties and responsibilities of a nurse at Doughty's Hospital.[180] In October 1894, when Mrs Risebrook was appointed nurse at a salary of 10s. per week, the following rules were adopted for the nursing staff:

1. Nurses shall attend to any inmate who is sick or infirm. The day nurse shall light fires and make the beds for those who are unable, shall see that the rooms are kept in a cleanly condition and generally shall promote the comfort and safety of the inmates.
2. The duties of the day nurse and the night nurse shall be taken alternately week by week but in the case of temporary indisposition they are expected to relieve each other.
3. The day nurse shall commence duty at 7am and work until 9pm. The night nurse shall commence at 9pm and work until 7am.
4. In case either nurse observes any indisposition in any of the inmates, she shall duly inform the other before going off duty and any serious change in symptoms shall be reported to the master.
5. The nurses are expected to work in harmony with each other and at all times show, by their patience and consideration of

---

177 NRO, N/CCH 113, 29 September 1882.
178 *Ibid.*, 15 May 1884.
179 *Ibid.*, 28 July 1886; 22 September 1886.
180 NRO, N/CCH 114, 19 September 1894.

the inmates, that they are striving for the comfort, cleanliness and happiness of those placed under their charge.

6. The master is empowered, in urgent or exceptional cases, to suspend the operation of these rules.[181]

This was the first instance of a written code of conduct for the nursing staff of the hospital and was far more in line with modern conceptions of nursing than the original rules dating from 1871.[182] The code also shows that the two nurses were now operating a system of shifts, one working in the daytime and the other at night, in order to effectively care for the elderly at the hospital. The shifts were very long – fourteen hours for the day shift and ten at night – and formal holidays and days off did not come into force until 1910.[183] Perhaps as a result of this, the staff turnover remained very high, with as many as nine changes of nurse in the sixteen years between 1894 and 1910.[184]

In 1901 the surgeon to the hospital, Dr Beverley, suggested that a head nurse and an assistant nurse should be appointed at weekly wages of £1 and 15s. respectively. By this point the master of the institution was receiving £2 10s. per week, so an increase in the two nurses' wages might have seemed appropriate.[185] Dr Beverley also recommended that cottage number 29 be reserved for the head nurse and that cottage number 30 be made into an infirmary for residents who were particularly unwell. He suggested that a door should be constructed between the two rooms and that a speaking tube should be placed between the head nurse's room and the one above, which should be reserved for the assistant nurse.[186] In June 1901 the trustees appointed a head nurse on a wage of £1 1s. per week – double the wage of the nurse just seven years before – and an assistant nurse on a wage of 15s. per week. They also appointed a third woman, to assist in nursing and carry out any menial tasks required.[187]

Following a report from the lady visitors to the hospital in December 1903, it was observed that the nurses of Doughty's spent some of their time administering to the wives of inmates, who – because they were not strictly on the foundation – should not really benefit from such care. They were particularly concerned about a certain Mrs Dix, who was very ill and took up a great deal of nursing resources,

---

181 *Ibid.*, 17 October 1894.
182 NRO, N/CCH 111, 23 June 1871.
183 NRO, N/CCH/117, 18 May 1910.
184 NRO, N/CCH 114, 19 September 1894; 17 October 1894; NRO, N/CCH 115, 16 October 1896; 20 December 1899; 19 June 1901; NRO, N/CCH 116, 17 June 1903; 15 September 1909; NRO, N/CCH 117, 18 May 1910.
185 NRO, N/CCH 115, 20 March 1901.
186 *Ibid.*, 20 May 1901.
187 *Ibid.*, 19 June 1901.

and recommended that the question of nursing the wives of inmates should be further considered.[188] In January 1904, the trustees resolved that medical care should extend to all the occupants of Doughty's Hospital, regardless of their status.[189] Dr Beverley wrote to the trustees explaining that he and the nurses had always considered the wives of inmates worthy of receiving care, but that the cost of medicine had by now far outstripped his salary. In consequence, Dr Beverley's wages were increased from £12 to £16 per annum.[190] In 1906, his salary was further increased to £20.[191] The medical officer continued, however, to be required to purchase medical supplies for the hospital out of his own salary, and this practice continued until November 1910 when the doctor was permitted to order some foods and medical comforts at the expense of the charity.[192]

Victorian almspeople

After the passage of the Municipal Corporations Act in 1835 Doughty's Hospital was administered by a new group of trustees. The clerk of the General List recorded the appointment of each inmate in the charity's minute books, the amount of information recorded changing through time. Sometimes the clerk would record the applicant's name, age and marital status, but at other times only the name of the new resident was entered. Between May 1837 and December 1897, 248 inmates were admitted to Doughty's Hospital. Of those admitted 162 were men and 86 were women. Ages are recorded for just 142 of the 248 applicants: the average age on entry into the almshouse was 71 years, the ages of men and women being identical.[193]

Between 1844 and 1890 the former occupations of some of the new residents were also recorded and these give an insight into the type of people admitted to the hospital. During this forty-six-year period 135 men and 65 women were elected. Unfortunately, only two of the women admitted had their former occupation recorded: on 30 June 1890, Jane Leech was listed as a second-hand clothes dealer while Sarah Gibson was identified as a nurse. Of the 135 men admitted, 52 had their former occupations recorded in the charity's minute books.[194] Of these 52, eleven were involved in the manufacture of cloth, including eight former weavers, one former worsted weaver,

---

188 NRO, N/CCH 116, 16 December 1903.
189 *Ibid.*, 17 February 1904.
190 *Ibid.*, 16 March 1904.
191 *Ibid.*, 16 May 1906.
192 NRO, N/CCH 117, 16 November 1910.
193 Not all applicants knew their ages, and some clerks failed to record ages regularly: NRO, N/CCH 110, 29 March 1848–28 September 1859.
194 NRO, N/CCH 110, 29 March 1848–28 September 1859.

one former dyer and one former comber. Norwich, as we have seen, had been a centre for the manufacture of textiles for many centuries, especially worsted cloth, and although the industry had been in slow decline in the area since the late eighteenth century it remained a significant employer down to the middle of the nineteenth century.[195] Seven of the men admitted to the hospital between 1844 and 1890 were former shoemakers and one was a former shoe mender. The shoe trade, as we have seen, had come to rival cloth production in Norwich by the mid-nineteenth century, with factories such as James Southall and Co. and Haldenstein & Sons employing large numbers of hands, both male and female.[196] To a large extent, therefore, the occupations of Doughty's male inmates reflected the occupational structure of the city. The majority of these new residents – thirty-four out of the fifty-two whose occupations are known – were skilled tradesmen, including a cabinet maker, a glazier, a tinplate worker and three former coopers. There were also men who had earned their living from working the land, including two gardeners, a farmer and a labourer. In addition to this, a few of the inmates had worked in positions requiring a high level of literacy, for example a lawyer's clerk and a land surveyor. This occupational information thus suggests that a wide range of applicants were admitted to the hospital, but also seems to indicate that they were not generally drawn from the very lowest socio-occupational groups.[197]

Further information on the profile of Doughty's residents is provided in the decennial census returns, available from 1841 through to 1911, and the results of an analysis of these returns is presented in Table 1.[198] Tracing Doughty's Hospital in the census is less straightforward than one might expect. In 1841 the whole institution is listed together, and its inhabitants are easy to reconstruct. From 1851, however, the main part of the hospital is included in the census return for St Saviour's parish, but another ten units are included in a quite different part of the census under the parish of St George Colegate, and hence both portions need to be consulted to get a complete picture. This practice continued in each census up to and including 1901, although by this

195 See above, pp. 38–9, 54.
196 Clark, 'Work and employment', pp. 390–1, 394.
197 NRO, N/CCH 110, 29 March 1848–28 September 1859.
198 1841 census: HO107/791, book 1, civil parish: St Saviour, County: Norfolk, Enumeration District: Doughty's Hospital, folio 41, p. 2; 1851 census: HO107/1813, folio 92, pp. 15–17; HO107/1812, folio 315, p. 42; 1861 census: RG9/1212, folio 90, pp. 27–8; RG9/1211, folio 14, p. 23; 1871 census: RG10/1809, folio 86, pp. 23–4; 1881 census: RG11/1939, folio 83, pp. 27–9; 1891 census: RG12/1520, folio 116, pp. 18–19; 1901 census: RG13/1836, folio 51, pp. 2–3; 1911 census: RG78/613, RD225 SD1 ED5 SN28. The 1911 census, oddly, was not governed by the 100 years rule, and hence a redacted version has been made available online ahead of the usual scheduled release date.

Table 1. The demographic profile of Doughty's almspeople, 1841–1911

| Date | Number of almspeople | | | Resident | Marital status | | | Age | |
	Total	Male	Female	relatives	Married	Widowed	Single	Average	Range
1841	36	28	8	7	–	–	–	73	63–87
1851	37	26	11	9	11	17	9	75	65–92
1861	39	26	13	14	14	21	4	74	63–89
1871	37	21	16	14	16	18	3	77	67–85
1881	36	20	16	7	10	24	2	76	69–87
1891	30	19	11	7	9	15	6	77	69–91
1901	29	14	15	10	9	18	2	76	66–91
1911	35	12	23	6	6	23	5	76	65–84

Notes: Marital status is not given in the 1841 census; in 1911 the marital status of one individual is unspecified.

date only two almsmen (in each case with their wives) were recorded in the latter parish.

We can immediately see from Table 1 that despite the financial problems which arose from the rebuilding of Doughty's in 1868–9, exacerbated by the impact upon Doughty's rents of the agricultural depression which began in the 1870s, overall numbers held up fairly well until the 1880s. Of course, the number of places available had expanded too, having risen to forty-two by 1847, so that at these snapshots provided by the decennial censuses (which counted the number of inhabitants on one night of the year only) Doughty's was operating close to, but not at, full capacity. Uninhabited dwellings were supposed to be identified by the census enumerators, but none are apparent in the return for 1851, even though the almshouse was not quite full. In 1861, however, three units (identified as numbers 8, 12 and 14) were empty, which with the thirty-nine resident inmates makes up the total number to forty-two. Similarly in 1871 five of the forty-four units that are identified were uninhabited (numbers 33, 35, 36, 39 and 42), all of them in the part of the hospital situated in the parish of St George Colegate, and as the two hospital nurses occupied a tenement each this, with the thirty-seven almspeople, again completes the requisite number. Even the seven-year embargo on new inmates imposed between 1877 and 1884 had a relatively limited impact on the figures in Table 1, for the thirty-six almsfolk resident in that year only suggests a shortfall of six (allowing for the nurses' accommodation), although it is noticeable that the number of resident relatives fell by half, possibly a reflection of cost-cutting measures.[199] The year 1901 represents the nadir of Doughty's fortunes in terms of the number of residents shown in the census. Even if two units are allocated to the one nurse listed and the laundress, this would still leave twelve of the forty-four tenements unoccupied. Numbers recovered once again at the start of the twentieth century, however, no doubt assisted by the new relationship forged between the hospital and the Town Close Estate and local Friendly Societies in the late 1890s, although there was a reduction in resident married couples to its lowest ever ebb by 1911, when just six were present.[200]

The range of relatives present at Doughty's also narrowed over time, while the way in which spouses were described changed also. In 1841 seven spouses are listed at the bottom of the return as 'Lodgers in the Hospital': that they were wives or husbands of almshouse appointees has to be inferred from their surnames. In 1851 six of the eight spouses are again listed separately and identified as inmates' wives, while the enumerator for that part of the almshouse in the parish of St George Colegate was less precise and failed to distinguish between almsfolk and their spouses. In this year, however, a 26 year-old unmarried daughter is present, as well as one Mary A. Robinson, described as 'servant to Miss Tubby'. A Charlotte Tubby had been nominated to the almshouse in the previous year, but was not present in the census, and it is possible that she had died in the interim, leaving her servant behind pending a new appointment.[201] Husbands and wives are again usually distinguished from inmates in 1861, but by now the range of relatives had expanded further, to include two daughters, two grandsons, a sister and a boarder, in addition to eight spouses. Among these was John Hedgeman, aged 83, a former carpenter, his wife Emily, aged 46, and grandson John Nichols, aged 5, described as a 'scholar', all living cheek by jowl in one small tenement.

Perhaps there was a crackdown after this, for while in 1871 there were fully eleven wives and two husbands present at the hospital, there was now only a single daughter, and from this date relatives apart from spouses were rarely found at Doughty's.[202] From 1881 onwards the census enumerators described all residents, apart from staff, either as inmates, or failed to distinguish between appointees and resident spouses. Not all married inmates brought their partners with them

---

199 Unfortunately, no information on uninhabited units is provided in any of the census returns after 1871.
200 See above, pp. 75-6.
201 The relationship of daughter to mother was inferred from relative ages and surname; NRO, N/CCH 110, 1 October 1850.
202 There was a single daughter in 1891 and an unspecified relative in 1901.

into the almshouse, however, and through to 1891 a small number were clearly described as married while living at Doughty's on their own. In the last two censuses, however, this ceased, and all inmates were either single or widowed, or lived in the almshouse with their husbands or wives. Of these categories, those who were single was always the smallest, and those who were widowed the largest, the widows and widowers increasingly dominating the institution by the early twentieth century.

In his will Doughty had specified that accommodation should be provided for twenty-four poor aged men and eight poor aged women. Expansion of the hospital by six units in 1791 allowed an increase on these numbers, but on census night in 1841 the gender balance remained heavily weighted towards men, just as its founder had prescribed, with twenty-eight male and eight female almspeople. During the course of the next seventy years that gender balance changed fundamentally, with – apart from an apparent blip in the year 1891 – an ever-increasing proportion of female inmates. By 1901 women outnumbered men for the first time, while at the next census there were almost twice as many female almspeople at Doughty's as there were men. Even this might be an underestimate for, as we have seen, it is impossible to distinguish appointees from their spouses in the census returns from 1881 on, and in compiling Table 1 it was simply assumed that the men (who were always listed first) were the inmates and the women their resident spouses. It is entirely possible, therefore, that the gender balance had shifted earlier than the statistics presented in Table 1 suggest.

The changing gender balance of residents in English almshouses is an interesting subject, both in the long and the short term. The research of Marjorie McIntosh, discussed in Part I of this book, suggested that more almshouse residents were men than women in her sample of 1,005 English institutions taken from the period 1350–1599, with 34 per cent of places dedicated to men, 24 per cent to women, and 42 per cent available to either sex.[203] A nineteenth-century sample taken from census returns between 1841 and 1901, however, comprising 7,655 census entries in nine English counties, produced very different results indeed. Although the sample was heavily skewed towards south-eastern England (and particularly the counties of Middlesex and Surrey), by this date almost 75 per cent of almshouse residents were women, and just 25 per cent were men. Even in Norfolk, the county with the least imbalance of the nine, almost two-thirds of almshouse inmates were

---

203 Again we are grateful to Professor McIntosh for permission to cite her unpublished figures, which must be regarded as provisional at this stage, and will be explained more fully in her forthcoming book.

women.[204] At the local level there is also evidence from Worcester that it was increasingly difficult to attract male almspeople towards the end of the nineteenth century, and it is possible that in both Norwich and Worcester rising living standards and a growth in alternative strategies for relief in old age were rendering almshouse accommodation decreasingly attractive to men – a topic that clearly deserves further exploration.[205]

The ages of men and women have not been distinguished in Table 1, simply because they were almost always very similar, apart from in 1841 when the men were on average four-and-a-half years older than the women, and in 1891 when the women were four years older than the men. In all other years there was barely more than a year between them. Nor was it thought necessary to present other measures of central tendency apart from the average, for calculation of the median (mid-point) age in each year produced results either identical with, or very close to, the average, indicating that the data was not skewed or distorted by extreme values at either end of the age spectrum. The average ages calculated from the census stand higher than the 71 years of age at entry established from the minute books, as one would expect given that many of those in the census returns would already have been resident for a number of years. The age ranges also show that Doughty's injunction to admit no-one 60 years or younger was followed to the letter, the youngest inmates found in any of the censuses being two individuals aged 63.

In 1856 it was decided by the trustees that the minimum age limit for nomination to Doughty's Hospital should be raised, and now no candidate under 65 years old would be accepted into the hospital.[206] Unfortunately, no explanation of this decision is recorded in the minutes. Clearly, however, one individual got through the net, for 63-year-old Samuel Stevens, a former dyer, was resident in tenement number 29 in 1861. After this date no-one below the age of 65 was found at Doughty's, while some inmates were very old indeed, and others handicapped. The 1851 return identifies two individuals as 'insane', one as 'blind', and another as 'deaf and dumb' – the latter being Charles Fulcher, former weaver, aged 92 years – which must have represented a significant challenge to nurse Harriet Stevenson. Two 91-year-olds were resident in 1891 and 1901 respectively, the first of these being Ann Love, widow,

204 N. Goose and S. Basten, 'Almshouse residency in nineteenth-century England: an interim report', *Family and Community History*, 12 (2009), pp. 68–70.
205 E. McGrath, 'The bedesmen of Worcester Cathedral: post-reformation cathedral charity compared with St Oswald's Hospital almspeople *c*.1660–1900', unpublished PhD thesis, University of Keele, 2009.
206 NRO, Case 20f/14, William Doughty's Will, 25 April 1687; NRO, N/CCH 110, 24 December 1856.

who had been there at least ten years in 1891, having featured also in the 1881 census. The other, in 1891, was Harriet Parish, widow, who entered the almshouse on 17 June 1880 and featured in the 1881, 1891 and 1901 census returns, and hence she was a resident at Doughty's Hospital for at least twenty-one years.[207]

Finally we can consider the occupations given in the census. Just as in the minute books, these are recorded erratically: none are given for inmates in 1841 or through 1871–1901, while in the three remaining returns the former occupations of men are generally recorded better than those of women. Only one female occupation is listed in 1851, that of dressmaker, a trade that also features at the next census along with two cooks, two laundresses, a charwoman, tailoress, baker, grocer and an annuitant – the latter being Ann Baker, a 71-year-old widow and, intriguingly, not described as 'late' annuitant, as all others attributed with an occupational designation are. By the 1911 census Doughty's similarly housed a number of women who had once been employed in what were usually fairly lowly branches of the service sector, including six former servants, two nurses, two charwomen, a laundress and a workhouse porteress, as well as a lodging housekeeper – an occupation that was often of dubious moral rectitude in nineteenth-century towns.[208] The traditional trades of the city are reflected in the presence of a boot closer and a shoe machinist, while the two caretakers – one in an office and one in a school – represent the emerging service sector. An unspecified factory worker, a shopkeeper and a woman formerly of 'independent means' make up the balance. While one can detect from these occupations a bias towards those trades that might be regarded as relatively lowly in the social scale, one must remember that it was to such occupations that women, in general, were largely confined. At the same time, far from all female almswomen at Doughty's conformed to this stereotype. The grocer, shopkeeper, annuitant and woman of independent means among them clearly suggest otherwise, the two caretakers must once have carried a fair degree of responsibility and even among the servants one proudly described herself as a 'lady's maid' and another as a 'housekeeper'.

A wide range of male occupations are represented among the inmates at Doughty's in 1851 and 1861, although of the forty-eight occupational labels attributed to them in these two years – unsurprisingly in view of the continued importance of textiles in the town and its extended decline – eleven were former weavers, while a dyer and a hot presser feature too. The remainder are not easily categorised, for they cover a

207 NRO, N/CCH 113, 17 June 1880.
208 B. Trinder, *The market town lodging house in Victorian England* (Friends of the Centre for English Local History: Leicester, 2001).

wide range of occupations, and only coopers (four), shoemakers (three), carpenters (two), cabinet makers (two) and hatters (two) feature at least twice, although the two carpenters, hatters and printers in fact refer to single individuals, John Hedgeman, James Orton and John Dawson respectively, who were all present in Doughty's at each census. There were no common labourers, however, and the great majority of those listed were skilled craftsmen who may well have been of respectable social standing – a stonemason, a brazier, a tinplate worker, a plumber and a glazier. Also included were a grocer, a publican, a maltster, a farmer, a gardener, a miller and a hairdresser, while perhaps the most surprising entry, found in 1851, was Levy Isaacs, an unmarried man of 75 years of age, 'teacher of Hebrew', who had been born in Holland. A similarly wide spectrum of trades was found among the twelve men present in 1911, ranging from a former railway navvy at one extreme to a hay merchant and an insurance agent at the other. Although it is very difficult confidently to convert these bald occupational titles to socio-economic status, it is quite clear that the male residents at Doughty's were generally respectable craft and tradesmen who found themselves in need of support in their old age, and certainly not the 'underclass' of Victorian and Edwardian Norwich.

Former employees often featured among almshouse residents, including Sophia Tuck, nurse to Doughty's in 1881 but an inmate in 1891, and Sarah Thirkettle, who had served as laundress to the hospital in 1891 but appears as an inmate ten years later. Indeed, in 1866 the trustees had agreed that long-serving masters, on their retirement, should themselves be offered accommodation in the institution, further underlining the respectability with which it was associated.

The behaviour of Doughty's residents, nevertheless, periodically caused problems for the hospital trustees. Although Norwich Corporation had stated in 1777 that any inmate of Doughty's Hospital who absented themselves from the institution for a period of time would be dismissed, in practice this was not always followed through.[209] Residents with health problems were able to live with friends or relatives and still collect their weekly stipend in the form of a pension. In December 1860 Mrs Rudd was permitted to live with her daughter and receive a weekly allowance from the hospital, but it was made clear that she would not be eligible for her clothing allowance unless she returned to Doughty's.[210] In September 1863 Maria Scott was allowed to live outside of the hospital with a weekly pension of 5s. 6d., as she was 'unable to maintain herself through infirmity'.[211]

209 NRO, Case 16a/34, MF 632.1, 24 December 1777.
210 NRO, N/CCH 110, 19 December 1860.
211 *Ibid.*, 14 September 1863.

However, not every case of absenteeism was received so favourably, and when Charles Raven applied to receive an out-pension of 5s. per week in June 1867 he was informed in no uncertain terms that if he did not come back to the hospital he would lose his place at the institution.[212] Mr Raven's case took some time to resolve, and in 1869, when he applied for leave of absence from the hospital for two nights per week, his request was again denied.[213] In September 1870, it was recorded that Raven had been absent from the hospital for almost twelve months, and the trustees finally resolved to expel him from the hospital, requesting that he remove all the furniture from his cottage in order that it could be allocated to a new inmate.[214]

Although the majority of residents obeyed Doughty's rule to 'live peaceably with one another', there were exceptions.[215] In August 1867 a complaint was made by Thomas Betts against a fellow inmate, Goldsmith Webb. Betts alleged that Webb had struck him across the head with a jug, broke the jug and wounded him with the broken part of it.[216] This was a serious allegation and Webb was brought before the trustees in order to speak for himself. The jury heard evidence from a medical attendant, Mr Cadge, who said that although Mr Betts' injuries were healing well the blow was inches away from severing one of his arteries and causing very serious physical harm. Three other inmates, Benjamin Barker, Philip Armes and Hezikiah Hill, all testified to Webb's constant use of violence and obscene language against them, Barker even claiming that Webb had abused him on a Sunday. The master confirmed these charges and Webb was asked to account for his actions. He proceeded to deny all the evidence and accused the other inmates of having led him 'a mad dog's life' ever since he entered the hospital.[217] The trustees resolved that Webb should be discharged for being 'a nuisance and [a] scandal', and he left in September 1867.[218]

Between 1870 and 1873, the trustees had to deal with instances of inmates tampering with the coal supplies, which, as we have seen, became an issue between certain residents and the master of the hospital, Mr Reeve.[219] In December 1870 the master complained that a resident, Mr Howard, was taking coals away from the hospital. Two

---

212 NRO, N/CCH 111, 21 June 1867.
213 *Ibid.*, 5 October 1869.
214 *Ibid.*, 28 September 1870.
215 NRO, Case 20f/14, William Doughty's Will, 25 April 1687. For an early modern example of unruly almshouse behaviour see S. Porter, 'Order and disorder in the early modern almshouse: the Charterhouse example', *London Journal*, 23 (1998), pp.1–14.
216 NRO, N/CCH 111, 12 August 1867.
217 *Ibid.*
218 *Ibid.*, 22 August 1867.
219 See above, p. 80.

other residents, Mr Bacon and James Thurtle, stood as witnesses to the fact, while Mr Moore testified that he believed both Mr Howard and Mr Davey were taking coal away 'as they never had fires in their rooms'. The implication would seem to be that these two residents were selling their coal allowance outside the hospital to make some pocket money. Both were reprimanded, and warned that if they again took coals away their coal allowance would be stopped.[220]

The issue of the coal allowance did not end there, however, for in October 1872 Mr J. Steward appeared before the trustees 'respecting missing coals'.[221] At first glance it would appear that John Steward had been stealing the coal in a similar manner to Mr Howard and Mr Davey. However, in August 1873 the trustees opened a sub-committee to look into the problem of coal in the hospital, and this sheds more light on Steward's actions.[222] Steward stood before the trustees and explained that it had come to his attention that both the inmates' and the nurses' allowances of coal were under weight. He had gone as far as to purchase a keel weight with which to weigh the coal in order to confirm his suspicions. He found that each bundle of coal weighed came up short of the allowance, sometimes by as much as eighteen pounds.[223] Other residents were examined during the course of the meeting and some agreed that they had seen Mr Reeve, the master of the hospital, apparently attempting to bring in coal from other companies in order to make up the short weight. It was implied that Mr Reeve might be siphoning off coal supplies for his own personal use, or perhaps was using this strategy in an effort to save money.[224] Eventually, the committee resolved to purchase a new machine for the weighing of coal, as the present machine was found to be inaccurate by around three pounds. They concluded, however, that there were no grounds for the complaints made against the master, and found that 'the statements made by John Steward as to the introduction of coals to the hospital stores in October last are distinctly contradicted by the persons referred to by him'. Mr Steward was warned not to take matters into his own hands in future.[225]

For other residents, misconduct was grounds for dismissal. The trustees, true to Doughty's original injunctions, did not take kindly to repeated instances of 'cursing, swearing, keeping bad hours [or] being drunk'.[226] Men and women found to have 'dirty habits' were also

---

220 NRO, N/CCH 111, 6 December 1870.
221 NRO, N/CCH 112, 31 October 1872.
222 *Ibid.*, 18 August 1873.
223 *Ibid.*
224 *Ibid.*
225 *Ibid.*
226 NRO, Case 20f/14, William Doughty's Will, 25 April 1687.

removed from the hospital. In June 1875 Mary Beales was cautioned for her dirty habits and one of the trustees was given the job of going to her cottage to speak with her personally about her unacceptable behaviour.[227] Evidently this did not have the desired effect, and Mrs Beales was dismissed in September of the same year for being 'incorrigibly drunk', 'dirty in her habits' and a danger to the hospital.[228] Dirty habits might also be a sign of mental instability, a condition that Doughty's was ill-equipped to deal with at this time. It is clear, however, that the well-being of the majority of residents was of paramount importance to the trustees. When, for example, in December 1877 Leggett Cobb was certified by Dr Beverley as 'very dirty in his habits', the trustees immediately arranged to have him removed from the hospital to the workhouse infirmary.[229]

Insubordination towards the master of the hospital was another undesirable characteristic of some Doughty's residents. In 1878 it was reported that 'inmate Howard' had given orders for the reparation of a truss without the permission of the master and, furthermore, that he was very rude to the master on being discovered. The trustees chose on this occasion simply to rebuke Howard for his behaviour rather than dismiss him from the hospital, which shows that they took each instance of misbehaviour on its individual merits.[230]

Drunkenness was also occasionally a problem among the inmates of Doughty's Hospital, and in January 1880 William Salter was reprimanded before the trustees for being intoxicated on three separate occasions.[231] However, the staff at the hospital appear to have had a more relaxed attitude to the consumption of alcohol than the trustees. In September 1901 Mrs Futter, who worked in the laundry at Doughty's, was fined by the local magistrate for drunkenness, as a result of which the trustees suspended her, and she claimed a month's wages in lieu of notice.[232] It seems that as well as having a relaxed attitude to their own drinking habits, some members of staff were also happy for the residents to indulge. In 1910 the rules for nurses at the hospital stated that staff were under no circumstances allowed to 'fetch stimulants from the public houses for the inmates', suggesting that perhaps this had been one of the nurses' more informal duties of care.[233]

---

227 NRO, N/CCH 112, 21 June 1875.
228 *Ibid.*, 28 September 1875.
229 *Ibid.*, 17 December 1877.
230 *Ibid.*, 20 September 1878.
231 NRO, N/CCH/ 108, 28 January 1880.
232 NRO, N/CCH 115, 18 September 1901.
233 NRO, N/CCH/117, 18 May 1910.

Doughty's in the early twentieth century

By 1908 Doughty's Hospital had grown and developed, both in terms of its administration and in terms of the building itself. Reorganisation of the trusteeship following the Municipal Corporations Act had coincided with the first inquiry of the Charity Commissioners, whose influence and support – though never paramount or heavy-handed – had henceforth to be taken into consideration by the trustees when taking major decisions. The nineteenth century had seen first some minor development of the accommodation at Doughty's and later the construction of a second storey over the original almshouse, which also allowed the expansion of each cottage. This meant that while the number of residents had not dramatically increased, the quality of their accommodation was much improved, and furthermore minor improvements to the hospital facilities continued into the early twentieth century. Its staffing complement had increased too, while a clearer division of labour had been established between those staff, and more professional terms of employment introduced.

By the end of the century the institution's clientele had changed fundamentally, not in terms of their social status – which had always been largely representative of the more respectable elements of the city's working class – but in terms of their gender. Originally intended by its founder as an institution which would be largely the preserve of elderly men, it had by now become an institution dominated by elderly women. The end of the nineteenth century also saw the hospital become more financially dependent upon other local charities, the Town Close Estate, Luke Fisher's and Cocke's Charities and local Friendly Societies each being given nomination rights in return for funds, all of which had been agreed in close consultation with the Charity Commissioners. Doughty's Hospital had successfully negotiated the various challenges that the nineteenth century had posed – economic, social, political and administrative – and emerged at the start of the twentieth century in good shape, and in financial health. The involvement of the state in the administration of charitable institutions would only increase as the twentieth century wore on, however, and the introduction of the government Old Age Pension in 1908 would fundamentally change the structure of finance at Doughty's Hospital.[234] The age of Victorian philanthropy was over.

---

234 NRO, N/CCH 116, 20 January 1909; NRO, N/CCH 124, 15 March 1944.

PART IV

The age of modern welfare, 1908–90

CHAPTER 12

Philanthropy in the age of modern welfare

The social welfare regime of the Victorian era would be wholly unrecognisable to the average English citizen of the second half of the twentieth century, while the champions of Victorian philanthropy would be appalled by the collectivism that is central to modern welfare. It has been suggested that the sums spent on private charity may have outweighed those spent on state-sponsored poor relief in mid-Victorian England, and this may have continued into the early twentieth century.[1] In 1911 the gross annual receipts of registered charities stood in excess of national public poor law expenditure, and this is to ignore the numerous unregistered charities, casual giving and the various self-help societies that also flourished at this time.[2] In 1893 it was estimated that 20,000 women worked full-time in various charities (excluding nurses), while perhaps 500,000 worked 'continuously and semi-professionally' as unpaid volunteers.[3] This was, perhaps, the height of the era of Victorian philanthropy, but already cracks were starting to appear in the edifice, while the early twentieth century was to produce more significant breaches which pointed the way to the future. The transition from one system to the other, and from one set of principles and values to another, however, was a gradual – if an inexorable – one. Furthermore, it would be wrong to dismiss the importance of state regulation and state welfare in Victorian England, just as it would be equally wrong to underestimate the continuing importance of private philanthropy in the modern era.

The underlying inclination of Victorian philanthropy was to treat social problems as the result of individual failings, and to attempt to remedy those failings through reformation of the character of the recipient, which could only be achieved by well-directed –

---

1   Best, *Mid-Victorian Britain*, p. 160; Kidd, *State, society and the poor*, p. 67.
2   J. Harris, 'Society and the state in twentieth-century Britain', in F.M.L. Thompson (ed.), *The Cambridge social history of modern Britain, 1750–1950, vol. 3* (Cambridge University Press: Cambridge, 1990), p. 68.
3   F. Prochaska, 'Philanthropy', in F.M.L. Thompson (ed.), *Cambridge social history*, p. 385.

not indiscriminate – charitable activity. This chimed well with the political and economic philosophy of *laissez faire*, which exalted the primacy of the market place and assumed that progress could best be achieved by allowing the free play of market forces and strictly limiting the intervention of the state.[4] However, the transition of the English economy from an agricultural and rural to an industrial and urban one between the mid-eighteenth and mid-nineteenth centuries, although it created enormous wealth, could not be achieved without considerable upheaval, economic disruption and social strain. The incidence of social problems – poverty, overcrowding, disease and unemployment – was now much more visible in the nation's growing towns and cities, while the 'Victorian statistical movement' – the activities of which were reflected in a succession of Royal Commission enquiries and reports – further served to identify and publicise the difficulties that were the result of such fundamental and sweeping social and economic change.[5] Despite its predilection to avoid undue government interference, therefore, successive governments were induced to regulate some forms of economic activity from early in the Victorian era – limiting the hours that children and women could work in factories (1833, 1844, 1847) and in mines (1842), introducing legislation on public health (1848) and, as we have seen, regulating the activities of Municipal Corporations (1835) – while even in the realm of education the voluntary religious societies that ran the system were in receipt of an annual grant of £20,000 from 1833 onwards.[6] The Youthful Offenders Act of 1854 extended the financial assistance of the state to the voluntary bodies established to deal with juvenile delinquents, while government grants were also provided to societies for aiding discharged prisoners.[7]

It was not until the final third of the nineteenth century, however, that the primacy of the voluntary and philanthropic solution to social problems started to be seriously questioned. The Forster Act of 1870 marked a fundamental turning point in government involvement in the sphere of education, while new public health legislation in 1866, 1871 and 1875 stimulated local authorities towards the more concerted action that was epitomised by, though by no means confined to, the activities

---

4   For a discussion of *laissez faire* and the degree to which it was put into practice see A.J. Taylor, *Laissez-faire and state intervention in nineteenth-century Britain* (Macmillan: London and Basingstoke, 1972).

5   M.J. Cullen, *The Victorian statistical movement in early Victorian Britain: the foundations of empirical social research* (Harvester Press: Hassocks, 1975).

6   J.F.C. Harrison, *The early Victorians 1832–51* (Panther Books: St Albans, 1973, first published 1971), p. 166. The grant was increased to £30,000 in 1839. Details of these various pieces of legislation can be found in any textbook on the period.

7   Owen, *English philanthropy*, p. 501.

of Joseph Chamberlain in Birmingham.[8] Indeed, as we approach the end of the nineteenth century, while central government expenditure in the United Kingdom was neither particularly high nor particularly low by international standards, local government expenditure was now rising significantly faster than that of the central state.[9] Nevertheless, at the very same time, in the realm of the poor law the government could initiate a 'campaign against out-relief' in 1869 which reasserted the fundamental determination to eradicate dependent pauperism that had been enshrined in the Poor Law Amendment Act of 1834, dramatically curtailing expenditure and radically reducing the numbers receiving relief outside of the workhouse.[10]

In 1869 too the Charity Organisation Society was founded – its acronym, COS, being represented as 'cringe or starve' among the poor – with a brief to introduce a more coordinated and 'scientific' approach to philanthropy, and above all to eradicate indiscriminate (and thus counter-productive) almsgiving.[11] It was, however, far less successful than its contemporary adherents claimed: under-funded, under-staffed and at odds with other local charities and Boards of Guardians, the COS singularly failed to transform charitable endeavour along the lines it intended and, for all the rhetoric of Victorian reformers, indiscriminate charity was never wholly suppressed, and inevitably re-emerged at times of exceptional economic distress. When faced with the rhetoric of COS adherents such as Bernard and Helen Bosanquet, C.S. Loch or Octavia Hill, therefore, one must remember that if these are the most strident voices of Victorian charity to echo across the centuries, they are far from wholly representative, and if discriminating charity appealed to many, there were lesser degrees of discrimination than even the Victorians would countenance.[12] It was the growing appreciation of the failure of philanthropy to eradicate poverty that was to lead to the search for new, very different, solutions.

Increased government involvement in social welfare, often preceded by Royal Commissions of enquiry, formed one part of the process; the sensational revelations of independent surveys of the social conditions prevailing in Britain's towns and cities formed another. In 1883 the Reverend Andrew Mearns published *The bitter cry of outcast London*, which sensationally laid bare the extent of continued urban

---

8   K.T. Hoppen, *The mid-Victorian generation 1846–1886* (Oxford University Press: Oxford, 1998), pp. 598–9; G. Kitson Clark, *The making of Victorian England* (Methuen: London, 1962), pp. 102–4.

9   Hoppen, *Mid-Victorian generation*, pp. 122–3.

10 Englander, *Poverty and poor law reform*, pp. 21–3.

11 Owen, *English philanthropy*, pp. 216–21; Prochaska, *Voluntary impulse*, pp. 70–1.

12 R. Humphrey, *Sin, organised charity and the poor law in Victorian England* (St Martin's Press: London, 1995).

deprivation, while in seventeen much more sober volumes Charles Booth's *The life and labour of the people of London* (1889–1903) dissected the living conditions of London's working classes, to produce the headline judgement that 30 per cent of Londoners were living below a bare level of subsistence. Perhaps even more surprisingly, Seebohm Rowntree's study of the very different city of York similarly revealed the failure of philanthropy to ensure a basic level of subsistence for a substantial proportion of its citizens.[13] But it was above all the work of Charles Booth that struck a chord, with his careful delineation of eight distinct economic classes, from Class A made up of 'the lowest class of occasional labourers, loafers and semi-criminals', to Class H the 'upper middle class'. This categorisation, allied to his estimates of the proportions that had fallen into poverty due to unemployment, low wages, large families, sickness and old age, represented an appraisal of the situation that appeared more scientific than it actually was, and emphasised the structural economic conditions that lay behind poverty as much as the culpability of individuals and their moral failings.[14] For all of the enormous charitable outpouring of late Victorian England, nowhere more generous than in the capital, about a million inhabitants of London in the 1890s were, according to Booth's statistics, dependent upon a family income of 20s. per week or less.[15]

Booth's major preoccupation was with the plight of the elderly. In the Stepney Poor Law Union, he estimated, old age was the principal cause of poverty in 33 per cent of cases, and sickness in 27 per cent more. Reform of the poor law, therefore, of necessity involved particular attention to the issue of old age, and he was quite sure that resolution of this problem would dramatically relieve the pressure under which both the poor law and private philanthropy currently operated. His proposal was for a non-contributory pension of 7s. per week payable to everyone 70 years of age or older.[16] The agitation he stirred up precipitated a full Royal Commission on the Poor Laws, appointed in 1905, to which Booth was invited to contribute. Its deliberations continued until 1909, and even then it failed to agree, producing Minority and Majority Reports that respectively advocated more and less reform of the current system. In the meantime, however, the Liberal government had started to put into place the piecemeal legislation that was to substitute for wholesale reform, central to which was the

---

13   Owen, *English philanthropy*, pp. 504–5; Prochaska, *Voluntary impulse*, p. 71.

14   A. Fried and R.M. Elman (eds), *Charles Booth's London* (Penguin edition: Harmondsworth, 1971), pp. 54–72; J.F.C. Harrison, *Late Victorian Britain 1875–1901* (Fontana Press: London, 1990), p. 191; Englander, *Poverty and poor law reform*, pp. 65–8.

15   Owen, *English philanthropy*, p. 505.

16   Englander, *Poverty and poor law reform*, pp. 68–72.

introduction of an old age pension in 1908 (to start in 1909), on a non-contributory basis, paying 5s. per week to individuals aged 70 or over whose income was less than £21 per annum, and 7s. 6d. per week to married couples. Those on slightly higher independent incomes were to receive a smaller pension, up to maximum earnings of £31 10s. per year, at which level of income all pension provision stopped. In 1909 the Trade Boards Act established boards to determine minimum wages in four trades, and this was extended to five additional trades in 1913. In 1911 the National Insurance Act provided for a vast compulsory contributory scheme to insure all manual workers against sickness, and a more limited compulsory scheme restricted to certain trades to insure against unemployment.[17] Despite the evident limitations of these provisions, and the fact that the poor law still remained in place, the age of modern welfare had begun.

The key feature of the inter-war years was the gradual extension of these forms of social welfare. The Unemployed Insurance Act of 1920 extended compulsory unemployment insurance to virtually all workers apart from those in agriculture, domestic service and the self-employed, while a separate scheme for agricultural workers was set up in 1936. Both the duration for which benefits could be claimed and the amounts to be paid were periodically increased. In the realm of pensions, rates were increased to 10s. per week for individuals aged 65 or over and £1 per week for co-resident married couples in 1925, while a contributory element was introduced which underpinned the long-term viability of the benefit. The new legislation increased the proportion of people over 70 who were eligible for the old age pension to 79 per cent, while on 1 January 1926 over 15 million people entered pensions insurance.[18] In addition, Housing Acts in 1919, 1923 and 1924 provided subsidies which allowed the construction of about 4 million homes between the wars, almost two in every five of them built by local authorities or with state subsidies.[19]

None of this immediately supplanted the poor law, but its relative significance did decline. In 1912, two years before the outbreak of the First World War, the number of workhouse residents reached an all-time high of 280,000, but the combined impact of pensions and sickness benefits was already reducing the overall burden, total numbers on relief falling from 916,377 in 1910 to 748,019 in 1913.

---

17   G.R. Boyer, 'Living standards, 1860–1939', in R. Floud and P. Johnson (eds), *The Cambridge economic history of modern Britain. Vol. II: economic maturity, 1860–1939* (Cambridge University Press: Cambridge, 2004), pp. 310–11; L.C.B. Seaman, *Post-Victorian Britain 1902–1951* (Methuen: London, 1966), p. 27.

18   Boyer, 'Living standards, 1860–1939', p. 311; P. Thane, *Old age in English history. Past experiences, present issues* (Oxford University Press: Oxford, 2000), p. 326.

19   Boyer, 'Living standards, 1860–1939', pp. 311–12.

Poor law infirmaries were rapidly improving and remained free of stigma, the category of 'able bodied poor' had been dropped by 1911 and workhouses were officially renamed 'poor law institutions' in 1913. On the eve of the First World War, poor law expenditure had declined to about £600,000, and was now dwarfed by expenditure on pensions which stood at £11.7 million nationally.[20]

Numbers of people on relief declined dramatically during the Great War, but rose rapidly thereafter due to post-war economic dislocation, to reach 2.5 million in 1926, the year of the General Strike. The 625 Boards of Guardians who ran the poor law could not cope, and gradually Neville Chamberlain, as Health Minister, strengthened his ministerial power over them, culminating in the Local Government Act of 1929 which abolished the Boards and replaced them with Public Assistance Committees, one for each of the 140 county councils and county borough councils. With the Boards of Guardians went, officially at least, the workhouse, Monday 31 March 1930 representing the last day of their legal existence, and in 1934 the Unemployed Assistance Board was established to further centralise the provision of poor relief. Although it took some three years to fully develop, soon the Public Assistance Committees were free to concentrate their efforts on supporting particularly vulnerable groups, notably children, the elderly and the sick. Still, however, the hated means test was retained for relief applicants. Nor did the workhouses immediately disappear, for if the intention was for them to develop their roles as specialist institutions – infirmaries, orphanages and the like – progress in this direction was slow. As late as 1939 almost 100,000 people remained in general institutions, in addition to 10,000 vagrant or casual poor, and their full transformation was not accomplished until after the Second World War.[21]

None of this activity had eradicated poverty, among the population in general or among the elderly in particular. The *New survey of London life and labour*, published in 1934, estimated that 10 per cent of the population of the capital remained in poverty, and many of these were elderly, while Herbert Tout's survey of Bristol produced identical conclusions with regard to the plight of the elderly there.[22] Nor did state-sponsored social welfare supplant philanthropy. While First World War drives for military support served to drain some of

20 A. Brundage, *The English poor laws, 1700–1930* (Palgrave: Basingstoke, 2002), pp. 142–3.
21 Brundage, *English Poor Laws*, pp. 147–52; J. Stevenson, *British society 1914–45* (Penguin: Harmondsworth, 1984), pp. 301–2; N. Longmate, *The workhouse. A social history* (Pimlico edition: London, 2003, first published 1974), pp. 276–83; M.A. Crowther, *The workhouse system 1834–1929. The history of an English social institution* (Methuen: London 1983, first published 1981), pp. 109–12.
22 Stevenson, *British society*, pp. 134–6.

the resources that might otherwise have found their way to charitable ends, the evidence from London suggests that here at least charities had recovered their pre-war financial position by the mid-1920s. For the remainder of the inter-war period, however, their incomes may have struggled to keep pace with rising costs, particularly in the case of the voluntary hospitals, and after the Local Government Act of 1929 gave local authorities increased responsibility for medical provision they became increasingly dependent on government support.[23]

In many other areas too there was increasing cooperation between the voluntary sector and the state, notably in family planning and infant welfare, where the state rapidly emerged as the senior partner.[24] The emerging relationship between the public and private sectors is reflected in the fact that by 1934 over one-third of the total income of English charities was being received as payment for services.[25] But new charities were emerging too, and some of them on a considerable scale. Among these were the National Council of One Parent Families (1918), the Save the Children Fund (1919), the Royal British Legion (1921), the Wellcome Foundation (1924), the Youth Hostels Association (1930), the King George Jubilee Trust (1935) and, most heavily endowed of them all, the Nuffield Foundation (1943).[26] The creation of the Unemployment Assistance Board, with its army of government social workers, did not spell the end of visiting societies and, indeed, much voluntary effort continued to be poured into helping the plight of the unemployed in the inter-war years.[27] Small-scale projects continued to abound, at the same time as the larger and better-endowed societies were coming to prominence. The more ardent advocates of voluntarist solutions may have begun to lose faith in the 1930s, but when Elizabeth Macadam, a leading social worker, announced in her book *The new philanthropy* (1934) the subjection of philanthropy to the state, she was foreseeing the post-war future rather than accurately representing the inter-war present.[28]

The foundation of a fully fledged welfare state was the achievement of the Labour government of 1945–51, although many of the ideas that underpinned it had emerged during the Second World War and were a response as much to the difficulties of the 1930s as they were to the war itself. The key document was without a doubt the Beveridge Report, published as early as December 1942, followed by the 1944 White Paper on Employment Policy. The Beveridge Report identified the

---

23   Owen, *English philanthropy*, pp. 529–31.
24   Prochaska, *Voluntary impulse*, p. 79,
25   Owen, *English philanthropy*, pp. 527–8.
26   Prochaska, *Voluntary impulse*, pp. 76–7; Owen, *English philanthropy*, pp. 568–9.
27   *Ibid.*, pp. 76, 78–9.
28   *Ibid.*, p. 80.

five 'giants' of deprivation as 'want', 'sickness', 'squalor', 'ignorance' and 'idleness', and recommended a comprehensive social security system covering every citizen, the institution of a system of family allowances, a national health service and an economic policy designed to obviate mass unemployment.[29] The White Paper on Employment Policy took up the last of these, while a 'caretaker' Conservative government introduced family allowances in 1945, payable at a rate of 5s. for second and subsequent children.[30]

It was the immediate post-war Labour government that put Beveridge's recommendations fully into practice, following his suggestions faithfully, if not to the precise letter.[31] The key pieces of legislation, all passed between 1946 and 1948, were the National Insurance Act, the National Insurance (Industrial Injuries) Act, the National Health Service Act – promising free health care for all at the point of delivery – and the National Assistance Act, which destroyed the last vestiges of the poor law. Reinforced by other legislation relating to – *inter alia* – education, child welfare, housing, town planning and legal aid, this represented a sea change in the degree to which the state was prepared to assume responsibility for social welfare, the provision of comprehensive welfare support for every citizen from 'the cradle to the grave', and an acceptance of the principles of collectivism over voluntarism that would have horrified our Victorian forebears.[32]

Many commentators also thought it sounded the death knell of private philanthropy, and predicted that the voluntary sector would quickly wither away.[33] Some socialists, in particular, welcomed the prospect of the demise of the independent charitable society: Aneurin Bevan was quite happy to see what he described as 'a patch-quilt of local paternalisms' replaced by 'intelligent planning'. Others, less hostile to private provision, felt that charitable funds would be much harder to come by in circumstances where the bulk of social welfare was already financed by personal taxation. Others still saw the new regime as a blessing in disguise, as it freed philanthropy from the thankless task of attempting to deal with issues that it was simply incapable of resolving, while offering new opportunities to which it was palpably better suited.[34] Beveridge himself, in his book *Voluntary action*, published in 1948, emphasised the importance of continued philanthropic activity,

29 A. Marwick, *British society since 1945* (Penguin: Harmondsworth, 1982), p. 50.

30 D. Fraser, *The evolution of the British welfare state*, 4th edition (Palgrave Macmillan: Basingstoke, 2009), pp. 270–1; Stevenson, *British society*, p. 305.

31 For the slight departures from its principles, see S. Pollard, *The development of the British economy 1914–67* (Edward Arnold: London, 1962), p. 399.

32 Marwick, *British society*, pp. 49–63; Owen, *English philanthropy*, pp. 531–2.

33 B. Knight, *Voluntary action* (Centris: London, 1993), p. 22.

34 Prochaska, *Voluntary impulse*, pp. 84–5; Owen, *English philanthropy*, p. 533.

and advocated new and vigorous cooperation between volunteers and statutory authorities. Voluntary activity, he felt, was one of the distinguishing marks of a free society. While celebrating the nation's long, voluntary tradition, however, far from turning back to a Victorian model of independent philanthropic activity, he now conceived of voluntarism working under the auspices of a 'Minister-Guardian of Voluntary Action'.[35]

There is no general study of charitable giving since the Second World War that allows even an approach to quantitative assessment. That said, all the available evidence points to the growing importance of grants from statutory bodies in keeping many charities afloat. The state itself, it has been suggested, has emerged as 'a major philanthropist and benefactor of the voluntary services'.[36] Of course, the benefit does not all flow in one direction, for the partnership has been a mutually advantageous one. The voluntary services provide staff, both professional and volunteer, equipment, financial resources and established expertise that saves the state money, and allows it to engage in a wider range of services than it would otherwise be able to encompass. Even in the realm of medical care, an organisation such as the St John Ambulance service could carry on much as it had done before the reforms of the post-war Labour government, while the King Edward's Hospital Fund – originally established in 1897 to help shore up the finances of the voluntary hospitals – found new uses for its money in enterprises such as staff colleges for hospital administrators, ward sisters and matrons, grants to hospitals for special purposes such as the provision of specialised equipment, and the establishment of recreation halls for staff and patients.[37]

Elsewhere in the voluntary sector there has been increased cooperation and collaboration with statutory bodies, while other charities whose essential purpose had been rendered redundant have had to redefine their objectives. As Prochaska has written, 'Voluntary action did not evaporate in 1948 as many commentators expected. It is perpetually discovering new needs and aspirations'.[38] Many charities are small in scale, local in both support and sphere of action, and diverse in nature, and this has been true of the voluntary sector throughout its history. Others are large and well-endowed, and have become etched into the fabric of contemporary life, such as Oxfam, the Royal National Lifeboat Institute (RNLI), the People's Dispensary for Sick Animals (PDSA) or the National Society for the Prevention

35   Harris, 'Society and the state', p. 104; Prochaska, *Voluntary impulse*, p. 85.
36   Owen, *English philanthropy*, pp. 538–41, quote on p. 541.
37   *Ibid.*, pp. 544–7.
38   Prochaska, *Voluntary impulse*, p. 88.

of Cruelty to Children (NSPCC). Others still are perhaps barely recognised as charitable organisations, such as Citizens Advice, which in 2009 operated 426 Citizens Advice Bureaux across England and Wales, and a further 22 in Northern Ireland, all of them independent registered charities. Each bureau is a member of Citizens Advice, the umbrella organisation and also an independent registered charity, and this provides training and support to member bureaux, and coordinates national policy work.[39] When the Nathan Committee met to discuss the voluntary services between January 1950 and December 1952, it found a sector in good health, virtually free from fraud or gross negligence, with trustees generally doing a creditable job, and obsolescence and redundancy rare. Above all it recognised voluntary action as an integral part of the machinery of the welfare state, a view that was endorsed when parliament rationalised charity law and its administration eight years later in passing the Charitable Trusts Act of 1960.[40]

All of this is reflected in the continued growth in the number of registered charities. In 1976 there were 122,000 registered charities, 157,000 in 1986 and 188,000 in 1998. In the latter year their aggregate income stood at £19.7 billion, and they remained active in all areas of welfare. Of course, this needs to be placed in perspective, for in 1999 UK government expenditure on social security amounted to £97 billion, while the Department of Health spent £48 billion.[41] The proportion contributed by the voluntary sector is therefore relatively small, and in this sense it is undoubtedly subordinate to state welfare. It does, however, still make a difference in local as well as national settings, and is often targeted at particular needs, such as medical research in general and cancer research in particular. Furthermore, as many of its staff are unpaid, its real income is actually higher than the bare figures suggest: a national opinion poll conducted in 1976 revealed that roughly five million British adults participated in some form of charitable work in that year, and in personal services their manpower outweighed that provided by the state.[42]

To come closer to our immediate concerns, voluntary activity has continued too in the sphere of care for the elderly, as was the specific intention of the post-war legislation. The National Assistance Act of 1948 assumed public–private collaboration, for local authorities were empowered to provide residential accommodation for the aged by giving subsidies to voluntary agencies or by employing them as their

---

39 www.citizensadvice.org.uk, consulted 31 July 2009.
40 Owen, *English philanthropy*, pp. 588–93.
41 J.R. Bryson, M. McGuiness and R.G. Ford, 'Chasing a "loose and baggy monster": almshouses and the geography of charity', *Area*, Vol. 34 (2002), p. 50.
42 Prochaska, *Philanthropy*, p. 391.

agents on locally agreed terms. Already during wartime the National Old People's Welfare Committee, founded in 1941, had obtained from the Assistance Board a supplementary allowance for old people resident in voluntary homes, allowing the number of such homes to expand and charting the pattern for the future, while a Nuffield Foundation Survey, published in 1947 as *Old people*, also assumed continued public–private cooperation. It also found that, on the whole, voluntary homes were superior to those established by public assistance authorities, and in the case of the former demand outran supply. The inquiry also resulted in the foundation of the National Corporation for the Care of Old People, designed to assist voluntary bodies by helping in planning, by operating pilot schemes and – most important of all – providing grants. In particular they helped almshouses. The Nuffield survey revealed that almshouses provided accommodation for more old people than did communal homes, both religious and secular, and when the National Assistance Act continued the payment of supplementary allowances to almshouse residents it proved possible for many to reduce residents' pensions and thus to accumulate small surpluses that could be spent on maintenance. 'In the rehabilitation of the almshouse', Owen writes, 'ancient charity, modern voluntary effort, and statutory stewardship have joined hands in fruitful partnership'.[43]

Although statutory provision for the residential care of the elderly has grown substantially since the Second World War, and the voluntary sector is clearly now by far the junior partner, the Nuffield Foundation Survey published in 1947 revealed nearly 1,500 almshouse charities accommodating over 22,000 people, of which endowed almshouses accounted for 12,000. By 1999 the Almshouse Association, founded as a national society in 1950, represented 1,748 member charities managing 2,599 groups of almshouses and providing accommodation for 31,241 residents. Between 1943 and 1999, therefore, the number of people living in almshouses increased by 43 per cent.[44] The latest figures available at the time of writing, published in 2009 on the Almshouse Association website, indicate a total of almost 1,800 separate almshouse charities, running 2,600 groups of almshouses, constituting over 30,000 almshouse dwellings, and providing accommodation for 36,000 individuals – a further growth of roughly 4,500, or 15 per cent, since 1999. The Almshouse Association proudly claims that, 'The support and help they provide is just as important today, in the twenty-first century, as it was over 1,000 years ago'.[45]

---

43   Owen, *English philanthropy*, pp. 547–52, quote at p. 552.
44   Bryson *et al.*, 'Chasing a "loose and baggy monster"', p. 51.
45   www.almshouses.info, consulted 26 August 2009.

CHAPTER 13
Twentieth-century Norwich

The progress of a nation

If Britain was the 'workshop of the world' in the mid-Victorian period, by the end of the twentieth century it had become just one among many developed nations, with an income level below that of North America, most of western Europe and parts of East Asia. Relative economic decline started in the latter part of the nineteenth century as Germany, the United States and France emerged as powerful rivals, first catching up and then overhauling the country that had been the world's first industrial nation.[46] Apart from problems in the agricultural sector, it was the old staple heavy industries that were struggling – iron and steel, shipbuilding, coal and textiles – as the levels of productivity they were able to attain started to lag behind our main rivals. At the same time those rivals were also developing new industries, particularly in the form of chemicals and electrical goods, and were overhauling Britain in their development of skilled engineering too. It was, of course, in the areas dominated by the old staple industries that unemployment reached such high levels in the inter-war years, precipitating the General Strike in 1926 and explaining the mass unemployment in parts of Wales and the north of England that persisted through the early 1930s, which in turn inspired the Jarrow March of 1936. At the same time new, light industries were beginning to make headway – car and cycle production, artificial fabrics, chemicals, rubber, paper and printing and electrical engineering, among others – and these exhibited higher levels of productivity in the inter-wars years, helping to sustain overall output and levels of employment. These, however, had a very different regional focus, and were more commonly situated in the south and the Midlands. In 1934, the year in which J.B. Priestley published his *English journey* depicting a nation divided between poverty and unemployment and industry and affluence, the level of unemployment in Jarrow was 68 per cent and in Merthyr Tydfil 62 per cent, but in Coventry just 5 per cent and St Albans 4 per cent. Overall, however, living standards

---

46 N. Crafts, 'Long-run growth', in Floud and Johnson (eds), *Cambridge economic history: Vol. II*, p. 2.

rose in the inter-war years, and the 1930s should be remembered as much as the age of the dance hall and the cinema as it was the age of the dole and the means test.[47]

Rearmament and the economics of total warfare provided renewed stimulus to a number of traditional industries, and further encouraged the development of newer ones. The index of production for the whole manufacturing sector (base 100 in 1907) stood at 171 in 1935, and had risen to 203 by 1948. The war also fostered new scientific discoveries, a new attitude to the application of science, and stimulated the development of new methods of mass production that were to have a lasting impact. Aircraft production, electrical and mechanical engineering, the chemical industry and agriculture were the main beneficiaries of wartime expansion and modernisation. The war also led to the nationalisation of certain key industries in 1945, the inspiration for which was the optimum deployment of resources rather than socialist reconstruction, while it was the wartime spirit that precipitated the Beveridge Report and the 1944 White Paper on Employment Policy. Despite its short-term – and human – costs, war produced long-term economic benefits. War had shown what was possible, allowed lessons to be drawn from the past and inspired visions of the future.[48]

The years 1950–73 have been described as the 'Golden Age' of the advanced capitalist economies, and as 'a period of secular boom on unparalleled scale'.[49] This era has also been dubbed one of 'growthmanship', 'the age of affluence' and – in the 1950s – a time when 'we've never had it so good'.[50] It was indeed an unprecedented period of long-term economic growth and – although the relatively poor performance of the UK is often contrasted with that of many of the other leading economic powers – gross domestic product (GDP, the total output of the economy) rose across this period by as much as 3 per cent per annum. The period saw a continued shift away from the old, heavy industries and towards new, more technological, consumer-oriented industries.[51] And while in the long term manufacturing was declining in relative importance, the service sector was steadily gaining

47 *Ibid.*, pp. 2–24; R. Floud, *The people and the British economy 1830–1914* (Oxford University Press: Oxford, 1997), pp. 3–21; Stevenson, *British society*, pp. 266–74, 395–7; Pollard, *Development of the British economy*, pp. 289–96.

48 *Ibid.*, pp. 308–321; A.S. Milward, *The economic effects of the two World Wars on Britain* (Macmillan: London and Basingstoke, 1970), pp. 34–5, 41–2.

49 A. Maddison, *Phases of capitalist development* (Oxford University Press: Oxford, 1982), pp. 92–3.

50 For growthmanship see M. M. Postan, *An economic history of western Europe 1945–64* (Methuen: London, 1967); J.K. Galbraith, *The affluent society* (Penguin edition: Harmondsworth, 1962, first published 1958). The final quote is, of course, from Harold Macmillan.

51 Marwick, *British society*, pp. 114–16.

ground, as indeed it had in all advanced economies.[52] This is particularly evident when one examines the occupational structure of so many of the nations' large towns towards the end of the twentieth century, Norwich included.

Across the twentieth century as a whole living standards had risen to unprecedented heights, notwithstanding the temporary interruption caused by further economic downturn after 1973, and no other century – with the possible exception of the fifteenth – had seen such elevation in the living standards of the average working Briton. That said, the distribution of both wealth and income remained highly skewed, and sociologists have not struggled to detect the persistence of poverty amidst affluence. Furthermore, there was also a demographic imperative that produced increased demand for welfare services, both medical and residential. For as levels of both fertility and mortality declined during the course of the century, the nation's population became progressively older, to the extent that the proportion of the population of pensionable age (65 for men, 60 for women) stood at approximately 18 per cent by 2007, compared with less than 7 per cent in the mid-Victorian era.[53] These economic developments provide the background against which we can consider the progress of twentieth-century Norwich, while the persistence of a highly skewed social distribution of wealth, allied to twentieth-century demographic change, provides the essential backdrop for the continued relevance of private philanthropy.

The development of Norwich

At the turn of the twentieth century, Norwich was a fairly prosperous and expanding city, its population growing particularly rapidly between 1891 and 1911, from 89,000 to 121,000.[54] Declining textile production had been replaced by a thriving boot and shoe manufacturing industry which had attained national prominence, especially in the production of women's and children's shoes, while it was a world leader in the sale of fire insurance and in the production of starch and mustard.[55] The outbreak of the First World War came as a shock, for immediately several Norwich firms lost their export markets and unemployment rose sharply, particularly among women. As in other towns and cities, war work provided some compensation. Both Harmers and Chamberlins quickly

52   R. Millward, 'The rise of the service economy', in R. Floud and P. Johnson (eds), *The Cambridge economic history of modern Britain. Vol. III: structural change and growth, 1939–2000* (Cambridge University Press: Cambridge, 2004), pp. 238–66.
53   www.statistics.gov.uk/cci/nugget.asp?id=2157, consulted 1 August 2009; E.A. Wrigley and R.S. Schofield, *The population history of England 1541–1871: a reconstruction* (Edward Arnold: London, 1981), Table A3.1, pp. 528–9.
54   Armstrong, *Population*, Table 1.2, p. 7.
55   R. Wilson, 'Introduction', in Rawcliffe and Wilson (eds), *Norwich since 1550*, p. xxvii.

1. *A Doughty's garden party, 1979*

2. *The men's choir perform at the tercentenary celebration, 1987*

3. Winnie and Fred Townsend, residents, celebrate their golden wedding, 1989

4. A gathering of friends outside Elsie Groom's flat

5. *Watching morris dancing. Four residents enjoy the entertainment*

6. *On the sea front at Gorlestone*

7.   Outside the Pier Hotel, Gorlestone

8.   Celebrating another 'Norwich in Bloom' award won by Geoff Beck, Doughty's gardener, early 1990s

9.   'Treading grapes'. Carol Hodge, cleaner, Diane Lee, care assistant, and Dorothy Ralph, keep-fit instructor, entertain the residents, 1992

10.   Gwen Bowen's Christmas choir, 1992

11. *Jean Whitlam, Matron, and her staff gather for a photo opportunity outside the staff room, early 1990s*

12. *'That hat'. Lady Benson reopens Doughty's after the refurbishment completed in 1995*

13.   *Royal visit, 1996. Her Majesty the Queen with Jean Whitlam, Matron, on Doughty's balcony*

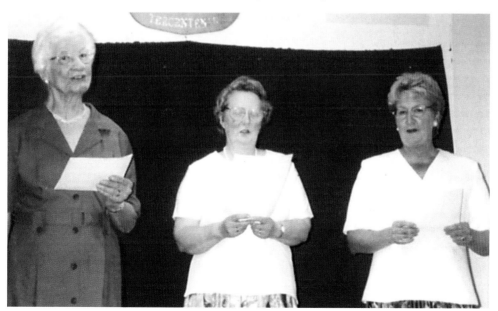

14.   *'The Three Matrons'. Gwen Bowen, Jean Whitlam and Freda Turner (née Holland) entertain the residents, 1997*

15. *Spring celebration featuring Harry Watson, Lord Mayor of Norwich and philanthropist, and Freda Holland, Matron*

16. *Doughty's Hospital, 2009, showing the reading room and Grace Jarrold Court*

turned their hands to the production of uniforms and waterproof clothing and oilskins, in great demand in support of the war effort, while during the war Howlett and White produced over half a million pairs of boots and shoes for the army and Allied forces. The engineering companies also turned their hands to production of munitions and aircraft, and both men and women workers found their hands full.

The end of the war proved to be just as much of a shock as its start, for contracts immediately ceased while export markets had been lost during the war years. By December 1920 there were 10,000 people out of work in the city. Slow recovery ensued, but Norwich – despite the fact that it had long since shed its reliance on textiles and played no part in the declining heavy industries – also suffered in the slump of the early 1930s. In 1931 14.8 per cent of its insured population was out of work, a figure that stood well below the unemployment hotspots of Wales and the north, but considerably above those found in many other southern and Midland towns and cities, such as the examples of Coventry and St Albans cited above. The way forward proved to be through ever greater reliance on shoemaking, which employed 17 per cent of the workforce by 1931, supported by mechanical and electrical engineering – an inter-war growth trade – and a wide range of other craft and service industries. Mergers and rationalisation helped, but although in 1934 Priestley could note that Norwich had 'escaped the full weight of the industrial depression', and the city was never classified as a distressed area, unemployment remained high, peaking at 20 per cent of the insured population in January 1933.

Notwithstanding the fact that the city was in the doldrums in the early 1930s, Norwich still impressed Priestley, and his impressions are worth quoting at length:

> In a very large slice of England, to thousands and thousands of good sensible folk who live and work there, Norwich is the big city, the centre, and has been these hundreds of years. My own native town is more than twice the size of Norwich, but somehow it does not seem half the size. This is not merely because Norwich has its cathedral and castle and the rest, but also because it has flourished as the big city in the minds of men for generations. It is no mere jumped-up conglomeration of factories, warehouses and dormitories. It may be minute compared with London, Paris, Rome, but nevertheless it lives its life as a city on the same level of dignity.[56]

---

56 Quoted in P.J. Waller, *Town, city and nation, England 1850–1914* (Oxford University Press: Oxford, 1983), p. 217.

After the depression of the first half of the 1930s slow recovery ensued, but the town failed to attract new industry. Inhibited also by a deeply depressed agricultural hinterland, the prosperity of which had for so long helped sustain its economy, it now felt the full effects of its geographical isolation compared with better-connected towns and cities elsewhere in southern and eastern England.[57] The population of the county borough of Norwich in 1939 stood at 121,700, which represented a decline of 4,500 compared with 1931, while no further growth was achieved between 1939 and 1951. In respect of aggregate population change 1931–51, Norwich occupied 133rd place among a sample of 157 towns. Equally as worrying, its infant mortality rate – often used by social historians as a surrogate measure of the standard of living – remained high in 1950–2, for although it was on a sharp downward trend, Norwich in the early 1950s remained in 112th position in terms of infant mortality amongst 157 large towns and cities in England and Wales.[58]

Again the exigencies of warfare between 1939 and 1945 propped up the economy of the city, but by now it had become clear to civic leaders that there was a need to diversify if Norwich was to keep pace with other English towns. Unemployment rates remained high while wages remained traditionally low, and the city council began to look for ways of encouraging new industries while at the same time improving basic amenities.[59] Housing was a primary concern after 1945. The large-scale damage that the city had suffered as a result of heavy bombing during the Second World War gave Norwich Corporation the impetus to clear areas of substandard and slum housing, while between 1945 and 1955 6,500 new homes were built by the city council on previously undeveloped greenfield land. Although the estimated population growth of the city itself was only 3,300 between 1951 and 1971, the population of the wider Norwich area grew much more significantly, fuelled by healthy levels of in-migration.[60]

As well as building new housing in the city, Norwich Corporation also sought to modernise its layout, and *The City of Norwich Plan* was set out in 1945. The plan indicated that, among other improvements, the city centre should be pedestrianised and an inner link ring road should be built around the city in order to facilitate travel and make Norwich more attractive to business investors. The need for the construction of a new dual carriageway was disputed by the Norwich

---

57   Clark, 'Work and employment', pp. 400–8.
58   Armstrong, 'Population', pp. 266–9.
59   P. Townroe, 'Norwich since 1945', in Rawcliffe and Wilson (eds), *Norwich since 1550*, pp. 461–3.
60   *Ibid.*, pp. 462–3; City of Norwich and Norfolk County Council, *A joint growth study* (Norwich, 1966); Townroe, 'Norwich since 1945', pp. 462–3.

Society, especially in the north of the city where it would destroy several historic buildings in Magdalen Street, including the matron's house at Doughty's Hospital. Despite these protests, these sections of the ring road were completed in the mid-1970s, providing markedly improved access to the city centre by road.[61]

In terms of employment, the boot and shoe making and clothing industries continued to dominate through to the early 1960s, whereafter both began to succumb to foreign competition. Standing at 10,000 in 1949 and 9,000 in 1961, by the 1980s employment in footwear had fallen to just over 3,000 and many companies had disappeared, either through bankruptcy or consolidation. Brewing, an industry with even deeper roots in Norwich, was also in decline, thanks to mergers and changes in production techniques. In the 1870s there had been five large breweries in the city and several smaller ones, but by 1985 there was only one, the King Street Brewery, which closed at the end of that year. Employment in both the railways and the gas industry were also on a downward path in these years.[62]

Despite contraction in a number of areas, however, there was expansion in others, and unemployment levels remained close to the low national rates that prevailed throughout the 'Golden Age' of the 1950s and 1960s. Manufacturing industry in the city diversified into light engineering, printing and publishing, and electronic components and plastics, and these were supported by the continuing strength of the food and chemical industries. Lotus cars became a key employer in the Norwich area by the late twentieth century, while British television screens reverberated to the unforgettable advertising campaigns of Bernard Matthews, whose 'bootiful' poultry products made a major national, and indeed international, impact. As in so many other towns, however, the real expansion came in the service sector – in insurance, banking, retailing and the provision of a wide range of personal services. By 1987 Norwich Union (in 2008 renamed Aviva) employed 4,500 people in Norwich. Both professional and more humble service employment was also buoyed up by the growth of education in general, and the establishment of the University of East Anglia in particular, while further hospital improvement and expansion provided yet further opportunities. Tourism became of increasing importance too, even if the city does not have the same appeal (or convenient location) as cities such as Cambridge, York or Bath. This activity has sustained a population consistently in excess of 120,000, the total for 1999 standing at 123,500. While across the twentieth century the City of Norwich

---

61   Townroe, 'Norwich since 1945', pp. 463-7; City of Norwich, *The City of Norwich Plan* (Norwich, 1945).

62   Townroe, 'Norwich since 1945', pp. 469-70.

had done little more than maintain its population when the national total had increased by approximately 60 per cent, there was substantial post-Second World War development in contiguous areas, with new or expanded housing investment at Earlham, Tuckswood, Lakenham, South Park Avenue, Mousehold, Thorpe St Andrew, Sprowston, New Catton, Hellesdon and New Costessy. In consequence, a 'joint growth study' conducted in 1966 could identify a 'city settlement area' with a population of 207,500. In both the rapid development of its service industries, and in the growing emphasis upon consumption rather than production, Norwich was typical of many large English towns and cities in the final third of the twentieth century.[63]

Philanthropy in twentieth-century Norwich

At the start of the twentieth century Norwich was relatively well endowed with charitable foundations. In 1895 the Royal Commission on the Aged Poor estimated that almshouses and pensions trusts accounted for a total income of roughly £660,000 per annum, but also noted that they were very unevenly distributed. Furthermore, they varied one from another in the form that endowments for the elderly took. Statistics compiled for the Royal Commission on the Poor Laws in 1905–9 bring this out well by contrasting two cities that were both very well endowed – Norwich and Coventry. In Norwich the funds available for almspeople stood at about £10,000, while there was just £480 for pensioners, and as much as £5,500 for doles. In Coventry, in contrast, the greatest sum by far, £9,500, was devoted to pensioners, with only £1,000 available for almspeople and £2,600 for doles.[64] Overall levels of support, while slightly in favour of Norwich, were of a comparable order of magnitude, but the means by which they were distributed were thus very different indeed. In the case of Norwich, of course, these figures stand as testimony to the success of its almshouse foundations, dominated by the Great Hospital, and supported by Doughty's.

The majority of the almshouses in the city – Doughty's Hospital, Cooke's Hospital, Pye's Almshouse and the cottages on Alms Lane – were amalgamated under the 1910 Norwich Charities Consolidation Act. This Act was passed to make the charities more efficient and to make it easier for people in the city to claim relief. Anguish's Boys' Hospital was incorporated into this scheme at the same time. In 1885 it sold its property in Fishergate for £550, and the Charity Commissioners suggested a new scheme whereby the money from

---

63   *Ibid.*, pp. 463–82.
64   Owen, *English philanthropy*, p. 507 and fn. 26.

Anguish's Educational Foundation would be used for scholarships for poor boys, and this scheme was eventually adopted in 1896. Boys receiving scholarships from the charity were entitled to one suit of clothes and two new pairs of boots per year and the guardians of boys, if they were boarded out, received £10 if the boy was under ten and £13 if he was over ten.[65] From 1910 the trustees of Norwich Consolidated Charities also administered Anguish's Educational Foundation, although its activities were separately minuted.[66] By the 1960s the scholarship fund, which now included provisions for school uniforms and educational trips and activities for children from poor families, was run from the same office in Bank of England Court as Doughty's Hospital and Norwich Consolidated Charities. The Town Close Estate Charity, which became known locally as the Freeman's Charity, was also reorganised under the 1910 Act. Although it was run separately under the new scheme, eight of the sixteen trustees of Town Close Estate were drawn from the trustees of Norwich Consolidated Charities.[67] The remaining eight trustees were representatives appointed from the freemen of the city.[68]

Despite the changes in the City of Norwich and the rise of state welfare charted above, private charity flourished, and anciently endowed philanthropic institutions like Doughty's Hospital continued to run parallel to the new state welfare system.[69] Doughty's, and the city's other almshouses, continued to provide affordable sheltered housing for the elderly. Furthermore, the formalisation of housing associations under the 1964 Housing Act gave the almshouses in Norwich the chance to expand through special grants and loans which funded social housing projects, particularly after 1974 when these grants became far more generous.[70] Many of the smaller loans and apprenticing charities were also able to survive into the twentieth century as a result of the consolidation of Norwich's charities.[71]

Early in the twentieth century Norwich also played host to new clubs and societies which were willing and able to raise funds on behalf of charitable organisations. For example, the Norfolk Federation of Women's Institutes was established in 1919, and at the time of writing is located at a property on All Saint's Green which the federation acquired in 1954.[72] The Norwich Round Table was established in the

---

65   Hooper, *Norwich charities*, p. 79.
66   NRO, N/CCH 117, 16 November 1910.
67   DOHI 015.
68   *Norwich charities: bill to confirm schemes of the Charity Commissioners,* BPP 1910, Vol. IV.35 (69), p. 12.
69   See above, pp. 101-11; Caffrey, *Almshouses*, pp. 16–18.
70   NRO, N/CCH 125, 21 November 1956; 17 July 1957; and see Part V, below, pp. 183-4.
71   NRO, N/CCH 117, 21 September 1910.
72   www.norfolkwi.org.uk, consulted 28 July 2009.

city in 1927 and has since spread around the world. The society still provides a forum for business people to meet and socialise.[73] Both the Round Table and the Women's Institutes are active in campaigning and raising money for charities in and around Norwich. Besides these and the long-established endowments, a vast range of new charitable institutions appeared in the city in the second half of the twentieth century. Smaller welfare charities began to appear in the city in the 1950s and 1960s and these survived by raising funds through charitable giving, rather than through the endowed property of the more established charities. For instance, in 1956 the Friends of the Old People of Norwich was established in order to give help, support and advice to the elderly population of the city.[74] The Norfolk and Norwich Spastic Association was first registered in October 1962 and aimed to raise funds for the support and relief of local people with cerebral palsy and their families.[75] The Association changed its name to Norfolk and Norwich Scope Association in 1994 and has continued to support both adults and children suffering from this condition.[76]

Foundations were also set up by prominent Norwich families: for example the John Jarrold Trust Limited, which was incorporated in March 1965 and registered as a charity in May of the same year.[77] The trust was established to promote, support and advance charitable purposes of all kinds, but particularly to aid projects in the areas of education and research in all or any of the natural sciences. Its focus was, and remains, upon projects which benefit the people of Norfolk, with donations also being made to a few select organisations working in developing countries.[78] The breadth and range of charity in the city in no way diminished in the twentieth century. Meanwhile the established charities in Norwich, such as Doughty's Hospital, have sought to improve and to develop, in an effort to remain relevant to, and to continue to meet the needs of, the community.

Medical charities in the city developed new systems of funding as a result of government intervention. The Norfolk and Norwich Hospital, which had been built in 1771 using subscriptions and bequests from wealthy benefactors, began to charge for care and treatment. In 1907

73 www.roundtable.org.uk/about.php, consulted 28 July 2009.
74 www.charitycommission.gov.uk/ShowCharity/RegisterofCharities/RemovedCharity Main.aspx?RegisteredCharityNumber=209721&SubsidiaryCharityNumber=0, consulted 28 July 2009.
75 www.charitycommission.gov.uk/ShowCharity/RegisterOfCharities/RemovedCharity Main.asp?RegisteredCharityNumber=210383&SubsidiaryCharityNumber=0, consulted 28 July 2009.
76 www.nansa.org.uk/html/history.html, consulted 28 July 2009.
77 www.jarrold.com/content/jjtrust.asp, consulted 29 July 2009.
78 www.charitycommission.gov.uk/SHOWCHARITY/RegisterOfCharities/Charity WithoutPartB.aspx?RegisteredCharityNumber=242029&SubsidiaryNumber=0, consulted 29 July 2009.

the hospital started to expect payment for out-patient care and by 1921 both out-patients and in-patients had to pay for their own treatment.[79] This gave rise to the Saturday Organisation, which made provision for people to pay a weekly contribution to the hospital in order to fund any future medical treatment. These insurance policies were formalised in 1911 under the National Insurance Act, which enabled most working men to pay towards their own health care.[80]

In 1925 the Norwich Eye Infirmary merged with the Norfolk and Norwich Hospital and continued to offer specialist eye surgery within the buildings of the Norfolk and Norwich. The Jenny Lind Children's Hospital continued to care for the children of Norwich separately from the main hospital, and remained at a site on Unthank Road until its demolition in 1975.[81] All these medical charities, as well as the dispensary on Pottergate, were absorbed by the state as a result of the creation of the National Health Service in 1946.[82] However, despite the emergence of a formal system of health care, which was free at the point of delivery, medical charities continued to be founded in the city. These were often established to meet needs that were not yet being fulfilled by the formal system of medical care. For example, the Big C Appeal is a charity which promotes and supports research into the treatment and cure of cancer. Established in 1980 in Norfolk and registered as a charity in February 1981, it makes grants to public, private and charitable organisations that undertake research into the causes, prevention, treatment and cure of cancer. The charity also provides support for those dealing with cancer diagnosis and aims to complement National Health Service facilities.[83] Another large medical charity in the city is the Norfolk and Norwich University Hospital National Health Service Trust Charitable Fund, which was registered in 1995 to raise money for the hospital. At the time of writing it consists of several subsidiaries, including the cancer charity, the patient charity, the equipment charity, the staff charity and the education, research and training charity.[84] Norwich charities, therefore, amply demonstrate the targeted nature of medical philanthropy that has become a general feature of the post-National Health Service period.[85]

---

79 Cherry, 'Medical care', p. 277.
80 *Ibid.*, p. 287.
81 *Ibid.*, p. 279.
82 *Ibid.*, p. 293.
83 www.big-c.co.uk/bigccentre.php, consulted 29 July 2009.
84 www.charitycommission.gov.uk/SHOWCHARITY/RegisterOfCharities/Charity
    WithPartB.aspx?RegisteredCharityNumber=1048170&SubsidiaryNumber=0, consulted 29
    July 2009.
85 See above, p. 110.

CHAPTER 14
Doughty's and the welfare state

In 1908, when David Lloyd George, the Chancellor of the Exchequer in Asquith's Liberal government, launched the old age pension for all those over 70 years of age and with limited additional income, it had immediate implications for the residents of Doughty's Hospital. In December 1908 the clerk to the hospital reported that almost all of the residents were eligible to receive this government pension. The implementation of the pension meant that the system of allowances for residents at Doughty's Hospital became much more complex. In order for residents over 70 years old to qualify for an old age pension, their weekly stipends had to be reduced from 5s. 6d. to 3s. per week, while those who did not qualify for the pension, by reason of age, were entitled to 8s. per week from the trustees.[86]

Those residents of the almshouse who were over 70, but who were not on the foundation and were being maintained by a weekly donation from a guarantor, would now be maintained by government pensions instead. As such, the introduction of the old age pension saw the disappearance of almspeople who were maintained solely by outside benefactors or Friendly Societies.[87] It took some time to create the right balance in the new system of allowances. In 1918 it was realised that while inmates on the old age pension received 7s. 6d. from the government and 3s. from the trustees, almspeople under 70 years of age only received 8s. per week. In consequence it was resolved that the almspeople under 70 be given 10s. 6d. per week, to bring them into line with old age pensioners.[88]

While the system of stipends was being restructured, the Charity Commissioners also sought to restructure the administration of charities in Norwich, a move that involved changes for Doughty's Hospital. An assistant Charity Commissioner, Mr A.C. Kay, made inquiries into the state of the charities in Norwich from 1905 to 1907

---

86 NRO, N/CCH 119, 14 March 1911.
87 NRO, N/CCH 116, 20 January 1909.
88 NRO, N/CCH 120, 19 June 1918.

and his subsequent reports recommended the consolidation of many of the city's charities.[89] The idea of the consolidation of the Norwich charities was first suggested by the Charity Commissioners in February 1909 but the trustees of the General List, who were responsible for the running of Doughty's Hospital, resisted. They reasoned that while it would be desirable to have the smaller loans and apprenticing charities grouped together, larger charities such as Doughty's would not benefit from the scheme.[90] However, the Charity Commissioners persisted and in November 1909 the clerk of the trustees received the draft scheme for the Consolidation of Norwich Charities as described in chapter 13 above.[91] The aims of the scheme were to ensure good management of the charities, to cut costs and pool resources and to make relief more generally available to the poor of the city.[92]

The trustees of the General List had several reservations and insisted that a master be employed to run Doughty's Hospital, rather than a matron as the Charity Commissioners scheme had specified.[93] A compromise was eventually reached, although the Commissioners refused to concede that a master should manage Doughty's. The Norwich Charities Scheme Confirmation Act was given royal assent on 26 July 1910.[94] The General List trustees remained in authority until 1 January 1911, after which the Norwich Consolidated Charities trustees assumed control.[95]

This new management consisted of sixteen representatives and eight co-opted trustees. Among the representatives there were eleven men from the city council, two from the Norwich Board of Guardians, one from the Norfolk and Norwich Hospital, one from the Norwich and District Trades and Labour Council and one from the Medical Board of the Friendly Societies of Norwich.[96] Power was delegated to three separate committees, the Estates and Finances Committee, the Loans and Apprenticeship Committee and the Almshouse Committee.[97] As well as a large group of parish loans and apprenticeship charities – including the small church charities, Balliston's Charity, Wingfield's Charity, James Elmy's Charity and Luke Fisher and Cocke's Charities – the new Consolidated Charities was also responsible for the majority of the city's almshouses. Doughty's Hospital, Cooke's Hospital and Pye's Almshouse, as well as several cottages in Alms Lane, were all

89   NRO, N/CCH 117, 17 November 1909.
90   NRO, N/CCH 116, 17 March 1909.
91   See pp. 118-19.
92   NRO, N/CCH 117, 17 November 1909.
93   *Ibid.*, 24 January 1910.
94   NRO, N/CCH 117, 21 September 1910.
95   *Ibid.*
96   Jewson, *Doughty's Hospital,* p. 23.
97   NRO, N/CCH 119, 31 January 1911.

now under the jurisdiction of the Almshouse Committee of Norwich Consolidated Charities.[98]

The growth of the welfare state on a national scale also had consequences for the inmates of Doughty's Hospital. In May 1943, as a result of the National Health Insurance Acts, insured almspeople were entitled to visits by their own doctors. The trustees asked Doughty's medical attendant, Mr Burfield, to apply to become a registered panel doctor so that the residents could continue to use his services under the new scheme. However, the Norwich Health Insurance Committee thought that these proposed plans interfered with the free choice of insured almspeople, and so contravened the rules of the insurance committee.[99] As a result of this, each almsperson was allowed to choose their own doctor, and the matron was required to keep a list of each resident's GP in case of emergencies. In May 1948, under the new National Health Service, all almspeople were free to register with any doctor, although Mr Burfield was kept on as medical attendant at Doughty's.[100] In 1951 it was suggested that the position of medical attendant be removed, as this would save an annual sum of £50. However, the trustees decided to keep Mr Burfield in his position as doctor to the almshouse, although he was now employed in a mainly advisory capacity.[101]

Not all of the changes in the 1940s were regarded favourably by the residents, including the gradual loss of the weekly stipend, a traditional part of life at Doughty's since the inception of the institution 250 years previously. This was a consequence of the new state supplementary allowances that had become available to the elderly residents in voluntary homes, introduced during wartime on the advice of the National Old People's Welfare Committee.[102] Because of the regular income which most pensioners now received, the trustees of Doughty's Hospital were able to phase out the payment of weekly allowances, with only two almspeople receiving money from the charity by 1943.[103] In March 1944 the last two stipends were discontinued when the residents reached pensionable age.[104] The trustees then brought in a weekly maintenance charge to ensure that facilities could continue to improve and to fund refurbishment and expansion of the buildings. In September 1954, this charge was 10s. per week.[105] In January 1955, changes to the national

98   *Ibid.*, 9 February 1911; 22 February 1911
99   NRO, N/CCH 124, 19 May 1943; 21 July 1943.
100 NRO, N/CCH 125, 19 May 1948.
101 *Ibid.*, 18 July 1951.
102 See above, pp. 110–11.
103 NRO, N/CCH 124, 17 November 1943.
104 *Ibid.*, 15 March 1944.
105 NRO, N/CCH 125, 15 September 1954.

assistance grants and old age pensions meant that Doughty's was able to increase the weekly contributions to 11s. 6d., although almspeople not yet in receipt of government assistance were exempt from the charge.[106] Like other almshouses, therefore, Doughty's Hospital was a beneficiary, not a victim, of the rise of state-sponsored social welfare in the first half of the twentieth century.

---

106 NRO, N/CCH 124, 19 January 1955.

CHAPTER 15

Finance and development, 1908–90

The development of Doughty's, 1908–39

As in previous centuries, it was endowments and monetary gifts that allowed Doughty's Hospital to expand in the twentieth century. In 1912 the hospital was the recipient of a substantial endowment that allowed the trustees to extend the hospital buildings for the first time since the 1860s. W. Magnus Pye, a local greengrocer, had spent a considerable length of time trying to acquire a place at Doughty's for an elderly relative, but without success. As a result of this fruitless endeavour Mr Pye resolved that the hospital was in desperate need of expansion. When he died in 1912, therefore, he left £976 to Norwich Consolidated Charities with the express wish that the money should be used to build more accommodation for the aged poor at Doughty's Hospital.[107]

In April 1914 plans for an extension to the institution were considered. Four new cottages were proposed in the south-east corner of the square and it was also suggested that a reading or recreation room might be housed comfortably on the south side of the square.[108] In November 1914 the specifications of the architect Mr Bond were considered.[109] The new buildings would not be cheap: £335 3s. 3d. was quoted for the new reading room and £424 6s. 3d. for the four new cottages.[110] However, thanks to Mr Pye, the money was available and the plans were approved. By 17 November 1915 the new cottages were built and ready for inspection and the reading room was formally opened on 6 February 1916, with a tea and concert provided for the residents and trustees.[111]

---

107 *Eastern Daily Press*, 9 February 1916.
108 NRO, N/CCH 120, 22 April 1914.
109 *Ibid.*, 14 October 1914.
110 *Ibid.*, 11 November 1914.
111 *Ibid.*, 17 November 1915; *Eastern Daily Press*, 9 February 1916.

Although the bequest of Mr Pye had given the hospital a substantial financial boost, 1912 was also a year of disaster for Doughty's and Cooke's Hospitals. On Monday 26 August 1912, Norwich experienced some of the worst floods in its history. All previous rainfall records were broken, with 6.59 inches falling in just twelve hours. Low-lying areas of the city were submerged as drains were clogged with debris and by 29 August the River Wensum had burst its banks, adding to the chaos.[112] The drains of Doughty's Hospital overflowed and rain drove under the roof tiles, causing water damage to the ceilings of six cottages. Cooke's Hospital fared far worse and was completely flooded, with multiple repairs necessary. During the reconstruction work, Reverend J.H. Griffiths and Mr R. Lincoln accommodated the residents of Cooke's Hospital in their own houses, a generous gesture much applauded by the trustees.[113]

Of course, any extensions or improvements to the buildings at Doughty's Hospital were dependent upon the institution's financial situation. After the completion of the new reading room and cottages, a modern laundry was considered in March 1916 and it was estimated that it would cost £230.[114] After applying to the Charity Commissioners for permission, work was started on the new laundry, which was fully operational by 1917.[115] At the same time, the six lean-to cottages in the courtyard were declared unsatisfactory and it was decided to move the residents as soon as other cottages became available. By December 1917 the lean-to structures had been vacated and the trustees ordered that the houses should be torn down and the area gravelled over.[116]

In 1914 the trustees agreed that the Town Close Estate sponsorship of residents was no longer necessary, as the hospital was now financially stable as a result of Pye's bequest. It was decided that residents currently being supported by the Town Close Estate would, upon their death or upon vacating their cottages, be replaced by nominees of Norwich Consolidated Charities.[117] This initiative, however, was short-lived and in 1917 the income of the Almshouse Committee had fallen by 10 per cent while expenditure had risen dramatically. The trustees needed to reconsider the finances of the hospital very carefully and it was decided to reintroduce the Town Close Estate's powers of appointment in return for an annual contribution of £35 per resident. The trustees also decided that no resident under the age of 70 should be admitted to the hospital. This was to ensure that all future residents would be

112 *Eastern Daily Press*, 27 August 1912, p. 5, col. C; *Eastern Daily Press*, 28 August 1912, p. 5, col. C.
113 NRO, N/CCH 119, 7 September 1912; NRO, N/CCH 119, 9 October 1912.
114 NRO, N/CCH 120, 20 March 1916; NRO, N/CCH 120, 14 June 1916.
115 NRO, N/CCH 120, 9 May 1917.
116 *Ibid.*, 12 December 1917.
117 *Ibid.*, 21 January 1914.

in receipt of the government old age pension and hence payment of stipends by Norwich Consolidated Charities could be reduced to a minimum.[118]

The problem of financial uncertainty at Doughty's Hospital continued. In January 1920 the clerk reported an overdraft of £120 18s. 11d. and the trustees reviewed the hospital's expenses in the hope of making savings where possible. Perhaps this was the reason why the trustees voted to dispense with the telephone line in 1921 after its installation just fourteen years earlier.[119] This was to prove a false economy, as the telephone was becoming an increasingly important form of communication and the trustees resolved to reinstall a line to the matron's cottage just three years later.[120] In May 1928 the telephone line was extended to include the laundry, so as to improve communication between the two buildings.[121]

The 10 per cent reduction in the income of Doughty's Hospital in 1917 had a lasting effect on the institution and, although the reintroduction of the Town Close Estate sponsorship helped to reduce anxiety, the problem of finance was far from resolved. In April 1921 the trustees discussed the idea of renting out vacant cottages for a fair price, but after much debate the proposal was dropped.[122] In 1931 rents were reduced at two rural properties owned by the charity, which left the hospital with a £40 deficit.[123] In 1939 the clerk reported on the financial situation of Norwich Consolidated Charities, informing the trustees that although the income had remained stable, the Almshouse and Pensions Committee – of which Doughty's Hospital was a part – and the Apprenticing Committee were both spending far beyond their allocation. The trustees of Doughty's rectified this problem by offering a further place to the Town Close Estate Charity, and restating their intention only to appoint residents who were over 70 years of age.[124]

Although the finances of Doughty's Hospital were not as healthy as they might be, the trustees maintained their interest in expanding the hospital and improving its facilities. The next building project to be considered for construction was a small 'emergency cottage'. This building was requested by the Almshouse Committee in October 1938 as a place to isolate residents in cases of infectious or difficult illness. The cottage was to be built in the north-east corner of the square and plans were made by Messrs Southgate and Sons for a bed-sitting room

118 *Ibid.*, 10 January 1917; 28 February 1917.
119 NRO, N/CCH 121, 14 January 1920; 13 April 1921.
120 *Ibid.*, 17 September 1924.
121 NRO, N/CCH 122, 9 May 1928.
122 *Ibid.*, 17 June 1931.
123 NRO, N/CCH 123, 9 October 1935.
124 NRO, N/CCH 124, 21 June 1939.

and a scullery with an outside toilet and a coal house. The building work was completed in January 1939 at a cost of £137 10s. 0d.[125]

Doughty's and the Second World War, 1939–45

Doughty's Hospital was not isolated from world events and in September 1945, when the Second World War began with the German invasion of Poland, the trustees were quick to react to protect the residents of the hospital. On 20 September the steward laid out air-raid shelter provisions for both Doughty's Hospital and Cooke's cottages. At Doughty's the reading room was strengthened and surrounded by sandbags for use in emergencies. At Cooke's Hospital one of the residents was relocated to a room at Doughty's and the spare cottage was sandbagged and strengthened for use as a shelter.[126] By April 1940 it was reported that a public air-raid shelter had been erected in the grounds of Doughty's Hospital and another had been built close to Cooke's. It was resolved that the sandbags be removed from both hospitals and that residents be instructed to use the public shelters in the event of an emergency.[127]

Bombing was a constant threat for the hospital during the first few years of the war. In March 1941 the Norwich Consolidated Charities minute books noted the bravery of a nurse, Mrs F. Thompson, in dealing with an incendiary bomb that had landed on the green at Doughty's Hospital.[128] The hospital sustained only minor damage as a result of these early air raids, but it was on 27 June 1942 that it suffered its worst damage when an incendiary bomb completely destroyed the reading room.[129] The resulting fire was so fierce that only a bound copy of the *Illustrated London News* and a single chair were salvaged from the wreckage.[130]

Cooke's cottages were also damaged by German bombing, the worst instance occurring on 2 August 1942 when an incendiary bomb landed on the hospital, damaging the roof of cottage number six.[131] However, by September 1944 work had begun on repairing the war damage at Cooke's and this was completed by October of the same year.[132] The reading room at Doughty's Hospital took considerably longer to repair. In March 1945 the steward was asked to write to the War Damages Commission in order to claim the money needed

125 *Ibid.*, 19 October 1938.
126 *Ibid.*, 20 September 1939.
127 *Ibid.*, 17 April 1940.
128 *Ibid.*, 19 March 1941.
129 *Ibid.*, 27 June 1942.
130 *Ibid.*, 15 July 1942.
131 *Ibid.*, 16 September 1942.
132 *Ibid.*, 20 September 1944.

to repair the buildings at Doughty's and to reimburse the charity for the money used to repair Cooke's Hospital.[133] By October 1945 the Commission had paid £379 18s. 10d. for damages incurred at Cooke's and £112 8s. 0d. to repair the damage to Doughty's reading room. However, it was resolved that the question of the reading room should be deferred until full thought had been given to the future development of Doughty's Hospital, and it would be six more years before a permanent new reading room was erected.[134]

Growth, modernisation and change, 1945–90

Like many other institutions, Doughty's Hospital emerged from the Second World War with a strong sense of the need to modernise its facilities. The trustees looked into providing machinery for the improvement of the laundry and a staff bathroom was recommended.[135] However, the hospital had to put its residents first and in July 1948 the steward reported on the desirability of providing each cottage with a tap and basin. The provision of running water for each resident was made a top priority, and in October of the same year a tender was accepted from Southgate's of Chatham Street of £532 18s. 0d. to place a basin and tap in each cottage. When the matron recommended that the basins ought to be placed on the side walls of each cottage, rather than on the back walls as planned, the costs increased by £138. Nevertheless, the work was approved.[136]

A full report was commissioned in 1950 to ascertain how Doughty's could best improve its accommodation. It was resolved that better bathroom, lavatory and cooking facilities were needed, as well as the reinstatement of the reading room. However, any new renovations would be difficult to undertake. Norwich Corporation was also considering modernisation, and plans were being discussed at City Hall for a new ring road for Norwich. The road, which had first been suggested in 1937, would run along the northern wall of the courtyard at Doughty's, parallel to the north wing of the square. This meant that the road would cut Cooke's cottages off from the main buildings and run directly over the matron's house and the laundry, which were both in the path of the proposed new structure.[137] The Corporation's plans were in their early stages in 1950 and the steward of Doughty's Hospital warned that it would be unwise to undertake large-scale improvements until they were finalised. In the meantime, a

---

133 *Ibid.*, 19 March 1945.
134 *Ibid.*, 17 October 1945.
135 NRO, N/CCH 124, 15 May 1946; NRO, N/CCH 125, 21 April 1948.
136 NRO, N/CCH 125, 20 October 1948.
137 NRO, N/CCH 123, 14 April 1937; NRO, N/CCH 125, 6 February 1950.

licence for the reconstruction of the reading room had been obtained and the work was completed on 7 July 1951, at a cost of £1,108 3s. 6d., all of which was recovered from the War Damages Commission.[138] In September 1951 the reading room was reopened and the trustees held a concert party to celebrate the occasion.[139]

Any further development of the hospital was postponed until 1953 when the trustees of Norwich Consolidated Charities discussed the need for Doughty's to undergo a complete rewiring to bring it up to standard with the mains electricity supply.[140] An Almshouse Improvement Fund was set up and in 1953 it yielded £1,000, which was set aside for the proposed rewiring. The trustees also found an annual surplus from the almshouse and pension committee of £370.[141] In September 1955 a gift of £1,000 was made to Doughty's Hospital by the Colman's House Trust, a local charity established in the Victorian era.[142] This charitable donation would be added to the money already available in the Almshouse Improvement Fund.[143] By January 1956, £2,500 was available in the fund and it was ordered that the money for improvements be placed in a special investment account at 3 per cent to accrue interest until it was needed.[144]

The large sum of money which had accumulated in the Almshouse Improvement Fund would be put to good use when the trustees agreed that the accommodation at Doughty's Hospital should be updated. It was decided to convert three cottages into two, making each tenement larger in the process. The conversion of the cottages began in May 1956.[145] The building work qualified for a 50 per cent local authority improvement grant, as a result of which £221 was provided for each conversion.[146] On 15 May 1956, work for the conversion of cottages one, two and three was begun.[147] The work was completed by 23 October 1957 and work began on the conversion of cottages thirty-four, thirty-five and thirty-six. During this time, the residents of the cottages that were undergoing conversion were moved to other cottages in the square and the nomination of new residents was postponed.[148] In May 1959 the second refurbishment was complete and plans had been made for the third conversion.[149]

---

138 NRO, N/CCH 125, 20 December 1950; 6 July 1951.
139 *Ibid.*, 19 September 1951.
140 *Ibid.*, 1 January 1953.
141 *Ibid.*
142 See above, Part III, pp. 55–6.
143 NRO, N/CCH 125, 21 September 1955.
144 *Ibid.*, 21 March 1956.
145 *Ibid.*, 16 May 1956.
146 *Ibid.*, 21 November 1956; 17 July 1957.
147 *Ibid.*, 15 May 1957.
148 *Ibid.*, 23 October 1957.
149 NCC Minute Book 8, 1958–70, 20 May 1959.

Although Doughty's had secured grants from the local authority and was able to use money from the Almshouse Improvement Fund towards the cost of the conversions, the finances of the hospital were still tight. The trustees sought to raise money for the construction work by increasing the contributions residents paid towards their housing and care. In February 1958 the trustees applied to the National Assistance Board, the government department responsible for the administration of old age pensions, for an increase in contributions to 13s. 6d. per week. This was agreed on the understanding that the money raised would fund the refurbishment of the residents' accommodation.[150] In 1959 the National Assistance Board raised the old age pension by 5s. per week and, to reflect this increase, Doughty's Hospital raised its contribution rate to 15s. per week.[151] In March 1961 the contributions were raised again to 16s. 6d. per week and in 1962, in line with the rise in pensions, contributions rose to 18s. per week.[152]

The issue of contributions was a contentious one and the trustees of Doughty's Hospital had to negotiate with both the National Assistance Board and the Charity Commissioners before any increase in payments could be implemented. In 1963 they decided to raise the contributions again to 19s. 6d. per week, and felt that this increase was justified because so much money was being spent on improving the facilities at the hospital. The Charity Commissioners were unwilling to give permission for another rise in contributions, however, and suggested that the trustees sell some of their property instead.[153] By June 1964 the Commissioners had been worn down, and now allowed Doughty's Hospital to apply the 19s. 6d. per week charge, but when the trustees tried in January 1965 to raise the contributions still further to 21s. 6d. they refused to give permission and the charge remained at 19s. 6d.[154]

As well as increasing the contributions paid by residents, the trustees also sought to reduce the number of staff at Doughty's Hospital in order to save money which could then be used to further improve the buildings. In 1957 the number of cleaners was cut from two to one and the nursing relief staff – part-time attendants Mrs Clasper and Mrs Laws, who were also residents at the hospital – were dispensed with in favour of a more centralised nursing structure.[155] In July 1958 the trustees agreed that the matron should be supported by three nursing attendants, who would live on the site at Doughty's and care for the residents.[156]

---

150 *Ibid.*, 24 February 1958.
151 *Ibid.*, 16 September 1959.
152 *Ibid.*, 15 March 1961; 19 September 1962.
153 *Ibid.*, 10 July 1963.
154 *Ibid.*, 24 June 1964; 17 March 1965.
155 NRO, N/CCH 125, 18 September 1957; 4 October 1957.
156 NCC Minute Book 8, 1958–70, 16 July 1958.

By June 1961 six sets of conversions had taken place and where there had been eighteen cottages, there were now twelve.[157] Work began on the seventh conversion in September 1961 and the trustees decided that, after this refurbishment, further reconstruction of Doughty's Hospital should be postponed. The reason for this abrupt change of plan was partly to do with the construction of the inner link ring road. Norwich Corporation had not yet made the trustees of Norwich Consolidated Charities aware of the details of their plans, which made it impossible for work to begin on the north side of Doughty's square which ran close to the proposed site of the road. Another reason for the break in the refurbishments was that the trustees considered the renovation of the bathrooms and lavatories at Cooke's Hospital to be a higher priority in terms of the welfare of the almspeople.[158] The architect for the improvements at Cooke's, Mr Gooch, estimated that each bathroom would cost £600, bringing the total cost of the project to £4,800. Deducting the estimated grant from the local authority, the net expenditure would be approximately £2,600. However, the lowest tender for the work, given by the building firm Ford and Carter, was considerably higher at £4,821 12s. 3d. for the entire refurbishment.[159] Despite the increase in estimated cost, the tender was accepted. Work began in May 1962 and the eight cottages were complete with their new facilities by the following January.[160]

During this time it became apparent that the path of the inner link ring road would indeed run straight through the laundry and matron's cottage, north of the courtyard at Doughty's Hospital.[161] The trustees would need to acquire more land in order to relocate the two buildings. Fortunately, land immediately to the south of Doughty's was owned by the Great Hospital and the steward of Doughty's Hospital was asked to negotiate the purchase of this property, which was currently in use by Messrs White's Bottle Company.[162] In September 1962 the Great Hospital and Doughty's reached an agreement whereby the latter would acquire the land to the south of its present site and in return the Great Hospital would receive a parcel of land in Mountergate belonging to Norwich Consolidated Charities. As the two plots were considered to be of equal value, no money would change hands in the exchange.[163] Mr White, the owner of Messrs White's Bottles, promised to vacate the

---

157 *Ibid.*, 15 June 1961.
158 *Ibid.*, 20 September 1961.
159 *Ibid.*, 17 January 1962; 21 March 1962.
160 *Ibid.*, 16 January 1963.
161 Townroe, 'Norwich since 1945', pp. 463–4; NRO, N/CCH 188, Doughty's Hospital Residents' Book 1893–1973.
162 NCC Minute Book 8, 1958–70, 24 May 1962.
163 *Ibid.*, 7 September 1962.

property in the spring of 1964 and the trustees of Doughty's Hospital brought in an architect, Mr Gooch, to begin drawing up the plans for the new staff accommodation.[164]

These plans had to be adjusted, however, when Norwich Corporation's plans for the inner link ring road produced a larger road than they had first anticipated, which meant that the plans for two staff cottages and an entrance to the almshouses on Calvert Street would no longer be feasible. Instead it was suggested that the entrance and houses be built on Golden Dog Lane, on land that the Great Hospital owned and was willing to sell for the project.[165] This revised plan was approved and the building of two new cottages, one for the occupation of the matron and a second for the deputy matron, started in September 1965.[166] The two new houses were completed in March 1966. The matron, Mrs Bowen, and the deputy matron, Mrs Fuller, were said to be 'delighted by the spacious new housing'.[167] The second phase of development, which began shortly before the completion of the matrons' cottages, was the construction of an administrative block, with a kitchen and staff room. This block was completed in July 1967.[168]

After the new houses had been built for both the matron and the deputy matron, the trustees felt it prudent to reconsider the salaries of the two women. This was because the deputy matron was now in receipt of a house and other emoluments (light, heating, laundry facilities and medical attendance) and this needed to be reflected in her pay. The trustees agreed that both women should have equal allowance for their houses, uniforms and interior decorating, and both were given £165 annually for these purposes. The matron's salary was £625 per annum and the deputy matron received £416 per annum.[169] In 1968 Mrs Bowen's salary, including the £165 emoluments, was increased to £842 a year and Mrs Fuller's rose to £633 per year.[170] By 1972 the salaries of the matron and deputy matron had risen to £1,075 and £800 respectively.[171]

During this period of structural improvement and expansion, Doughty's Hospital was also responsible for keeping its standards of care high, and this involved internal improvements. The Almshouse Association was established in 1950 with the aim to represent the interests of almshouses to the Charity Commissioners, housing

---

164 *Ibid.*, 18 September 1963.
165 *Ibid.*, 18 March 1964.
166 *Ibid.*, 15 September 1965.
167 *Eastern Daily Press*, 20 April 1966.
168 NCC Minute Book 8, 1958–70, 12 January 1966; 12 July 1967.
169 *Ibid.*, 2 February 1966.
170 *Ibid.*, 13 March 1968.
171 NCC Minute Book 9, 1971–9, 12 January 1972.

associations and other governmental departments, as well as to give advice and guidance to individual almshouses.[172] In 1963 the Association circulated a publication calling for a need for almshouses to be centrally heated. The trustees felt unable to deal with this problem immediately as the matrons' cottages were in the construction stages, but resolved to review the matter once all other building works were complete.[173] In 1968 they were finally ready to deal with modernisation of the heating system and the steward was asked to look into methods of centrally heating Doughty's Hospital, Cooke's Hospital and the two matrons' cottages.[174] It was decided to install oil-fired central heating in Doughty's and Cooke's at a combined cost of £12,216.[175]

The central heating systems were functional in both hospitals by March 1969, but the fuel used in the new system proved expensive and the trustees were at a loss as to how to cope with the steep increase in costs. On average, a week's supply of coal had cost Doughty's £13 and Cooke's £5 10s., while oil was now costing Doughty's £36 per week and Cooke's £16 per week. To combat this problem, the trustees were forced to introduce a heating charge of 15s. per week for each resident. This was separate from the contributions charge, which remained at 19s. 6d. in 1969. The charge was approved by the Charity Commissioners, given the huge increase in costs that the charity now had to bear.[176] Having learned their lesson, when it came to central heating for the matrons' cottages, the trustees chose to install gas-fired heating instead.[177]

The trustees continued to focus on the expansion of Doughty's Hospital and in 1965 they bought a property to the south of the reading room at a cost of £7,250.[178] In December 1968 the *Eastern Evening News* described how the trustees of Doughty's had purchased the former site of Anglia Glass Company, which gave them a large area of land south of the reading room upon which more accommodation could be built at a later date.[179] In 1970, a property at 17 Golden Dog Lane was purchased by the trustees for £10,000. This latest purchase meant that Doughty's Hospital now owned land that stretched from the south side of the reading room down to Golden Dog Lane, and was large enough for the trustees to consider building a new almshouse block.[180]

---

172 Howson, *Houses of noble poverty*, p. 166.
173 NCC Minute Book 8, 1958–70, 17 July 1963.
174 *Ibid.*, 8 May 1968.
175 *Ibid.*, 11 September 1968.
176 *Ibid.*, 12 March 1969; 14 May 1969.
177 *Ibid.*, 8 July 1970.
178 *Ibid.*, 13 October 1965.
179 *Eastern Evening News*, 12 December 1968.
180 NCC Minute Book 8, 1958–70, 8 July 1970.

The architect for the new almshouse buildings, Mr Hastings, sought permission to demolish the buildings on the site south of Doughty's Hospital, in order that new accommodation could be built.[181] The plans for twelve new units of accommodation – eight double flats and four single bedsits – were discussed in 1972, along with a proposed extension of the reading room. The architect estimated the cost at £74,100.[182] However, the construction process was not without incident. The Norwich Society, a local group which advocated the preservation of historic buildings, protested at the demolition of numbers 17 and 19 Golden Dog Lane, which they argued were both significant seventeenth-century buildings. The society even drew up its own set of plans showing how to modernise the buildings without the need to tear them down.[183] The steward of Doughty's Hospital, Mr Sam Hornor, argued that the costs of conversion would be prohibitive and, due to the varying floor levels throughout the buildings, they would anyway be unsuitable for occupation by the elderly. The Norwich Society and the Norwich Preservation Trust appealed against Norwich Consolidated Charities' plans to bulldoze the site and, when their appeals were rejected, accused the trustees of putting cost before heritage. Mr Hornor categorically rejected such an accusation, arguing that 'money has never been the major factor. Our main consideration has always been the care of old people'.[184]

The buildings were demolished on 8 May 1972 and the lowest tender for building the new accommodation was accepted from John Youngs Ltd for £101,402, some £27,000 more than originally specified by the architect.[185] Nevertheless the construction work began. In 1973, when a long-serving committee member died suddenly, the trustees decided to name the new almshouses after her, in recognition of her devotion to Doughty's Hospital. Grace Jarrold had been a trustee of Norwich Consolidated Charities for twenty-three years and chairman of the Almshouse Committee since 1959.[186] Grace Jarrold Court was completed in August 1974 and officially opened in April 1975 by Mrs Jarrold's husband, John Jarrold.[187] Having initially considered funding the project with a loan from Norwich District Council, the Estates and Finance Committee of Norwich Consolidated Charities eventually secured a Housing Association Grant for the project from the Housing Corporation, which required registration with the Corporation

---

181 NCC Minute Book 9, 1971–9, 12 May 1971.
182 *Ibid.*, 12 January 1972; 5 January 1972.
183 *Eastern Daily Press*, 12 May 1972.
184 *Eastern Daily Press*, 13 May 1972.
185 NCC Minute Book 9, 1971–9, 10 May 1972; 4 April 1973.
186 *Ibid.*, 17 October 1973.
187 *Ibid.*, 13 March 1974; *Eastern Evening News*, 7 April 1975.

as a Registered Social Landlord.[188] The grant secured amounted to £70,000.[189]

In July 1974 the extension of the reading room, which had first been considered in 1972, was discussed, the justification being that the building was now too small to accommodate the growing almshouse population. The trustees of Doughty's Hospital decided to apply to Anguish's Educational Foundation, for the full £4,100 grant for the work.[190] The grant was approved and construction began in January 1975, with the extension completed in April 1975.[191] It was after the completion of these renovations that the trustees were able to go back and convert the last eight cottages to the north of the courtyard. The number of tenements in the courtyard had now been reduced from thirty-six to twenty-four.[192] The process was finally completed in 1977, having taken approximately twenty years to complete.[193]

By the late 1970s the long waiting lists for entry to Doughty's and the high demand for housing among the elderly in Norwich put pressure on the trustees to expand the hospital once again.[194] Problems had also arisen as a result of the new ring road. The residents of Cooke's cottages were only able to access Doughty's Hospital by means of a subway under the flyover, and many residents were anxious about the journey, especially at night.[195] The position of Cooke's Hospital was also difficult for members of staff. Mrs Whitlam, the matron from 1980 to 1997, recalled that it was awkward to tend to the residents of Cooke's Hospital, especially at night, as the matron on duty would have to make the journey through the subway.[196] In March 1976, the architect for Doughty's Hospital, Mr Hastings, argued that there was no future in Cooke's Hospital and that a new site should be found for the residents living there.[197] In 1978 a site on Golden Dog Lane was developed, and in 1980 the new Cooke's Court was opened by the Lord Mayor of Norwich, Valerie Guttsman.[198]

In March 1978 the residents of Cooke's Hospital were told that they would soon be moving to the main site at Doughty's Hospital and most were happy to go. One resident, however, was unwilling to

188 NCC Minute Book 9, 1971–9, 15 January 1975; 2 April 1975.
189 *Ibid.*, 14 May 1975.
190 *Ibid.*, 10 July 1974.
191 *Ibid.*, 8 January 1975; 12 March 1975.
192 NRO, N/CCH 188, Doughty's Hospital Residents' Book, 1893–1973.
193 Jewson, *Doughty's Hospital,* p. 27.
194 DOHI 013; DOHI 014.
195 DOHI 015.
196 DOHI 001.
197 NCC Book 9, 10 March 1976.
198 *Eastern Evening News*, 22 April 1980; Jewson, *Doughty's Hospital,* p. 29; NCC Minute Book 9, 1971–9, 18 October 1978; 3 October 1979.

leave his cottage.[199] In November 1979 the almsman concerned was still stubbornly refusing to move and the trustees authorised their solicitors, Cozens-Hardy and Jewson, to begin eviction proceedings against him. Despite these legal proceedings, the trustees decided to offer this resident a cottage at Doughty's Hospital in return for him vacating the property at Cooke's.[200] On 2 January 1980, all the residents of Cooke's Hospital made the move to the newly built Cooke's Court, apart from the man who refused to leave, who stubbornly remained in the old accommodation.[201] It was clear that a harder line would have to be taken, and the trustees told the gentleman in question that services to the site would be cut off after 8 January, but for practical, moral and legal reasons they were unable to leave him without basic water and electricity. He then spoke to the local media about the situation, giving an account of the affair which caused a good deal of difficulty and embarrassment to the staff at Doughty's Hospital.[202] On 26 February he was served with a notice warning him to vacate the property within thirty days.[203] On 25 April 1980, twenty-eight days after the end of the final notice, our reluctant-to-move resident finally vacated Cooke's Hospital.[204]

While Cooke's Court was being constructed between 1978 and 1980, the trustees continued to purchase property and convert it into suitable accommodation for the elderly. The house at number 12 Golden Dog Lane was acquired from Anguish's Educational Foundation, as the tenant, Mrs Watson, was no longer able to maintain the house by herself. She was given a place at Doughty's Hospital and the house was converted into four flats in January 1979.[205] There was difficulty in converting the house, however, and the trustees found it hard to obtain planning permission to convert the stairs in the old property. They wanted to build a landing, so as to split the stairs in two and make them easier for the elderly to climb. Eventually they obtained permission and the conversion went ahead.[206] These flats were named Mottram House, after the late R.H. Mottram, an author and trustee of Norwich Consolidated Charities. Mottram House and Cooke's Court were officially opened in April 1980 by the Lord Mayor, Mrs Valerie Guttsman, who told the *Eastern Evening News* that she would be glad to end her days in a 'happy, homely environment' such as Doughty's (Figure 6).[207]

---

199 NCC Minute Book 9, 1971–9, 8 March 1978.
200 *Ibid.*, 21 November 1979.
201 NCC Minute Book 10, 1980–6, 2 January 1980.
202 *Ibid.*, 9 January 1980.
203 *Ibid.*, 12 March 1980.
204 *Ibid.*, 25 April 1980.
205 NCC Minute Book 9, 1971–9, 10 January 1979.
206 DOHI 014.
207 *Eastern Evening News*, 22 April 1980.

Figure 6.   Opening of Mottram House by Valerie Guttsman, Lord Mayor of Norwich, 1980 (by kind permission of Archant publishing)

The architect was given yet more work in 1979 when the trustees asked him to make plans for the conversion of numbers 4 and 6 Golden Dog Lane into three new flats.[208] However, the Housing Corporation refused to provide a grant for the project, on the grounds that it would only produce a small number of tenements, and was hence not cost-effective.[209] By 1981 Norwich Consolidated Charities had also acquired number 2 Golden Dog Lane and therefore now owned three adjoining properties, numbers 2, 4 and 6. They applied to the council for permission to demolish the buildings and build almshouses on the site.[210] However, due to a further refusal of funding from the Housing Corporation in 1982 and delays in the Housing Corporation accepting the tender for the work from contractors in 1983, building at the site did not start until 1984.[211] The four new flats were completed in March 1985 and were named Hesketh Court after another trustee, Mr Stanley

208 NCC Minute Book 9, 1971–9, 11 July 1979.
209 NCC Minute Book 10, 1980–6, 12 March 1980.
210 *Ibid.*, 3 June 1981.
211 *Ibid.*, 6 January 1982; 11 May 1983.

Figure 7. Opening of Hesketh Court by Stan Petersen, Lord Mayor of Norwich, 1985 (by kind permission of Archant publishing)

Hesketh.[212] Stan Petersen, Lord Mayor of Norwich, performed the opening ceremony (Figure 7). The trustees also bought an eighteenth-century building to the south of Grace Jarrold Court, number 20 Golden Dog Lane, and converted it into four flats in 1985.[213] During these building works, the reading room was extended for the second time.[214] Doughty's Hospital now had fifty-four units of accommodation, including eight double flats.

The clerk, Mr Matthew Martin, and the steward, Mr Nick Saffell, were both responsible for the skilful way in which the trustees took advantage of all the available grants and funds in order to pay for the various extensions of the hospital in the later twentieth century.[215] However, the increasing cost of amenities, coupled with the improved facilities as a result of the refurbishments, caused Doughty's trustees to apply for an increase in sponsorship money for each of the Town Close Estate's nominated almspeople. The Town Close Estate Charity, as

212 *Ibid.*, 6 March 1985.
213 *Ibid.*, 9 January 1985.
214 *Ibid.*, 9 May 1984.
215 DOHI 008.

discussed above, had been given the power of nomination of freemen to Doughty's Hospital in 1892 and had continued to provide for the financial welfare of its nominees since that date.[216] In May 1977 the trustees of the Town Close Estate agreed to pay £400 per annum for each of its almspeople and in 1980 that maintenance cost rose to £750 per person per annum.[217] By 1981 the charity had agreed to provide £1,000 per annum for each of its nominees.[218]

Throughout the twentieth century, Doughty's Hospital continued to receive bequests and monetary gifts, and although these were no longer the very large amounts that the charity had received in the eighteenth and nineteenth centuries, the money was still very welcome. Most gifts came from the wills of grateful former residents or their relatives, and the money was used in various ways to benefit the almspeople. For example, in 1960 Mrs Maria Cromer left Doughty's £132 17s., of which £100 was put into a 5 per cent mortgage loan while the remaining money was used to fund a private telephone line between Doughty's and Cooke's Hospitals.[219] In 1968 Mrs Riley left £250 for the benefit of Doughty's Hospital. The trustees resolved to invest the money, but later decided to make it available for use by the residents, and the bequest was used to finance a central television aerial.[220] £100 from the late Mr Parnell was used to provide facilities in the newly extended reading room in 1974, and in 1984 the residue of Miss Turner's estate, a substantial sum in the region of £12,000, was spent on a minibus for the institution.[221]

The Marion Road Day Care Centre and the site at Cadge Road

By 1983 Norwich Consolidated Charities was on a stable financial footing, so much so that there was actually money to spare. The projected surplus income for 1983 was estimated at £107,767 and for 1984 at £45,852.[222] The chairman of Norwich Consolidated Charities, Mrs Claire Frostick, remembers how the Charity Commissioners were keen to see this money spent on charitable projects rather than simply reinvested.[223] In February 1983 the trustees formed a working party to discuss ideas for new projects, and these deliberations produced a proposal to fund the creation of a second almshouse complex in Norwich.[224] Two possible sites for the buildings were discussed, but one

---

216 NRO, N/CCH 114, 17 August 1892; and see above, Part III, p. 75.
217 NCC Minute Book 9, 1971–9, 11 May 1977; NCC Minute Book 10, 1980–6, 12 March 1980.
218 NCC Minute Book 10, 1980–6, 13 May 1981.
219 NCC Minute Book 8, 1958–70, 18 May 1960.
220 *Ibid.*, 10 January 1968; 8 January 1969.
221 NCC Minute Book 9, 1971–9, 11 September 1974; NCC Book 10, 9 January 1985.
222 NCC Minute Book 10, 1980–6, 18 February 1983.
223 DOHI 017.
224 NCC Minute Book 10, 1980–6, 18 February 1983.

– the St Helen's Wharf site – was considered too small, while the other proposed site – at Courtauld's factory – was unavailable.[225] The trustees envisioned creating a modern hospital similar to Doughty's, with fifty units of accommodation, a reading room, a communal kitchen and staff accommodation for a matron and a deputy matron. In July 1985 a site at Cadge Road was considered, which was big enough to erect the proposed fifty units of accommodation.[226]

In February 1987 the clerk outlined plans to fund the project, with the Town Close Estate Charity willing to offer annual grants of between £50,000 and £60,000 towards the new almshouses. The clerk also resolved to see if a Joint Funding Grant could be secured for the communal facilities.[227] Applications to the Housing Corporation were made in 1985, 1986 and 1987 but each application was rejected on the basis that Norwich was not a high priority area and was not in desperate need of affordable housing. The clerk of the charities was also unable to secure a Joint Funding Grant. The trustees would have been able to take the project forward without a grant, by borrowing money or by using some of their accumulated funds, but this meant they would only be able to complete thirty-two units of accommodation. The trustees were adamant that the new almshouse should contain fifty units and, if they were unable to secure outside funding, decided that the project would have to be completed in two phases, with the remaining eighteen cottages being delayed until appropriate financial backing could be obtained.[228]

There was also concern over the cost of running the new almshouses. Ideally the trustees were looking to create an institution which would provide facilities on a par with Doughty's Hospital, with twenty-four-hour support and a high standard of care. This would mean substantial running costs. If the trustees could not obtain grants for the project, they would not be able to run the almshouse to a suitable standard, and residential care would have to be provided by Social Services, Home Help and other nursing organisations. Despite this, it was decided to go ahead without grant backing in July 1986.[229] The lack of financial assistance from the Housing Corporation was compounded in December 1987 by city council resistance. The council insisted on nomination rights to the new almshouses, despite the fact that they were unwilling to compromise on the sale price of the land or to grant any money towards the project. When the council

---

225 NCC Minute Book 11, 1986–9, 20 April 1988.
226 NCC Minute Book 10, 1980–6, 3 July 1985.
227 NCC Minute Book 11, 1986–9, 4 February 1987.
228 NCC Minute Book 10, 1980–6, 26 November 1986.
229 NCC Minute Book 11, 1986–9, 20 April 1988.

further informed Norwich Consolidated Charities that a cycle track needed to be provided around the perimeter of the almshouses, the trustees questioned the stipulation, arguing that a cycle path would increase worries over the privacy and security of the site. The city council refused to compromise, however, and this small disagreement proved to be the last straw. The trustees, defeated by a lack of support from all sides, abandoned their designs on the land at Cadge Road.[230]

Despite the failure of the trustees to create a second Doughty's Hospital, the surplus funds were put to good use in an inventive way. The trustees were determined to create new facilities to help vulnerable groups of people in Norwich. In 1983, in parallel with the inquiries into the second almshouse, the trustees began to consult various parties on the best use of the money. In interview Mrs Frostick recalled that the trustees were keen to 'fill the gaps' left by other organisations in the city, and they consulted the local authorities, the Social Services, the Health Authority and Age Concern in order to determine what facilities would be most beneficial to the community.[231] After meeting with these groups, it was clear that the possibility of a day centre for the elderly, and especially elderly people with degenerative mental conditions, should be explored, and the city council suggested a site in Marion Road that was fit for purpose.[232]

The Health Authority and Social Services agreed to help fund the day centre through a Joint Funding Scheme and £151,000 was secured from the two authorities towards the cost of the project.[233] It was also agreed that a new trust should be established for the Marion Road Day Care Centre, consisting of eight trustees from Norwich Consolidated Charities and one trustee each from the county council, Age Concern and Social Services.[234] This meant that, although the buildings and maintenance of Marion Road would be the responsibility of Norwich Consolidated Charities, the Marion Road Day Care Centre Trust would be responsible for the day-to-day management of the establishment. The aim of the centre was to provide care and social opportunities for the elderly and frail, with a special emphasis on those with mental illness and degeneration.[235] Work began on the building in October 1985 and the site was handed over to the Marion Road Day Care Centre Trust on 23 June 1986.[236]

---

230 NCC Book 11, 15 December 1987.
231 DOHI 017.
232 NCC Minute Book 10, 1980–6, 11 May 1983.
233 *Ibid.*, 4 March 1984.
234 *Ibid.*, 4 March 1984; 3 May 1984.
235 *Ibid.*, 10 June 1985.
236 *Ibid.*, 2 July 1986.

CHAPTER 16
Staffing Doughty's

The number of staff at Doughty's Hospital increased over the course of the twentieth century, while the various roles developed too. In the 1911 census, the hospital was employing two sick nurses, a laundress and a 'help to laundress', and the running of the hospital was overseen by Benjamin Inwood, the master, a married man whose wife, Maryann Inwood, was described as the 'mother' of the institution.[237] By 1981 Doughty's Hospital employed a matron and a deputy matron instead of a master. The hospital no longer employed its own laundry staff and four carers took the place of the sick nurses, along with three permanent cleaners.[238] But it was not simply a case of a steady increase in the number of staff, and the financial circumstances of the hospital and the personal circumstances of the residents played a large part in the hiring and firing of staff at Doughty's Hospital.

In the few years before the Norwich Charities Consolidation Act of 1910 the trustees of the General List spent much of their time reforming the structure of nursing at Doughty's Hospital, perhaps in a last-ditch attempt to show the efficiency of the old system.[239] In March 1909, Mrs Darkin, the wife of a trustee, advised that a change of nurse would be beneficial as Nurse Aldham had 'become stout and was quite short and unable to lift and turn patients'. She had also, according to Mrs Darkin, become 'more irritable'. Mrs Darkin suggested that in Mrs Aldham's stead they should employ a 'tall, capable, kind and sympathetic woman with tact to comfort and help the infirm'.[240] There was no doubt about it, at least to Mrs Darkin's mind: Nurse Aldham had neither the physicality nor the disposition for the job. She was asked to hand in her resignation, to which request she duly complied.[241] Mrs Darkin also recommended the occasional help of a district nurse in extreme cases, and the Norwich District Nursing Association agreed to provide a relief nurse for one year at a cost of £2 2s.[242]

---

237 1911 census: RG78/613, RD225 SD1 ED5 SN28.
238 DOHI 004.
239 NRO, N/CCH 117, 21 September 1910.
240 NRO, N/CCH 116, 17 March 1909.
241 *Ibid.*, 17 March 1909.
242 NRO, N/CCH 117, 21 April 1909.

In May 1910 it was agreed that both the night nurse and the day nurse ought to help in making the beds, and bathing and preparing breakfast for those who were unable to look after themselves. Before this point these activities had been solely the job of the day nurse. The trustees also decided that each nurse would be allowed to have one day off per week, from 10 am to 10 pm. However, at all other times nursing staff were unable to leave the hospital, apart from Sunday mornings for church service, unless given express permission by the master. The most interesting of these new rules, already noted in chapter 11, was that the nurses were not allowed to fetch 'stimulants from the public houses for the inmates'.[243] There is no evidence to suggest that this was a frequent occurrence, but the fact that it was prohibited implies that it had indeed happened.

In September 1910 a charwoman was employed for two hours each day, from 1 October to 30 May each year, in order to help with the cleaning and maintenance of the hospital.[244] In November 1910 further reforms were made in the nursing system and the nurses were required to keep a logbook of all residents requiring medical attention. The nurses were also authorised to cook for residents in special cases, and Mrs Phillips, an almsperson who had previously assisted the nursing staff, was able to continue to do so. The charwoman was to be engaged under the supervision of the nurses from 7am each day at an hourly rate of 3d. The clerk also reported that a doorway had been built between the head nurse's room and the infirmary room, and it was resolved that a second room be opened up onto the head nurse's room in the same way.[245]

Under the 1910 scheme of Norwich Consolidated Charities, the Charity Commissioners had identified the need for a matron instead of a master to manage Doughty's Hospital.[246] The trustees of the General List had strongly resisted this change in management, arguing that it was 'absolutely necessary' to have a master at the hospital.[247] But the Charity Commissioners refused to compromise.[248] So, when Benjamin Inwood was pensioned off as a result of ill-health in February 1912, the trustees advertised for a head nurse, aged no less than 35 years, to reside in the present master's house and oversee the running of the hospital.[249] In March 1912, Mrs Rosanna Ann Oliver was offered the position at

243 *Ibid.*, 18 May 1910.
244 *Ibid.*, 21 September 1910.
245 *Ibid.*, 16 October 1910.
246 *Ibid.*, 24 January 1910.
247 *Ibid.*
248 *Ibid.*, 16 February 1910.
249 NRO, N/CCH 119, 22 November 1911; 16 February 1912.

Figure 8.
Benjamin Inwood, Master of
Doughty's Hospital 1896–
1912, and subsequent
resident (died 1929)
(by kind permission of
Archant publishing)

a weekly wage of 15s. for a six-month probationary period.[250] The low wage and insistence upon a probationary period were clear signs of the trustees' scepticism of the ability of a woman to run the almshouse effectively. Mrs Oliver was destined to prove them very wrong indeed, for she held the position, which became known as matron, for the next thirty-nine years.[251]

On 12 September 1928, it was reported that Benjamin Inwood, the former master of Doughty's, had been knocked down by a car and was unable to continue his duties as inquiry officer to Norwich Consolidated Charities.[252] The trustees resolved that Mr Inwood should be admitted to the hospital as a resident. It was also agreed that he would receive 7s. per week, and that these benefits were in satisfaction of his pension of £48 per annum. On 2 March 1929, Mr Inwood died at Doughty's Hospital and, having spent sixteen years as master to the institution from 1896 to 1912, special recognition of his service to the charity was recorded in the minute books by the trustees.[253]

---

250 *Ibid.*, 20 March 1912.
251 NRO, N/CCH 124, 27 August 1941.
252 NRO, N/CCH 122, 12 September 1928.
253 *Ibid.*, 13 March 1929.

In May 1938 staff wages were discussed. By this time the matron received 35s. per week, the day nurse 26s. per week and the night nurse 30s. 6d. per week. All three positions also included the emoluments of a furnished cottage, light, fuel, laundry, medical attendance and clothing.[254] The nursing committee decided that these wages were acceptable but that, instead of having separate day and night nurses, each nurse in turn should work nights for four consecutive weeks, and receive extra remuneration of 4s. 6d. per week while so engaged. As a result, the position of night nurse was no longer necessary. It was also decided that each nurse should be provided annually with a uniform consisting of one pair of black shoes, three pairs of black stockings, two white overalls and two white caps.[255]

Not all nursing staff were suitable for the job, or capable of carrying out their duties to the high standard expected by Doughty's trustees. Nurse Thompson appeared before the nursing committee in May 1938 and was asked by the chairman to aim to be neater in her person and tidier in her cottage arrangements, and also to be more dignified and sympathetic in her dealings with the almspeople.[256] She appears to have heeded this warning, as no further action was taken against her. However, in November 1938, Nurse George was reprimanded for her slackness of duty and general attitude.[257] In March 1940 Mrs Oliver reported that Miss George continued to be negligent and refused to get up early to attend to a dying inmate. She clearly did not have what it took to be a nurse at Doughty's Hospital, and her employment was terminated.[258]

Although Mrs Oliver proved to be a capable matron, her health was not particularly good and in July 1934 she was given a month's leave due to a suspected nervous breakdown.[259] In September of the same year she was again confined to her bed, this time with phlebitis and pleurisy.[260] Two months later she was still receiving medical treatment for these conditions.[261] In November 1939, Mrs Oliver suffered an attack of bronchitis and was granted a fortnight's leave of absence in order to recover.[262] Her recovery was relatively short-lived, however, and she died on Wednesday 20 August 1941.[263]

---

254 NRO, N/CCH 124, 18 May 1938.
255 *Ibid.*
256 *Ibid.*
257 *Ibid.*, 16 November 1938.
258 *Ibid.*, 20 March 1940.
259 NRO, N/CCH 123, 11 July 1934.
260 *Ibid.*, 12 September 1934.
261 *Ibid.*, 10 October 1934.
262 NRO, N/CCH 124, 15 November 1939.
263 *Ibid.*, 27 August 1941.

Following the death of Mrs Oliver, the trustees sought once more to reform the staffing arrangements at Doughty's Hospital. They resolved that the contracts of present nursing staff should be terminated forthwith, and in their place a head female attendant and two female attendants with home nursing experience should be appointed. They also wrote to the Charity Commissioners asking that the scheme for the hospital be changed so as to permit the appointment of a master or warden to the hospital.[264] This may have been a reaction to Mrs Oliver's failing health, and was coupled with the trustees' residual belief that a man would be better placed in the managerial role at the institution. The trustees also resolved to employ a permanent cleaner to the hospital and to raise the wages of all staff. It was decided that the warden and his wife should be employed at a joint salary of £3 5s. per week, the head attendant at £1 15s. per week, and the two attendants at £1 12s. per week.[265] However, the Charity Commissioners remained unwilling to sanction the employment of a warden in place of a matron.[266] As a result, Miss Mildred M. Hemmings, formerly of Hull Trained Nurses Association, was appointed matron of the hospital on 12 November 1941 at a yearly wage of £156.[267]

While the trustees were expanding the nursing and cleaning staff at Doughty's Hospital, other staff members found themselves surplus to requirements. The hospital had employed laundrywomen at the institution since 1876.[268] But in September 1946, as a result of the increased costs of staff and resources, the trustees voted that the laundry work be contracted out to an external company. The tender of City Laundry Limited was taken up, at an annual cost of £256.[269] The contracts of the two laundrywomen were terminated on 31 August 1946 and one of them, Mrs Anderson, was admitted to Doughty's Hospital as a resident on the condition that she continued to sort the incoming and outgoing laundry.[270] By January 1947 it was apparent that the fortnightly laundering system was unsatisfactory and was not running to schedule.[271] In March, City Laundry Limited agreed to make weekly visits to the almshouse, to collect and drop off the laundry.[272] In March 1948 the laundry service had lost a number of items of clothing belonging to residents, and in May of the same year

264 *Ibid.*
265 *Ibid.*, 11 September 1941.
266 *Ibid.*, 17 September 1941.
267 *Ibid.*, 12 November 1941.
268 NRO, N/CCH 112, 30 March 1876.
269 NRO, N/CCH 124, 18 September 1946.
270 *Ibid.*, 20 November 1946.
271 *Ibid.*, 15 January 1947.
272 *Ibid.*, 19 March 1947.

the hospital terminated its contract with City Laundry and began to use Frairscroft Laundry in Wymondham instead.[273]

In 1957, as a result of the high costs of the refurbishments of the accommodation at Doughty's and Cooke's Hospitals, the trustees cut the number of cleaning staff from two to one and dispensed with the part-time relief staff, both of whom were residents at the hospital, in order that they might be replaced with more professional nursing staff.[274] In July 1958 it was agreed that the matron should be supported by three nursing attendants, who would live on site at Doughty's and care for the residents.[275] However, the two women who were eventually employed, Mrs Fallon and Miss Tortice, were both unwilling to take up residency at the hospital and the trustees struggled to find adequate staff.[276] They decided that able-bodied almspeople should be 'encouraged to give assistance' to the attendants wherever possible, which contradicted the earlier policy of discouraging residents from participating in paid work at the hospital.[277] In November 1959 advertisements for resident attendants were posted in the newspapers, but no suitable applicants came forward.[278]

In July 1961 Miss Hemmings announced her intention to retire, and in December of the same year interviews were held to find her replacement. The trustees saw seven candidates and Mrs Gwendoline Maude Bowen was offered the position of matron, which she accepted. The trustees were also impressed by the interview of Mrs Margaret Violet Fuller, and created the new role of deputy matron especially for her.[279] The two women began their duties on 1 April 1962 and the appointment of a deputy matron seemed to ease the previous staffing problems.[280] However, although the trustees offered Mrs Fuller and her husband the use of one of the cottages at Doughty's, the couple declined, saying that the house was unsuitable to their needs.[281] Mrs Bowen was now the only member of staff to reside at the hospital, in the house situated to the north of the courtyard cottages. She was supported by full- and part-time attendants, as well as a night sister and a full-time cleaner.[282]

Mrs Bowen proved to be very popular with the residents of Doughty's Hospital, and organised several concerts and specialist

273 NRO, N/CCH 125, 17 March 1948; 19 May 1948.
274 *Ibid.*, 18 September 1957; NRO, 4 October 1957.
275 NCC Minute Book 8, 1958–70, 16 July 1958.
276 *Ibid.*, 20 November 1958.
277 *Ibid.*, 16 September 1959.
278 *Ibid.*, 18 November 1959.
279 *Ibid.*, 14 December 1961.
280 *Ibid.*
281 *Ibid.*, 17 January 1962.
282 Jewson, *Doughty's Hospital,* p. 29.

evenings, utilising the reading room and creating a sense of community among the residents. She even moved her own piano into the reading room in order that the residents could have more social gatherings there.[283] In 1969 Mrs Bowen suggested a summer party for the residents, staff and trustees and this was arranged for 10 June 1969. Reporting after the event the matron offered a vote of thanks to the trustees, saying that the residents had 'very much enjoyed' the afternoon tea party, after which it became a regular fixture in the social calendar at the hospital.[284]

In 1963, less than a year after she had been appointed to the position, the courage of the matron was tested when a resident, Mrs Elizabeth Baxter, accidentally set fire to her bedclothes. Mrs Bowen put out the fire with buckets of water, but by the time Mrs Baxter had been taken to hospital it was too late to save her life. A senior fire officer praised Mrs Bowen's quick thinking in dousing the flames and stopping the spread of the fire to other cottages in the building.[285] The coroner recorded a verdict of death by misadventure and offered the assurance that Mrs Baxter's death in no way reflected on the precautions taken by staff and trustees. The trustees also praised Mrs Bowen, noting that if the fire had indeed spread, the situation could have been very much worse.[286]

By the 1960s, Norwich Consolidated Charities employed a secretary to deal with the running of their affairs. Mrs Vera Cary started working at their office in Queen Street in 1961 and was responsible for the administration of all the charities amalgamated under the 1910 Consolidation Act. Mrs Cary distributed money for school bus tickets and school uniforms on behalf of the Anguish Educational Foundation, as well as overseeing the administration of Doughty's Hospital. The office, which was located in Bank of England Court, was also responsible for ordering coal for the fires at Doughty's Hospital before the advent of the oil-fired central heating system. Staff wages were also distributed from the offices.[287] In interview Mrs Cary remembered collecting the contributions from each resident, a task she performed every Monday morning.

The administrative office also had a novel way of distinguishing the needs of each resident, through a unique system of classification. Mrs Cary drew up a chart with residents grouped in order of age: 60–70 years old, 70–80 years old and 80–90 years old. The residents were then

---

283 NCC Minute Book 8, 1958–70, 21 November 1962.
284 *Ibid.*, 8 January 1969; 9 July 1969.
285 *Ibid.*, 20 March 1963.
286 *Ibid.*, 20 March 1963.
287 DOHI 015.

split into further categories according to their respective degrees of dependency. For example, 'no help needed' was the group to which the fit and healthy members of the hospital belonged, followed by 'some cleaning necessary' for the slightly less fit residents, and the classification continued up to those who were completely dependent.[288] This system was still being used when Mrs Cary left in 1986. The administrative staff had to add an extra column when one resident reached her 91st birthday, an age that Mrs Cary says 'was much rarer' during the twenty-five years that she worked for the charity than it was later to become.[289]

The deputy matron, Mrs Fuller, retired in September 1978 and was replaced by Mrs Jean Whitlam.[290] When Mrs Bowen retired as matron in September 1980, the trustees agreed to appoint Mrs Whitlam in her place, and she moved into the matron's cottage along with her husband and four teenage sons.[291] Mrs Whitlam recalled moving house, from the deputy matron's cottage to the matron's cottage, saying that all she had to do was lift the fence and move all her things from one back garden to the next. This was partly as a time-saving exercise, and partly to stop the residents spying on their belongings as they marched from one house to the other.[292] Mrs Whitlam's salary was £3,894 annually plus £171 in recognition of her nursing qualifications.[293] In 1978, when Mrs Whitlam first joined the hospital, the institution was run with only five members of staff, the matron and deputy matron, an attendant, a cleaner and a night attendant.[294] By 1981, this number had risen, and there were four carers and three cleaners, as well as the matron and deputy matron.[295]

Mrs Parkes replaced Mrs Whitlam as deputy matron in May 1980 but was only with the hospital for three years before she tendered her resignation.[296] In March 1983, Miss Muriel Smith was appointed deputy matron, and went on to hold the position for fourteen years.[297] The small circle of staff was described as 'caring yet organised' by Mr Harry Boreham, a former trustee. Mr Boreham was convinced that because the almshouse was run as a charity it was able to focus completely on the care of the elderly, without worrying about profit margins as a commercial organisation might.[298] Mrs Claire Frostick,

---

288 *Ibid.*
289 *Ibid.*
290 NCC Minute Book 9, 1971–9, 11 January 1978; 10 May 1978.
291 DOHI 001.
292 *Ibid.*
293 NCC Minute Book 10, 1980–6, 9 January 1980.
294 DOHI 001.
295 DOHI 004.
296 NCC Minute Book 9, 1971–9, 14 May 1980; 12 January 1983.
297 *Ibid.*, 9 March 1983; DOHI 002.
298 DOHI 008.

a former chairman of Norwich Consolidated Charities, explained that under Mrs Whitlam the hospital was run like a large family unit, with staff caring for residents' social and emotional needs as well as nursing them through any illness or infirmity.[299] Miss Smith was often known to sit with dying residents through the night, to make them feel as comfortable as possible. Very few residents moved out, and when one did it was usually as a result of a physical or mental problem that needed specialist care that Doughty's was unable to provide.[300] Mrs Frostick remembered that one resident left the hospital in order to get married, but that she and her new husband remained on the applicants' list, waiting for a double flat to become free at the hospital. It was a testament to the high standards of Doughty's Hospital that even those who left the institution were keen to come back.[301]

For the trustees, working on behalf of Doughty's Hospital was virtually a full-time job. Mr Boreham recalled being at the hospital almost every day of the eighteen years that he was chairman of the trustees. Each trustee was allocated several residents with whom they would meet on a regular basis. This was a practice that enabled residents to communicate with an independent person should they have any worries or grievances. However, Mr Boreham 'can't remember anyone ever complaining', as the residents benefited from subsidised rents and a high standard of care and support.[302] There was a chain of communication for any instances in which the residents felt ill-treated, and residents could approach the matron with any concerns. If the matron was unable to resolve any problems, then the issue would be put to the trustees. Mr Boreham could not recall a single situation where a resident was asked to leave, and reported that any problems that did arise were usually dealt with swiftly and sympathetically.[303]

Changes in the structure of the nursing staff were again considered in the 1980s. This time, as a result of the illness and infirmity of a few particularly elderly residents, a full-time night attendant was appointed in 1986.[304] In interview Mrs Whitlam explained that the neighbourhood in which Doughty's Hospital was situated was not a particularly safe one at this time, with a clutch of nightclubs close by in Anglia Square. This made the role of a night attendant difficult, particularly when she had to attend to residents in Calvert Court, which was several hundred yards away from the main buildings of the hospital and on a public road. As a result of security worries a second night nurse was

---

299 *Ibid.*; DOHI 009.
300 DOHI 008.
301 DOHI 009.
302 DOHI 008.
303 *Ibid.*
304 DOHI 001; NCC Minute Book 9, 1971–9, 5 November 1986.

employed shortly after the first.[305] There were also changes in terms of the meals cooked for residents. The nursing staff had been authorised to cook meals for the almspeople since 1910, and had done so on a stove in a small kitchen in one of the staff flats.[306] By the 1990s this was no longer a viable option and one carer, Mrs Sue Hills, recalls how health and hygiene rules made it increasingly difficult for carers to cook main meals for residents.[307] The trustees agreed that improvements to catering facilities were indeed needed, and between 1996 and 1998 a new modern kitchen was built. Two chefs were employed to prepare meals for residents, enabling the carers to continue with their primary duties, while at the same time giving residents more flexibility with respect to their meals.[308]

305 DOHI 001; DOHI 005.
306 NRO, N/CCH/117, 16 October 1910.
307 DOHI 004.
308 NCC Minute Book 13, 1996–9, 19 June 1996; DOHI 003; DOHI 004.

CHAPTER 17
Doughty's residents

Doughty's almspeople – in general

No census data on individuals is available after 1911 due to closure under the 100-years rule, but in the case of Doughty's we are fortunate that a Residents' Book survives from 1893 to 1973, recording names, date of appointment, age at appointment, date of removal or death, as well as a range of subsidiary information such as nominating individual or body, stipend (if any) health and conduct record, whether or not they had been a Doughty's employee, or whether they had been transferred from another institution.[309] A total of 356 entries appear in the book, but many of these are multiple entries which are usually the product of internal transfers from one cottage to another, although Rosa Maud Thurstons's name appears three times because on 6 June 1958 she declined the nomination of W.E. Walker only to accept that of Mrs C.G. Garrold on 17 May 1961, and then moved from number 7 to number 12a in February 1962. As many as forty-four Doughty's residents moved once between cottages, fourteen moved twice, two moved on three occasions while one particularly peripatetic inmate moved a total of four times over a ten-year period. This was Mrs Ethel Martha Nash, who was appointed on 21 September 1955 aged 68, and took up residence in cottage number 29. In November 1957 she moved to number 24, in March 1960 to number 27, in June 1962 to number 22a, and her meanderings were completed in December 1965 when she came full circle to return to where she had started her Doughty's career, in number 29. How long she remained there is unknown, as no date of removal or death is given. Another example is that of a particularly long-lived resident, Alice Wilson, who was appointed at the age of 71 on 9 October 1935 to number 8 Cooke's Cottages. She transferred to number 28 at Doughty's on 28 March 1939, to number 29 on 12 July 1950, went back to number 28 in August 1955, and remained there until her death on 12 August 1961, by when she had achieved the ripe old age of 97 years.

---

309 NRO, N/CCH 188, Doughty's Hospital Residents' Book 1893–1973.

Once these multiple entries have been stripped out, 277 discrete appointments remain, and these can be used to gain some insight into the demographic profile of the almspeople, just as we were able to use the census for this purpose in chapter 11 above.[310] Information on numbers of entries, gender, marital status and age are presented in Table 2. In terms of the number of appointments, we can see some general correspondence between numbers admitted, changing financial conditions and periods of expansion or consolidation. Eleven new appointments were made in 1909 – the year in which old age pensions were payable for the first time – which compares with an annual average of just under two per year during the previous decade. Numbers grew further during the 1910s, no doubt facilitated by the availability of pensions as well as by the expansion that had been made possible by the bequest of Magnus Pye. Tight financial conditions during the 1920s produced a decline in intake during that decade, while the increased number of appointments made in the 1930s might explain why it was reported in 1939 that the Almshouse Committee of Norwich Consolidated Charities was spending in excess of its allocation. Numbers fell back somewhat in the years during and after the Second World War, no doubt reflecting the emphasis upon modernisation rather than expansion that characterised this period, as well as the reduction in the number of cottages that accompanied the conversion of three into two to produce larger, more comfortable units of accommodation from the 1950s. Unfortunately the Residents' Book comes to an end in 1973, and thus fails to reflect the building programme that began in the mid-1970s.

Table 2 clearly shows that the gender bias in favour of women – already evident from our analysis of early twentieth-century census returns – continued unabated, the stipulations of William Doughty's endowment notwithstanding. Almost two almswomen were appointed for every man up to the end of the 1930s, after which the number of men plummeted to new depths, to the extent that appointments to Doughty's were almost totally dominated by women thereafter, only seven men in all being appointed from 1945 through to the early 1970s compared to ninety-one women. The great majority of Doughty's inmates also appear to have lived on their own, and there is no sign of a return to the mid-Victorian policy of allowing a range of relatives to live-in. Indeed, the Residents' Book suggests that fully 90 per cent of all residents across this period lived alone, just 9 per cent with their wives (not a single female is recorded as living with her husband), and just over 1 per cent with other relatives (two sisters, one mother and one daughter).

---

310 See Part III, pp. 87–92.

Table 2.   The demographic profile of Doughty's almspeople on admission, 1893–1973

	Number of almspeople			Residential companions				Age at appointment	
	Total	Male	Female	Alone	Husband	Wife	Other	Average	Range
1893–9	3	0	3	3	0	0	0	78	70–83
1900–9	30	11	19	27	0	3	0	76	68–84
1910–9	45	16	29	41	0	3	1	71	54–87
1920–9	31	12	19	24	0	6	1	72	61–85
1930–9	52	20	32	41	0	9	2	69	52–81
1940–9	37	8	29	34	0	3	0	72	62–86
1950–9	44	2	42	43	0	1	0	70	59–80
1960–9	28	1	27	28	0	0	0	71	59–80
1970–3	7	1	6	7	0	0	0	72	60–84
Total	277	71	206	248	0	25	4	72	52–87

Of course, the information in Table 2 is not strictly comparable in all respects with the census data, for the Residents' Book gives individuals' details on admission, while the census is a snapshot at one point in time that includes inmates at various stages in their residential lives, and this will inevitably produce a lower age profile. Apart from during the period 1893–1909, average ages shown in Table 2 are significantly lower than those found in the Victorian and Edwardian censuses, some five years or so on average, and this is in spite of the fact that the twentieth century has witnessed a significant ageing of the British population. The difference is, however, entirely an artefact of the different profiles the two sets of data represent, and does not allow us to conclude anything at all about the average age of twentieth-century residents. All we can say is that from 1910 to 1973 there was virtually no change in the average age at which almsmen and women were appointed, the overall average for 1893–1973 standing at 72 years. Nor was there any significant difference by gender, for the average of men across the period as a whole stood at 71.9 years and that for women at 71.3. The age range at entry was a wide one, however, usually lying between 59 and 87, and this stayed very much the same throughout the period too.

Occasional instances of considerably lower ages at entry are invariably due to special circumstances. Hence Letitia Low, widow, who was appointed on the nomination of the committee on 14 May 1913 at the age of 54, was a former nurse at Doughty's, and was also granted the generous pension of 10s. 6d. She remained at the hospital for a further fifteen years, until her death in 1928. Similarly Emily Took, appointed on 9 January 1938 at the age of 52, was a former laundress. Her stay was short-lived, however, for on December the same year she left to live with her sister due to the onset of paralysis. The tradition of caring for ex-employees, which had been established in the nineteenth century, was clearly continued, therefore, and in total eight were appointed at various dates between 1913 and 1958 – three former nurses, two laundresses, one master, one head attendant, and the widow of a former trustee.

A more exceptional case is that of Emma Eliza Phillips, who was appointed on 10 February 1932 at the age of 54, and is identified as the daughter of Emma Ann Phillips. Emma Ann Phillips had been admitted to Doughty's at the age of 65 in 1910, and appears in the census for the following year, living alone.[311] However, her daughter must have come into the hospital to live with her at some point between 1911 and 1932, for on her appointment it is noted by way of explanation of her admission that she had 'lived with her mother for some years before her own appointment'. Emma Eliza was either entirely institutionalised, or simply happy in her accustomed home, and she remained at Doughty's for a further twenty-nine years until her death on 13 October 1961, which made her one of the longest-serving residents in the hospital's history.

From the dates of death provided for a number of Doughty's inmates in the Residents' Book it is possible to calculate age at death for a total of 169 individuals, which gives a much clearer perspective on the problem faced at the institution as a result of the longevity of its inmates. It is also possible to calculate the length of stay of residents whose date of death is recorded, and this information is presented in Table 3. One interesting sidelight is the fact that men's ages at death were far more commonly recorded than were those of women – 56 out of 71 (79 per cent) as compared to 113 out of 206 (55 per cent). The high average ages at death shown in Table 3 reflect the fact that Doughty's almspeople were a distinctive sub-set of the total population, a sub-set that had to live to a reasonable age in order to qualify to enter Doughty's in the first place. For while there are various ways to measure expectation of life (commonly based upon either a 'period' or a 'cohort' perspective), whichever method is used Doughty's residents emerge – on average – as particularly long-lived in comparison with the population at large.[312] Average ages at death shown in Table 3 also reflect the fact that women in the twentieth century, as indeed in

---

311 1911 census: RG78/613, RD225 SD1 ED5 SN28.
312 A. Hinde, *England's population. A history since the Domesday survey* (Hodder Arnold: London, 2003), pp. 259–61.

Table 3.   Age at death and length of residence of Doughty's almspeople, 1893–1991

| Date appointed | Sample size | | Average age at death | | | Average length of residence | | |
	Male	Female	Total	Male	Female	Total	Male	Female
1893–9	0	3	83.7	–	83.7	17yr 2m	–	17yr 2m
1900–9	7	12	84.4	83.1	85.1	12yr 2m	10yr 6m	13yr 1m
1910–9	12	22	81.9	77.8	84.1	11yr 3m	7yr 6m	13yr 3m
1920–9	12	13	80.2	79.3	81.1	6yr 11m	7yr 1m	6yr 9m
1930–9	17	23	79.8	78.4	80.8	9yr 7m	6yr 3m	12yr 1m
1940–9	7	18	81.4	77.1	83.0	8yr 5m	7yr 1m	8yr 11m
1950–9	1	16	77.7	77.0	77.8	5yr 9m	5yr 9m	5yr 9m
1960–9	0	6	82.5	–	82.5	7yr 0m	–	7yr 0m
Total	56	113	81.0	78.8	82.0	9yr 4m	7yr 4m	10yr 3m

previous centuries, had (and continue to have) a distinct advantage over men in terms of longevity.[313] There is, however, no reflection of the more general ageing of the population that the twentieth century has witnessed, once again probably because this is anything but a representative sample of the population, and its composition will no doubt be affected by changing admissions policies to the hospital as much as by anything else. On the evidence available here, if anything Doughty's residents were dying slightly younger on average towards the middle of the century compared to the earliest cohorts in Table 3, but the differences are small, the data erratic and the sample sizes small.

Furthermore, while these figures are averages only, further consideration of the changing proportions dying in the higher age groups suggests that there were fewer rather than more over time. If we divide the sample between those appointed on or before 1930 and those appointed after, then 10.3 per cent of the earlier sample lived into their nineties, compared with 8.5 per cent in the later period. The oldest resident of all, however, whose age is highlighted in the Residents' Book, was Florence Beatrice Dewing, who died on 16 June 1986 having lived to 101 years and 11 months, the last twenty-two years and eleven months of which had been spent at Doughty's. As we saw when considering the changing staffing needs of Doughty's, it was the care needs of the very elderly residents such as Mrs Dewing that posed an ever-growing challenge towards the latter years of the twentieth century.

---

313 *Ibid.*, Table 15.1, p. 259.

Figure 9.   Florence Dewing's 100th birthday celebration, 1984

With regard to length of residence, the averages figures tended to decline from their late Victorian and Edwardian peak to settle at around seven to nine years, with women tending to stay a little longer than men – no doubt reflecting the fact that they were more long-lived. The averages, however, hide enormous differences from individual to individual in each decade, for they range from those who died just a month or so after their appointment to others who stayed on for twenty years and more. Indeed, across the period as a whole thirteen residents could boast a stay of twenty years plus, while a further eighteen lived at Doughty's for between fifteen and twenty years. These differences were simply serendipitous, though none were so unfortunate as Thomas Lincoln, who came to the end of his time at Doughty's at the age of 80 as a result of being 'knocked down by a motor car', subsequently dying in hospital on 22 December 1931.

Doughty's almspeople – in particular

In the early years of the twentieth century the poor health of residents was a constant problem, with some suffering from ailments and difficulties with which Doughty's Hospital was simply unable to cope. In February 1907 Mrs Foulsham was certified by Dr Beverley as unfit to be an almsperson at the hospital due to her frequent delusions and the fear that, if left unaided, she might burn down the building. Dr Beverley recommended that she be placed in the workhouse infirmary.[314] In March 1910, Mr Robert Clears was similarly afflicted with 'mental aberration' and Dr Beverley recommended his removal.[315] The process would prove to be complicated, and involve controversy over the inter-related matters of medical opinion and jurisdiction. In April 1910 Mr Clears' condition appeared to have improved and Dr Beverley recommended that he should be permitted to stay in the hospital.[316] However, in February 1912 his condition had again deteriorated and Dr Beverley now urged the trustees to remove him to the asylum. The poor law medical examiner, however, examined Mr Clears and thought him fine to remain at Doughty's.[317] In May 1912 the trustees of Doughty's Hospital wrote to the workhouse Board of Guardians with a view to placing Robert Clears with them. The Guardians declined, claiming that as Mr Clears was not destitute he could not be placed in the workhouse.[318] Despite this, the minute books show that Robert Clears died at the workhouse infirmary in November 1912.[319]

There were also instances of insubordination among the residents. In September 1911, the trustees' attention was called to the atmosphere of 'unwholesome gossiping' that prevailed in Doughty's Hospital, and Mrs Mortar and Mrs Gardiner were both called before the committee and informed that repetition of such behaviour was grounds for dismissal.[320] For some residents, poor behaviour was a result of underlying mental conditions. Others, it seemed, were just cantankerous. For example, Mrs Perryman was reprimanded in May 1920 for causing a disturbance to the other residents and Dr Burfield was called to look into her

---

314 NRO, N/CCH 116, 20 February 1907.
315 NRO, N/CCH 117, 16 March 1910.
316 *Ibid.*, 20 April 1910.
317 NRO, N/CCH 119, 16 February 1912.
318 *Ibid.*, 8 May 1912; NRO, 12 June 1912.
319 *Ibid.*, 13 November 1912.
320 *Ibid.*, 29 September 1911.

mental condition.[321] No mental abnormalities were recorded, but Mrs Perryman continued to make a nuisance of herself, appearing in the minute books in June, July and November because of her poor behaviour.[322] In December 1920 she was moved to a smaller almshouse in the city, St Swithins, but in May 1921 she was still causing trouble and the trustees resolved to remove her to the workhouse.[323] In June 1921 Mrs Perryman was asked to leave the almshouse with a pension of 5s. a week for the next twelve months.[324] However, four weeks later, she had still not left St Swithins and fellow residents continued to complain of her bad language and behaviour.[325] Finally, in September 1921, the trustees resolved that if Mrs Perryman did not vacate her cottage within seven days, they would take possession of it without due notice, and she left.[326]

Cleanliness remained a problem for some of the residents of Doughty's Hospital, despite the fact that a bath had been installed at the hospital in 1922.[327] In November 1924, the clerk called attention to the poor personal hygiene of some of the male residents and it was resolved that the assistant clerk speak to these inmates about the necessity of washing at least once a month.[328] In October 1930 two inmates were sent written warnings regarding their lack of cleanliness and told that, if the situation did not improve, they would be removed from the institution.[329] In November 1931, Mr Stubbs was removed from Doughty's Hospital because his cottage was unkempt and he was unable to look after himself properly.[330]

The trustees of Doughty's Hospital also had to deal with the occasionally poor behaviour of relatives of the residents of the hospital. In January 1928 Mrs Oliver, the matron, reported to the trustees about the behaviour of the daughters of Mrs Ames. Mrs Oliver had witnessed the daughters removing coal, calico, food and other items from the cottage belonging to their mother.[331] The two daughters were questioned about this and, as a result, Mrs Ames left the hospital shortly thereafter to stay with the two women.[332]

The drinking habits of some residents continued to cause problems. In June 1932 Mr J. Taylor was cautioned after his drinking

---

321 NRO, N/CCH 121, 12 May 1920.
322 *Ibid.*, 9 June 1920; 14 July 1920; 10 November 1920.
323 *Ibid.*, 11 May 1921.
324 *Ibid.*, 8 June 1921.
325 *Ibid.*, 18 July 1921.
326 *Ibid.*, 14 September 1921.
327 *Ibid.*, 12 April 1922.
328 NRO, N/CCH 122, 12 November 1924.
329 *Ibid.*, 8 October 1930.
330 *Ibid.*, 11 November 1931.
331 *Ibid.*, 11 January 1928.
332 *Ibid.*, 8 February 1928.

had caused disturbances among his neighbours at the cottages.[333] On 19 June 1939, a special sub-committee met to hear the case of Elizabeth Hansell and Charles Woodcock, two inmates who had arrived home intoxicated a few nights before. Mrs Hansell had received facial injuries as a result of falling while incapacitated and it was the belief of Dr Burfield that her case was a chronic one and that she was not, therefore, a suitable almsperson. The trustees agreed, ordering Mrs Hansell to leave the almshouse within fourteen days and banning her from visiting Doughty's at any time after this period. In contrast, Dr Burfield characterised Mr Woodcock as a weak man who was easily led and, because he had caused no trouble despite being under the influence of alcohol, the trustees allowed him to remain at the almshouse upon the condition that nothing of the like should happen again.[334]

In March 1936, a report, signed by trustee John Watling, was commissioned into the age and condition of the inmates at the hospital. The report stated that since the consolidation of the charities in 1910, Doughty's Hospital had cared for 170 almspeople. It recorded that the average age on arrival was 70 and the average age at death was 80, with inmates being housed at the almshouses for an average of seven years – figures that compare fairly well with those presented in Tables 2 and 3 above. The report also lists the seven long-term inmates of the institution, with the longest serving almswoman, Mrs Phillips, residing at the cottages for twenty-six years. Also listed are twelve former inmates who had been removed to the Norwich Infirmary between October 1912 and March 1936. A third of these former residents had been removed due to 'dirty habits', while a quarter were suffering from various delusions and mental decay. A further three out of the twelve had been removed due to violent or abusive conduct towards the nurses or other residents. Of the final two, one left at her own request, while the other was moved because of a critical operation.[335]

The report encouraged the trustees to further consider the question of what to do when residents became mentally or physically incapable. The clerk suggested that, in most cases, the poor health of a resident was apparent before they entered the almshouse. The trustees agreed that the health of an inmate should be a factor in deciding their suitability. It was agreed that Dr Burfield, the medical officer, should examine each candidate and report on the state of their health before any future appointments were made. In 1941 following the death of one elected inmate and the subsequent poor medical report of a second, it was resolved that medical examinations should be carried out on all

---

333 *Ibid.*, 8 June 1932.
334 NRO, N/CCH 124, 19 June 1939.
335 Almshouses: report signed by J. Watling, dated 7 March 1936.

candidates before an election was called.[336] It was probably this medical examination that, in November 1948, led to one prospective candidate being refused entry to the almshouse due to her previous admissions to Hellesdon Hospital suffering from melancholy and depression.[337]

Due to better living conditions and a higher quality of free health care as a result of the National Health Service Act of 1946, the trustees of Doughty's Hospital found that their residents were living longer towards the later years of the twentieth century, as indeed was the case among the country's population at large. For example, in May 1968 one resident, Mrs Rix, reached her 94th birthday, while another – as we have already seen – was recorded as 101 years and 11 months when she died on 16 June 1986.[338] Many of the older residents were frail and needed a substantial amount of specialist nursing care for which the nursing staff were unqualified, and hence the trustees moved to try to further regulate the conditions of entry. In November 1968 the trustees placed an advertisement in the local newspapers for new applicants to the almshouse, and this specified that potential candidates must be between the ages of 60 and 70 as well as 'active and in good health'.[339] However, this did not stop potential almspeople who were unwell from applying to the hospital. In January 1977 two new female residents were both found to be suffering from mental illnesses that had not been disclosed during their application process. One had been suffering from depression while the other was described as a victim of 'mental confusion'.[340] As a result of this, the trustees decided that in future potential candidates to the almshouse should be asked to sign a letter allowing the charity's medical attendant to consult with candidates' doctors on their medical history.[341] The trustees also reaffirmed their rule that no person over the age of 80 years old should be admitted to the hospital, unless under exceptional circumstances.[342]

Applications to Doughty's were also regulated through periodic closure of the waiting list. The increasing longevity of residents often meant that there were fewer vacancies becoming available at the hospital and July 1981 was one of the occasions when the register, on which potential candidates hoping to acquire a cottage at the almshouse were placed, was closed.[343] Three years later, the list of potential residents

---

336 NRO, N/CCH 124, 16 July 1941.
337 NRO, N/CCH 125, 17 November 1948.
338 NCC Minute Book 8, 1958–70, 8 May 1968.
339 *Ibid.*, 13 November 1968.
340 NCC Minute Book 9, 1971–9, 12 January 1977.
341 *Ibid.*, 12 January 1977.
342 *Ibid.*, 11 May 1977.
343 N.C.C. Minute Book 10, 1980–6, 8 July 1981.

had been significantly reduced and the register was opened once more.[344] However, just one year later still, in March 1985, the assistant clerk reported that the list of names on the register had risen to well over 100, and it was again closed until further notice.[345] In 1988 it was resolved that the list, which now contained thirty-three single and ten couples' applications, should remain closed.[346]

One of the care assistants, Mrs Sue Hills, who worked at the hospital during the 1980s and 1990s, explained the problems that were often involved with caring for the elderly. Although many came into the hospital when they were 'fit and healthy' their health often deteriorated as time went on, and age-related illnesses prevented them from being able to look after themselves properly. The carers would then take over, preparing meals, helping the resident to wash and bathe, and a cleaner would come into the flat once a week to clean.[347] However, this support, she reported, was only given if the almsperson asked for it, and nothing was ever forced upon the residents.

Mrs Hills also recalled a change in the emergency call system. When she first began working for Doughty's Hospital in 1980, the call system was a series of lights that would flash above the door of the flat and block that required assistance. Mrs Hills said that under this system it was often difficult to see which flat needed help, so she welcomed the improvement to the call system which was put into place in November 1988.[348] The almshouse had been due for improvements to its smoke alarm system and the trustees decided to update the call system at the same time. An intercom system was installed and residents were then able to pull a red cord and speak directly to a carer by way of several hand-held mobile devices.[349] This system, recalled Mrs Hills, was much more convenient and allowed action to be taken much more quickly in the event of any emergencies.[350]

Another problem that the carers found when dealing with residents was that, in cases of dementia or mental decay, residents might become difficult, spiteful or uncooperative. This was particularly problematic, Mrs Hills remembered, when dealing with residents who were suffering from senility. She recalls one occasion where an almsperson accused her and a colleague of stealing, only to find that the resident had the items in her handbag all along. Mrs Hills said that it was this problem that led to the decision that carers should only enter residents' flats in

344 *Ibid.*, 7 March 1984.
345 *Ibid.*, 6 March 1985.
346 NCC Minute Book 11, 1986–9, 22 June 1988.
347 DOHI 004.
348 NCC Minute Book 11, 1986–9, 9 March 1988.
349 *Ibid.*, 11 May 1988; 22 June 1988; 14 September 1988.
350 DOHI 004.

pairs – a policy that was as much for their own security and to prevent claims of theft, as to help care for the elderly themselves.[351]

Residents' perquisites

As we have already seen, the residents of Doughty's Hospital lost their weekly allowance of money during the course of the 1940s, with the last two weekly stipends being discontinued in March 1944 when the residents reached pensionable age.[352] In the 1950s the residents were also to lose their allowance for clothing, a tradition that had been established in Doughty's will in 1687. In the eighteenth century the residents of the hospital were given a gown or cloak of purple cloth upon entry to the almshouse, and this item of clothing was replaced every two years.[353] In April 1710 a bill for six gowns for the old women at 6s. and nine coats for the old men of the hospital at 18s. was recorded in the hospital minute account books, showing that each coat would cost 2s. to make and each gown 1s.[354] In 1835, Mr Thomas Allen was employed to provide purple cloth for the hospital, at 3d. per yard.[355] However, the colour of the uniforms changes between 1835 and 1845, when William White lists the annual clothing allowance for each inmate as follows: one pair of shoes, blue clothing and linen for shirts and shifts.[356] This change may have occurred because the other large almshouse in Norwich, the Great Hospital, dressed its inmates in blue and the trustees may have wanted to create a sense of uniformity across all the almshouses.[357] However, the reason for the change is not recorded, and it may have simply been due to the fact that blue cloth was less expensive than purple cloth before the development of aniline dyes after 1856.

In November 1903 Hotblack Brothers won the tender to make suits for the men of Doughty's Hospital at 23s. 11d. per suit and 37s. 6d. for a suit for the master. It is noted in the minute book that from this date on residents at Doughty's would be allowed the option of blue or black material for their suits.[358] In December of the same year female inmates were also given the choice of black or blue material for their dresses.[359] In 1911 the allowances for clothing were extended to all inmates at the hospital, not restricted to those receiving a stipend from the charity, and in September 1913 this privilege was also extended to

---

351 DOHI 004.
352 NRO, N/CCH 124, 15 March 1944.
353 NRO, Case 20f/14, William Doughty's Will, 25 April 1687.
354 NRO, N/MC 2/3, Hospital Committee Minute Book 1708–20, 7 April 1710.
355 NRO, N/MC 2/8, Hospital Committee Minute Book 1826–36, 10 December 1835.
356 White, *White's Norfolk directory*, p. 136.
357 NRO, N/MC 2/8, Hospital Committee Minute Book 1826–36, 10 December 1835.
358 NRO, N/CCH 116, 18 November 1903.
359 *Ibid.*, 16 December 1903.

the wives of inmates who were not on the foundation themselves.[360] In 1917 the annual income of the Almshouse Committee was cut by 10 per cent and the trustees had to make cuts in expenditure. As a result they resolved only to grant clothing allowances when new clothes were needed, rather than annually as before.[361] In 1942 the benefit system was changed, and each female inmate received a £5 voucher with which to purchase her own clothes and household linen, while each male inmate received a suit at a cost of £4 5s. 6d.[362] In 1944 this system was refined, and each almsperson was given a £5 clothing voucher, to be used in one of six local clothing shops.[363] However, the clothing allowance was discontinued in 1950, as a result of 'administration costs outweighing the income of the institution'.[364] After 1950, the residents of Doughty's Hospital would never again have an annual clothing allowance.

Social life at Doughty's

The first written record of organised entertainment at Doughty's Hospital does not occur until 1897. In commemoration of Queen Victoria's Diamond Jubilee, a tea was provided for the inmates of Doughty's Hospital, Cooke's Hospital, the Girls' Hospital and Pye's Almshouse, as well as the pensioners and exhibitors of the Town Close Estate Charity and those on the foundation of, and exhibitors to, Anguish's Boys' Charity.[365] This is not to suggest that there had been no entertainment at all at Doughty's prior to this, as it may have been informal and so went unrecorded. However, from this time the instances of celebration and entertainment at Doughty's Hospital became increasingly frequent and well documented.

In June 1908 the inmates of Doughty's Hospital were invited by one Mr Mack of Hellington to spend the afternoon at his farm, the cost of which was defrayed by the trustees, and in October 1909 the residents, along with those from the other almshouses in Norwich, were invited to St Andrew's Hall to witness a visit from the King.[366] In 1911 the chairman arranged for the inmates to have a tea in commemoration of the coronation of George V and the trustees also authorised the inmates to have a drive around the city.[367] The construction of the reading room in 1916 must have rendered Doughty's Hospital a better environment in which to have concerts and parties.[368] Certainly the

360 NRO, N/CCH 119, 10 September 1913.
361 NRO, N/CCH 120, 10 January 1917; 11 July 1917.
362 NRO, N/CCH 124, 21 January 1942.
363 *Ibid.*, 15 March 1944.
364 NRO, N/CCH 125, 15 March 1950.
365 NRO, N/CCH 115, 17 March 1897.
366 NRO, N/CCH 116, 17 June 1908; NRO, N/CCH 117, 20 October 1909.
367 NRO, N/CCH 119, 21 June 1911.
368 NRO, N/CCH 120, 17 November 1915; *Eastern Daily Press*, 9 February 1916.

reading room was utilised for occasions like the King's Silver Jubilee in 1935, which was marked by a drive around the city, followed by tea and entertainments in the reading room.[369]

Entertainments provided for the residents during the first forty years of the twentieth century were usually arranged to coincide with national celebrations, such as a coronation or jubilee.[370] So after the victorious conclusion of the Second World War in Europe in May 1945 the trustees again decided to celebrate with an excursion. The clerk invited the almspeople to his home at Letheringsett near Holt, and an excursion by motor coach, via the coast, was planned for 10 August.[371] However, the weather did not hold and the trip was cancelled.[372] On 1 October 1945, the victory excursion was rescheduled and the residents of Doughty's were treated to a trip to Great Yarmouth by motor coach.[373]

In September 1951 the reading room, having been destroyed by wartime bombing, was reopened and the trustees held a concert party to celebrate the occasion.[374] Now that there was once more a permanent room at the hospital for recreation, organised entertainments became more frequent, and in March and July 1952 two children's singing troupes came to entertain the residents.[375] In August 1954 the Eaton Afternoon Townswomen's Guild invited the residents of Doughty's to Eaton Parish Hall for entertainments, and in November 1955 the Lonsdale House School invited residents to a party in the grounds of the school.[376] In November 1957, £25 was allocated by the trustees for a 'festive party'.[377] In May 1960, Miss Hemmings, the matron, suggested that the residents might enjoy a television set in the reading room if one was provided for them.[378] In September of the same year Norwich Relays Limited offered the rental of a television set, with installation costs, at £21 10s. 0d. for the first year and £18 per annum for subsequent years. The trustees accepted and the television was duly installed.[379]

In the later years of the twentieth century regular coach outings were arranged, with contributions to the cost being made by the residents. In the later 1980s and early 1990s the favoured destination

---

369 NRO, N/CCH 123, 13 March 1935.
370 NRO, N/CCH 115, 17 March 1897; NRO, N/CCH 116, 17 June 1908; NRO, N/CCH 117, 20 October 1909; NRO, N/CCH/119, 21 June 1911.
371 NRO, N/CCH 123, 18 July 1945.
372 *Ibid.*, 19 September 1945.
373 *Ibid.*, 21 November 1945.
374 NRO, N/CCH 125, 19 September 1951.
375 *Ibid.*, 19 March 1952; 16 July 1952.
376 *Eastern Evening News*, 27 August 1954; NRO, N/CCH 125, 16 November 1955.
377 NRO, N/CCH 125, 20 November 1957.
378 NCC Minute Book 8, 1958–70, 18 May 1960.
379 *Ibid.*, 20 September 1960.

was the seaside town of Gorleston, and Plates 6 and 7 are photographs taken during the course of these visits. The Pier Hotel, featured in Plate 7, was a regular destination, where a late lunch of fish and chips was invariably the order of the day.[380] A wider variety of seaside attractions were visited subsequently, including Great Yarmouth, Lowestoft and Southwold.[381]

The year 1987 saw the 300th anniversary of William Doughty's bequest of £6,000 to build an almshouse in the City of Norwich. The trustees decided that something should be done to commemorate the event and the Lord Lieutenant of Norfolk, Sir Timothy Colman, was invited to unveil a plaque at the hospital.[382] The festivities were timed to coincide with Doughty's annual garden party, which was attended by residents, staff, trustees and their families. One woman, who at the time of writing is herself a resident of Doughty's Hospital, remembered attending the celebration as a guest of her mother, who was an almswoman at Doughty's in 1987. This lady recalls that she and her sister both attended and were impressed by the wonderful strawberry teas they were served.[383] The mayor and mayoress of Norwich, Mr and Mrs Wheatley, were also invited to attend, and a marquee was erected on the lawn to shelter the guests in case of inclement weather. Luckily it was a glorious sunny day. After the plaque was unveiled, the assembled crowd enjoyed sandwiches, cakes, tea and fresh strawberries and cream.[384]

After the formal service, which had taken place in the afternoon, the matron had arranged a more informal evening barbecue for staff, residents and their friends and relatives. The party continued in the reading room, with singing and performances by staff and residents. Mrs Whitlam had found a song about Doughty's Hospital, written by a resident and to be sung 'to a popular melody'. Mr Harry Boreham remembers helping Mrs Whitlam to scour local second-hand book shops in search of a tune for the song. After finding an appropriate melody, *To be a farmer's boy*, in a nineteenth-century song book, Mr Boreham wrote a final verse to the song to commemorate the tercentenary of the hospital, and all the eight gentlemen residents sang the song to a very favourable reception.[385] After this Miss Muriel Smith, the assistant matron, and Miss Rachel Hills gave an amusing rendition of a song recorded in 1960 by Harry Belafonte and Odetta – 'There's a hole in my bucket' – while wearing appropriate costume. This too was

---

380 Following p. 114.
381 These are discussed below, Part V, p. 229.
382 *Eastern Daily Press*, 15 July 1987.
383 DOHI 011.
384 DOHI 004; DOHI 005; DOHI 008.
385 H. Boreham, *Doughty's Hospital tercentenary celebrations: a record* (July 1987), p. 2; DOHI 008.

warmly received. The night was rounded off by the playing of records, and residents were given the chance to dance and sing along as they wished.[386]

Doughty's song
So, after threescore toilsome years,
How sweet it is to come,
Divested of all worldly cares,
To a snug and peaceful home.
A house to shield us from the storm,
To us a minor heaven,
With clothes and coals to keep us warm,
And freely, nobly given.
And freely, nobly given.

A weekly pension, duly paid,
To us a mine of wealth,
A doctor when we need his aid,
To keep us in good health,
Let Doughty's name – a name most dear –
With Cooke's be ever joined;
Their noble acts must all revere,
So gen'rous and so kind.
So gen'rous and so kind.

Three hundred years have passed away,
But still lives Doughty's dream,
For that same care is giv'n today,
Brought by a loving team.
With quiet calm we view the years,
And bless retirement's ease,
Advancing age presents no fears,
Each day is sent to please.
Each day is sent to please.

Chorus:
So raise your glass to Doughty's toast,
Let banners be unfurled,
It is our very proudest boast,
It's the best in all the world![387]

---

386 DOHI 004; DOHI 005; DOHI 008.
387 DOHI 008; H. Boreham, *Doughty's Hospital tercentenary celebrations*, p. 4.

This event spawned two new social activities for Doughty's Hospital. Firstly, the sketch performed by Miss Smith and Miss Hills evolved into an annual event, with residents, staff and trustees all participating in singing, dancing and performing sketches. The Music Hall, as it came to be known, continued just into the early twenty-first century, but has since fallen from popularity as a result of the advancing age and frailty of residents, who are increasingly unable to participate.[388] Lady Hopwood, the chairman of the Almshouse Committee, remembers that members of staff were still performing at social functions when she came to the hospital. In January 2002, at Lady Hopwood's first Christmas dinner as chairman, she recalls Geoffrey Beck, the gardener, and Christine Share, the deputy matron, with others, performing a most entertaining sketch after the meal.[389] A choir was also established by Mr Boreham, as a result of the keen interest shown in Doughty's song. The numbers in the choir rose from the original eight men in 1987 to around twenty-five to thirty members of both sexes, who would regularly perform to the other residents and at other venues around the city (see Plate 2). Sadly this too has suffered as a result of the age and ill-health of residents, and the choir fell from popularity in the late 1990s.[390]

Doughty's at the start of the twenty-first century

The twentieth century was a period of considerable change and development at Doughty's Hospital and all aspects of the institution were affected. There were administrative changes in the form of the consolidation of the Norwich charities and the introduction of maintenance charges for the residents. The hospital also experienced unprecedented expansion, with six new accommodation blocks being built or converted between the 1960s and the 1990s. The original courtyard buildings of the institution were refurbished and a reading room was built and extended. The increase in tenements meant an increase in residents and this in turn meant an increase in staff. More staff were also needed due to the increasing age and frailty of the residents who were admitted to the hospital, as medical and social changes meant that people were living longer. The replacement of the master with a matron was resisted by the trustees but, after finding the Charity Commissioners unwilling to compromise, the idea of a woman running the hospital was finally accepted. Above all Doughty's, like almshouses everywhere, had been deeply affected by the rise of state welfare, and the hospital had proved to be highly successful in integrating its charitable activities with both the personal and

---

388 DOHI 004; DOHI 005; DOHI 008.
389 Correspondence from Lady Hopwood, 28 July 2009.
390 DOHI 008; DOHI 013.

institutional funding that, particularly after the Second World War, had become so readily available.

The twenty-first century would bring with it increased government controls and regulations as systems of social care were increasingly formalised. New government and independent initiatives and grants would soon require Doughty's not only to maintain its high standards, but also to prove that these standards were being consistently reached. An era of enhanced governmental regulation was approaching.

PART V

Into the twenty-first century

CHAPTER 18

Housing policy and the rise of the voluntary sector

Housing in Britain in the later twentieth century

If the Victorian era was the golden age of philanthropy, the period from the later 1940s to the 1970s was the golden age of state welfare, sometimes described as the 'classic' era of the welfare state.[1] Of course, in all periods of our history a variety of welfare provisions have existed, which has included private market solutions as well as state welfare and philanthropy. While the balance between the three has clearly changed over time, as John Stewart has recently remarked, welfare 'has always been delivered by a range of agencies and institutions – there is, and always has been, a mixed economy of welfare'.[2] Nevertheless, the extraordinary expansion of welfare services by the central state on the basis of the blueprint set out in the Beveridge Report of 1942 and the White Paper on Employment in 1944 marks out the four post-Second World War decades as an era of collectivism on a scale hitherto unimaginable. While, as discussed above, voluntary provision by no means disappeared, it was now that the predictions voiced as early as the 1930s – that philanthropy would become supplementary to state welfare – came to be realised.

In the realm of housing policy and provision, the classic era of the welfare state witnessed a clash of ideologies which was largely absent from other spheres of welfare, where a high degree of consensus prevailed. Indeed, it has been suggested that 'housing policy enjoyed little wartime consensus and remained throughout the postwar years at the heart of party conflict'.[3] Through the late 1940s and well into the 1950s the Labour Party supported, as it had done before the war, the provision of council housing controlled by local authorities, while the

1 B. Lund, 'State welfare', in M. Powell (ed.), *Understanding the mixed economy of welfare* (The Policy Press: Bristol, 2007), pp. 41–60.

2 J. Stewart, 'The mixed economy of welfare in historical context', in Powell (ed.), *Understanding the mixed economy of welfare*, p. 24.

3 P. Thane, *Foundations of the welfare state* (2nd edition, Longman: London, 1996), pp. 193–5; R. Lowe, *The welfare state in Britain since 1945* (Palgrave Macmillan: Basingstoke, 2005), p. 247.

Conservative Party – in theory if not always in practice – positioned itself as the champion of a 'property-owning democracy'. While the Addison Housing Act of 1919 had kick-started council house building, it was the Labour government's Housing Act of 1924 that had ensured that council housing would have a permanent future, for it gave local authorities the leading role as providers of rented housing, supported by subsidies from central government.[4] Labour voices were also raised in the mid-1930s in opposition to the conclusions of the Moyne Committee on housing policy, for in tandem with local authorities they strongly objected to the enhanced role that this committee's report envisaged for private housing associations, which in consequence remained marginal to housing provision and policy in Britain for forty more years.[5]

The main concern of successive post-war governments was to rectify the existing housing shortfall, for the almost complete cessation of building during the war, the complete loss of 450,000 houses to bombing and damage to three million more had been accompanied by a population increase of one million people, to create the worst housing shortage the century had witnessed.[6] Housing standards were also remarkably poor, nearly half of all houses lacking sole use of a bathroom, two in every five without a bathroom at all and nearly one-quarter lacking exclusive use of a lavatory.[7] Aneurin Bevan was enthusiastically attracted to the socialist idea of building good quality council housing accessible to everyone, although expenditure cuts that were necessary to fulfil the conditions of the Marshall Aid provided by the United States, allied to shortages of building materials, placed limits on what could practically be achieved in the short term.[8] Nevertheless, while only 122,000 local authority houses had been built in the pre-war peak year of 1938, in 1948 the total reached 217,000, an achievement that was facilitated by retention of wartime controls over building materials and the introduction of far more generous subsidies. This figure was, however, partly at the expense of the building of private houses, the number of which fell from 237,000 in 1938 to a paltry 34,000 in 1948, and it was not until the mid-1950s that private house building again began to rival the total achieved by local authorities.[9] Norwich was a notable beneficiary of council house construction, creating a very high

4   N. Ginsburg, 'Housing', in R.M. Page and R. Silburn (eds), *British social welfare in the twentieth century* (Palgrave Macmillan: Basingstoke, 1999), p. 229.

5   P. Malpass, *Housing associations and housing policy. A historical perspective* (Macmillan: Basingstoke, 2000), pp. 95–102.

6   *Ibid.*, p. 117.

7   H. Glennerster, *British social policy 1945 to the present* (3rd edition, Blackwell: Oxford, 2007), pp. 65–6.

8   Ginsburg, 'Housing', p. 230.

9   Malpass, *Housing associations*, p. 117; Lowe, *Welfare state,* pp. 257–8.

proportion of public sector housing compared with other British cities of a similar size, and both reflecting and contributing to the dominance of the local Labour Party in city politics through from 1934 to 2002.[10]

When the Conservatives came to power in 1951 one of their central commitments was to build 300,000 houses a year, effectively out-bidding their Labour opponents. This they achieved through the adoption of a pragmatic policy that continued the council house building programme – indeed, the period 1952–6 produced the largest number ever constructed in a four-year period – while simultaneously encouraging private building through the removal of restrictions on land use and the abolition of building licences.[11] In consequence private house building recovered to 109,934 dwellings in 1955, 146,476 in 1959 and 179,366 in 1961, by when the private sector was building almost twice as many houses per annum as were local authorities. By the mid-1950s the immediate housing shortage had effectively been solved, the only cost being a reduction in size and a drop in quality of the units built, with terraces replacing semi-detached housing in the public sector and average house sizes falling by 10 per cent.[12] It was then that a new relationship between public and private provision was developed, with tax concessions stimulating the private sector while the generous subsidies once offered to local authorities were reined in, cheap loans abolished and preferential land prices withdrawn.

In 1956 subsidies were restricted to meeting the needs of the elderly, slum clearance and new town development, and were withdrawn for general housing. The basic Conservative instinct to favour private property and a free market was thus asserting itself, which was further reflected in the increased pressure placed upon local authorities to sell council houses after 1959. At the same time, through the Rent Act of 1957, they decontrolled overnight half a million private tenancies, laid the groundwork for the ending of rent controls when tenancies changed, and allowed rent increases to permit essential repairs. The failure of the private rented market to revive led to a reversal of policy with regard to council house building in 1962, when general purpose building was again allowed, while the Housing Corporation was established in 1964 specifically to encourage the provision of rented accommodation by not-for-profit housing associations but, initially, creating for them a far more limited role than that suggested by the Moyne Committee in 1933.[13]

---

10   Townroe, 'Norwich since 1945', p. 463.
11   Lowe, *Welfare state*, p. 258.
12   *Ibid.*; Malpass, *Housing associations*, Table 6.1, p. 120.
13   Lowe, *Welfare state*, pp. 259–60; Ginsburg, 'Housing', pp. 234–5; Glennerster, *British social policy*, pp. 84–5.

When a Labour government was returned to power in 1964 it was immediately apparent that the old ideological commitment to local authority housing in preference to owner occupation had gone, reflecting the realisation that both standards of living and aspirations had changed fundamentally. Their first major policy statement, *The housing programme, 1965–70*, accepted the idea of a mixed economy in housing, through which it aspired to build 500,000 houses a year – a figure that was never achieved. In an effort to get close to this figure, and influenced also by the new technological solutions proposed by the major building companies, some councils began to build high-rise accommodation, which just a decade later was widely regarded as unsuitable for the development of sustainable communities.[14] In 1968, when house building peaked at 426,000 units, construction was shared almost equally between the public and private sectors. Owner occupation was now considered the norm by both major political parties, and the 1960s saw the introduction of substantial financial support to owner occupiers, most significantly in the form of exemption from capital gains tax on the family home, the removal of taxation on the imputed rent of owner-occupied dwellings and the introduction of much more substantial tax relief on mortgage payments.[15]

After some retrenchment in the face of the economic difficulties of the 1970s, which saw a switch from redevelopment to renovation, the next major policy departure was the concerted drive to extend home ownership initiated by the Thatcher government in 1979, through a policy of de-regulating mortgage finance and introducing the right to buy local authority rented housing. Between 1979 and 1989 the number of owner-occupied dwellings in Britain increased by over 4.5 million, followed by a further 1.1 million from 1989 to 1995. Discounts on local authority property of up to 70 per cent were offered by 1989, and between 1979 and 2000 the share of total housing owned by local councils fell from nearly a third to under one-fifth.[16]

A glance back across the twentieth century shows the remarkable transformation that has taken place in the distribution and occupation of the nation's housing stock. In 1914 approximately 90 per cent of the housing stock was privately rented, 10 per cent owner-occupied, and less than 1 per cent was in either the public or voluntary rented sectors. By 1971 only 19 per cent was privately rented, 52 per cent was owner-occupied, 28 per cent was council housing and 0.9 per cent was in the voluntary rented sector. By 1989 the transformation in the major

---

14 Glennerster, *British social policy*, p. 145; Lowe, *Welfare state*, pp. 264–5.
15 Lowe, *Welfare state*, pp. 260, 266–7; Ginsburg, 'Housing', p. 235.
16 *Ibid*. pp. 237–8; Glennerster, *British social policy*, p. 188.

forms of occupation was complete, for in that year only 7 per cent of property was privately rented, 68 per cent was in owner occupation, 21 per cent was public-authority rented, and 2.8 per cent was in the voluntary rented sector.[17] While the most significant long-term shift has been from private renting to owner occupation, therefore, we can also detect within these figures the beginnings of the rise of the voluntary sector in housing provision, which formed part of a more general shift in social policy that occurred towards the end of the twentieth century.

The rise of the voluntary sector

Defining the voluntary sector is fraught with difficulty, simply because of its innate diversity. In his recent book on the subject, Jeremy Kendall offers two approaches to definition. The broad voluntary sector (BVS) includes all formal organisations which are constitutionally independent of the state and are self-governing, not-for-profit, and involve some degree of voluntarism (excluding political parties and religious congregations). The narrow voluntary sector (NVS), on the other hand, excludes organisations not usually construed as part of the voluntary sector, because they are viewed as effectively part of the state or are not wholly oriented towards public benefits. Such a definition would exclude, for example, schools, universities, sports and social clubs, trade unions and business associations, and is perhaps the preferred common-sense view of what comprises the voluntary sector.[18] Unfortunately, international comparisons can only be made for the BVS, and this, as calculated in 1995, was quite modest in size for a developed democracy, accounting for 6.2 per cent of total paid employment, compared to a 22 country average of 4.8 per cent, and standing behind the Netherlands, Ireland, Belgium, Israel, the United States and Australia. On this broad measure, in 1995 there were 3,137,000 full-time equivalent paid and voluntary employees in the sector, accounting for 9.2 per cent of GDP, and with a total expenditure of £47.1 billion, or 6.6 per cent of GDP. On the narrower, more satisfactory, NVS measure, there were 1,277,000 full-time equivalent employees (paid and volunteers), accounting for 3.4 per cent of GDP, and with a total expenditure of £15.4 billion, or 2.2 per cent of GDP. Whether broadly or narrowly defined, therefore, the voluntary sector was making a significant contribution to economic activity in the UK in the middle of the last decade of the twentieth century.[19]

What is even more significant, however, is the rapid growth of the sector during the first half of the 1990s. Between 1990 and 1995

---

17   J. Kendall, *The voluntary sector* (Routledge: Abingdon, 2003), Table 7.1, p. 135.
18   Kendall, *Voluntary sector*, p. 21.
19   Kendall, *Voluntary sector*, Table 2.1 and Figure 2.4, pp. 22, 30.

paid employment in the BVS grew from 4 to 6.1 per cent of national employment, although a significant proportion of this was due to the transformation of educational institutions into self-governing, non-profit-making bodies. Nevertheless, NVS employment grew rapidly too, with paid employment increasing by 29 per cent from 390,000 to 503,000 during the same period. Equally significantly, and whichever definition is used, the voluntary sector by 1995 relied ever more heavily upon public sources of finance, which had by now become the most important single source of income. By 1995 the income of the NVS was made up of 19 per cent private giving, 36 per cent private earned income and 45 per cent government income. The most rapidly growing sectors within the NVS were personal social services, development and housing, and international activities.[20] It also appears that this growth has continued into the twenty-first century. Although the following figures are not strictly comparable, in that they are calculated on a different basis by the National Council for Voluntary Organisations, they should roughly correspond with Kendall's NVS measure. Even though they exclude many smaller community-based organisations, the data for 2003/4 reveal that the voluntary sector now had a total income of £26.3 billion, assets worth £70.1 billion, and a workforce of 608,000 paid employees – each of these measures suggesting considerable further growth since 1995.[21]

We have discussed in a previous chapter how Beveridge had foreseen a significant and continuing role for voluntary action within the new welfare state of which he was chief architect, but for both ideological and practical reasons that role had not developed into the prominent one that he had envisaged, and voluntary provision remained strictly supplementary for much of the later twentieth century.[22] However, where it was once regarded as paternalistic, undemocratic, unaccountable and patchy in its coverage, the voluntary sector has been embraced by successive governments in the past thirty years or so as a means to facilitate the introduction of market principles and 'consumer choice' into social welfare.[23] The sector had been far from moribund before that, with new groups such as Gingerbread, the Child Poverty Action Group and Shelter, together with the Pre-school Playgroups Association, emerging in the 1960s, while its growing confidence was reflected in the establishment of the Volunteer Centre in the 1970s and a new coordinating body, the Voluntary Services Unit, within the

---

20   *Ibid.*, pp. 24–7.
21   P. Alcock and D. Scott, 'Voluntary and community sector welfare', in Powell (ed.), *Understanding the mixed economy of welfare*, p. 86.
22   See above, Part IV, pp. 108–9.
23   Stewart, 'Mixed economy of welfare', p. 35.

Home Office. Tax concessions were also offered during the 1980s, but it was only towards the end of that decade that governments started actively to promote voluntary organisations as a component of a more truly mixed economy of welfare, with a view to achieving greater cost effectiveness and enhanced quality of provision. From being for so long regarded as strictly supplementary in the role that it was expected to perform, the voluntary sector suddenly found itself thrust into 'the forefront of many of the developing debates about the reform and delivery of public services'.[24]

The greatest impact upon the sector was the introduction of new community care legislation in 1990, under which Social Services departments and National Health Service agencies were required to look to public, private and voluntary organisations to deliver both health and social care, entering into contracts with these bodies to deliver specific outcomes as deemed appropriate. This, of course, was an entirely new relationship, one that involved a shift from support to regulation and control.[25] In consequence, those organisations that for so long had relied upon government grants to supplement their own income and private donations – those grants usually being given for general purposes which might include service provision, advice, administration and campaigning – were now required to enter into specific contracts to deliver measurable outcomes within specified time constraints, which both formalised and rendered more bureaucratic the relationship they enjoyed with the state.[26] This, of course, also involved enhanced inspection and evaluation which, as we shall see, was a feature that extended also into the realms of almshouse provision, and was to present a challenge to Doughty's.

In stark contrast to the prejudices and preferences of 'old Labour', 'new Labour' has embraced the notion of the mixed economy of welfare, offering a new commitment to the role that voluntary activity plays within society in general, and its potential as a partner in the delivery of public services. At the annual conference of the National Association of Voluntary Organisations held in 2004, Gordon Brown spoke of the 'transformation of the third sector to rival the market and the state, with a quiet revolution in how voluntary action and charitable work serves the community'. Five years previously, in 1999, the Voluntary Services Unit in the Home Office had been expanded and re-launched as a new Active Communities Unit (ACU), with an enhanced budget and a commitment to the modernisation of the sector.

---

24 Alcock and Scott, 'Voluntary and community sector welfare', p. 88.
25 *Ibid.*, p. 89.
26 J. Lewis, 'Voluntary and informal welfare', in Page and Silburn (eds), *British social welfare*, pp. 266–7.

The notion of a formal Compact between the sector and the state was taken up, and is being developed both nationally and locally. In its Comprehensive Spending Review published in 2002, the following statement addressed the position of the voluntary sector:

> The Government needs a voluntary and community sector that is strong, independent and has the capacity, where it wishes, to be a partner delivering world-class public services. To help achieve this, the Government will increase funding to build capacity in the sector and increase community participation.

These were not empty words: the review proposed increases in funding for the ACU from £35 million in 2002/3 to £65 million in 2005/6. A new Futurebuilders investment fund was also established to help modernise the sector, promising £125 million over three years, while another initiative was introduced in 2004 called ChangeUp, designed to develop expertise within the sector, which included £80 million funding to support a capacity-building framework, followed by £70 million over the two years from 2006 to 2008.[27] It is this fundamental transformation in the status, funding and political perception of the role of the voluntary sector that underpins the rapid expansion of both employment and income that the last decade of the twentieth century and first decade of the twenty-first century have witnessed.

The voluntary housing sector

Part and parcel of the rise of the voluntary sector was the growth in provision of voluntary housing. In recent years this has mainly been achieved through the agency of housing associations. Peter Malpass's recent survey of their history reveals that the term 'housing association' was first widely adopted in the mid-1930s, when they generally took the form of a 'copartnership society', which generally catered to the better-off sections of the working class, or an inner-city society where tenants were commonly among the poorest. Although the National Federation of Housing Societies was formed in 1935, it was far from representative of housing associations as a whole, and the movement only really came into its own during the 1960s and 1970s.[28] 'The simplest way to describe housing associations', Malpass suggests, 'is probably to say that they are voluntary organisations whose main purpose is to provide rented housing at affordable rents on a not-for-profit basis'.[29] This very broad definition disguises a wide variety of different forms,

27   Alcock and Scott, 'Voluntary and community sector welfare', pp. 90–3.
28   Malpass, *Housing associations*, pp. 105–7.
29   *Ibid.*, p. 4.

however, one of which would be the traditional almshouse. While most housing associations have governing boards and shareholding members, the latter's role being to elect the board members rather than to profit financially from their shareholding, associations which are endowed charities (such as almshouses) tend not to have shareholding members, and instead their board members are appointed as set out in the original deed of trust.[30] Furthermore, housing associations range from very small, local organisations to large regional or even national societies, some with turnovers in excess of £50 million annually.[31]

Housing associations grew in response to government efforts – at first half-hearted but later much more concerted – to find a non-governmental solution to the problem of the provision of affordable social housing. The Housing Corporation was first set up in 1964 to coordinate this policy, and to provide loans to cost-rent and co-ownership societies, though not to housing associations more generally. Cost-rent schemes struggled from the outset, and were officially converted to fair rents in 1972, which made them indistinguishable from the general run of housing associations. Although the raising of funds proved difficult, co-ownership schemes built over 36,000 dwellings across Great Britain, mostly before 1973, at which date new schemes began to be converted to fair rent.

Notwithstanding their exclusion from the attentions of the Housing Corporation, new housing associations were formed during the 1960s, stimulated by a wave of fund-raising by various religious organisations, the activities of Shelter and increased support from local authorities, most notably the Greater London Council. These aimed to ameliorate the perceived failings of government policy, especially in the inner cities, while at the same time many of them directed their attention to the problem of housing the elderly, in consequence receiving higher levels of government subsidy. From 1967 increased funding was made available to housing associations for the purposes of improvement. The result was a slow but steady growth in activity, housing associations having built 1,638 dwellings in 1961, rising to 10,667 in 1971, followed by slight decline in the early 1970s to produce a total of 9,920 in 1974, alongside which there were 4,132 renovations.[32] The fact that housing association projects were generally small in scale also weighed in their favour in this period, for 'there was a fortuitous coincidence between intensifying policy interest and the rejection of "mass" models' as pursued by British local authorities, while the humane intentions of voluntary housing contrasted with

---

30 *Ibid.*, p. 5.
31 *Ibid.*, p. 6.
32 *Ibid.*, pp. 137–51.

the scandals of landlord exploitation and cupidity in the private rented sector that had recently received much public exposure.[33] While their growth to date had been modest, the year 1974 was to prove a turning point in housing association history.

The transformation in the fortunes of housing associations was a product of the passage of the Housing Act of 1974, which introduced a wholly new regulatory and financial regime. Under this Act the Housing Corporation assumed a central role as promoter and regulator of all housing associations, and would henceforth act as the agent for the Secretary of State in considering applications for Housing Association Grants (HAG). The Act provided for the registration of associations as Registered Social Landlords (RSLs), and those that had registered then became eligible for HAG, which could be used for building, renovation or conversion, and was designed to cover any deficits on projects that were designed to provide subsidised accommodation for people in need. Capital grants typically covered 80–90 per cent of allowable costs, which was supplemented with a small residual loan that could be financed from rental income, and hence the 1974 Act effectively created for housing associations 'a risk-free environment'.[34] We will see shortly that Doughty's Hospital was an early beneficiary, forming part of a general upsurge in activity, with new building by housing associations rising from 9,920 dwellings in 1974 to 25,091 in 1977, and renovations from 4,132 to 19,630 over the same period, after which public expenditure cuts resulted in a slight decline in the overall numbers of dwellings built or renovated in the next two years.[35] By 1979, however, housing associations managed 400,000 dwellings, which was roughly twice the number at the start of the 1970s.[36] While both the number of new builds and renovations fell back in the following decade while the Conservative government pursued its policy of council house sales and encouragement of owner occupation, by the end of the 1980s public expenditure on housing association investment was now running at over six times the sum devoted to local authority housing, over 12,000 dwellings were being built per annum and over 13,000 renovated.[37]

The 1974 Housing Act dramatically elevated the profile of housing associations in the political sphere, and created a platform for future developments. Those developments were ushered in by the Housing Act of 1988, for since this date housing associations 'have become

33 Kendall, *Voluntary sector*, p. 138.
34 Malpass, *Housing associations*, pp. 160–4, quote at p. 164.
35 *Ibid.*, Table 8.2, p. 169.
36 *Ibid.*, p. 176.
37 *Ibid.*, Tables 8.4 and 8.5, pp. 175–6.

the dominant providers of new rented housing and the main vehicle for the break up of the local authority sector'.[38] Under this Act direct government subsidies to local authorities were ended and council tenants were required to pay full economic rents. Rent controls on private lettings were removed and new forms of tenancy created. Both private landlords and housing associations were to be encouraged to bid for the right to manage council estates, subject to agreement by ballot of existing tenants. Construction of new property was to be the responsibility of the 34,000 or so not-for-profit housing associations, not that of local councils. To facilitate this HAG was retained, but was set at new lower levels, with a requirement for housing associations to enter private finance markets, and also to plan ahead to cover long-term borrowing and maintenance costs.[39] In 1988–9 housing associations' total capital expenditure stood at £1,009 million, of which a mere £100 million was private finance. Four years later total expenditure was £3,604 million, of which £900 million was private finance, a ninefold increase. Despite a reduction in total expenditure of the order of one-third by the end of the decade, the quantity of private finance was maintained at roughly the same level.[40] By this time also 352,000 dwellings had been transferred from eighty-six local authorities to RSLs, while the programme for 1999–2000 contained over 140,000 more. At this rate of growth the voluntary rented sector was threatening to overtake local authority housing as a form of property tenure, and to position itself as second only to owner occupation.[41]

Given these developments, it is not surprising to find such rapid development of the voluntary sector in terms of employment and expenditure that we discussed above, for it was social care and social housing that were in the forefront of that expansion throughout the 1990s.[42] While the voluntary sector in England accounted for only 2 per cent of housing stock in 1988, that proportion had increased threefold to 6 per cent by 2001/2, and remained on an upward trajectory.[43] The cost was higher rents (supported by housing benefits paid by the state), increased bureaucracy and government control, and a growing skew towards larger, more impersonal organisations at the expense of the smaller, more humane operations that had once characterised the sector.[44] Indeed, these changes have proceeded so far and so fast that the historian of housing associations has been led to the conclusion that

---

38   *Ibid.*, p. 183.
39   Lowe, *Welfare state*, pp. 368–9; Malpass, *Housing associations*, pp. 201–3.
40   *Ibid.*, Table 10.1, p. 204.
41   *Ibid.*, p. 237.
42   Kendall, *Voluntary sector*, pp. 26–7, 38.
43   *Ibid.*, Table 7.1, p. 135.
44   Malpass, *Housing associations*, pp. 11–12, 240–1.

'the price of growth has been loss of autonomy, and ... associations have been used as convenient mechanisms for the pursuit of government objectives', while 'RSLs at the end of the century are little more than agents of the state, and ... the voluntary element has been reduced to only marginal and largely symbolic importance, providing a fig-leaf for those who really hold the power'.[45]

At the time of writing Norwich City Council is working in partnership with eleven local housing associations under the Home Options Scheme.[46] This scheme gives people waiting for council housing the option of registering with selected housing associations and acquiring a place in one of their social housing schemes. Priority is given to vulnerable people, those who are unintentionally homeless, those threatened with immediate violence or those with serious or complex medical complaints.[47] In addition to these main RSLs, there are other housing associations in Norwich which cater to specific groups of people. For example, Housing21 and Anchor Trust are both national housing associations with facilities in Norwich. Both associations provide rented accommodation specifically for elderly residents. Housing21 began as an arm of the Royal British Legion, but changed its name in 1992 with a view to providing services for all elderly people, not just those from an armed services background. The association currently manages over 16,000 sheltered, extra-care apartments and bungalows throughout the country.[48] Anchor Trust has four sites in Norwich, which provide rented retirement accommodation for people aged 55 and over.[49] Norfolk and Norwich also benefit from the services of smaller housing associations which work exclusively within the county and city boundaries. One such association, the St Martin's Housing Trust, is specifically tailored to the needs of the city's homeless and vulnerably housed. St Martin's was originally the Norwich Night Shelter Project, which ran a night shelter in St James' Church on Barrack Street from 1972. In 1976 the shelter relocated to the disused St Martin at Oak Church in Oak Street. In 2001 the night shelter closed and was replaced by purpose-built, instant access accommodation for up to ten people at Bishopsgate House. The trust

45 *Ibid.*, p. 259.
46 Peddars Way Housing Association; Hastoe Housing Association; Habinteg Housing Association; The Guinness Trust; Saffron Housing Trust Ltd; Cotman Housing Association Ltd; Orwell Housing Association; Places for People; The Wherry Housing Association; Orbit Housing Association; Broadland Housing Association. Source: www.norwich.gov.uk/webapps/atoz/service_page.asp?id=1321, consulted 4 September 2009.
47 www.gnhomeoptions.org.uk/Data/ASPPages/1/32.aspx, consulted 4 September 2009; www.norwich.gov.uk/webapps/atoz/service_page.asp?id=1629, consulted 4 September 2009.
48 www.housing21.co.uk/about-us/quick-facts/, consulted 4 September 2009.
49 www.anchor.org.uk/OurServices/Servicesearch/Pages/Default.aspx?DisplayResult=true&Location= NR4+6DD&SubCat=Housing+for+rent, consulted 4 September 2009.

also has thirty-three beds at Highwater House and twenty-two beds at Carrow Hill House, and the two houses provide residential care for people with mental health issues, or drug or alcohol dependencies.[50] In total there are over thirty housing associations, both locally and nationally based, operating in Norwich. As we will shortly see, while Doughty's Hospital took advantage of the funding available through registration with the Housing Corporation as a Registered Social Landlord, to date it has not entered into partnership with any of these locally based housing associations.

Almshouses into the twenty-first century

Almshouses form part of the housing association movement, broadly defined, but although new foundations continue to be endowed their numerical significance has declined in relative terms as the housing association movement has expanded. The data is as complex as the voluntary housing movement itself, and different measures can be produced by reference to the figures available from different umbrella organisations. In 1997, for example, there were 2,446 social landlords (RSLs) registered with the Housing Corporations of England, Scotland and Wales, but as many as 4,000 housing associations listed by the Registrar of Friendly Societies. Helpfully, the Housing Corporation distinguished almshouses from other types of social landlords, and counted 612 among its membership in that year out of 2,249 separate organisations, or 27 per cent. However, while most almshouses and many housing associations managed a relatively small number of dwellings, the total housing stock is dominated by a small number of very large RSLs. Indeed, while 1,600 small associations (with up to 100 dwellings, which included virtually all of the almshouses) owned less than 3 per cent of the total housing stock, just 338 associations owned 95 per cent of housing stock, and a mere 16 owned fully one-quarter, with over 10,000 dwellings each.[51] Although far from all almshouses, as we will shortly see, are registered with the Housing Corporation, even these partial figures show that the provision made by almshouses is now – in purely quantitative terms at least – a small proportion of the total available stock of social housing.

The number of almshouses charities and dwellings is constantly changing, but we have already seen in a previous chapter that their number continued to grow in the later twentieth century.[52] In a very valuable report written in 1999, Jenny Pannell and Caroline Thomas noted that almshouse charities provided over 3,000 new dwellings in

---

50   www.stmartinshousing.org.uk/services.htm, consulted 4 September 2009.
51   Malpass, *Housing associations*, pp. 9–11.
52   See above, Part IV, p. 111.

the period 1986–96, as well as modernising and upgrading over 5,000 more. In 1999 they identified 1,729 member charities managing 2,288 groups of almshouses with over 32,500 almshouse dwellings in current use. Allowing for those inhabited by couples and families, there were probably of the order of 35,000 almshouse residents in that year.[53] The *Annual report* of the Almshouse Association for 2008 numbers its member charities as 1,717 at 31 December in that year, managing 2,622 groups of almshouses made up of 30,988 dwellings.[54] The Association's website, which provides more rounded numbers, suggests that there are now approximately 36,000 almshouse residents.[55] Just two new members joined during 2008, while there were sixteen mergers – eleven with other almshouse charities and five with other providers of sheltered housing.[56] These figures would appear to indicate, therefore, that in the early years of the twenty-first century the almshouse movement, in terms of bare numbers, remains in a steady state. The data available from the Association's *Annual report* also confirms that almshouse charities remain mostly small in scale, particularly if compared to the larger housing associations. Only 2.7 per cent of almshouse groups consist of fifty-one or more dwellings, which means that the recent expansion of Doughty's, discussed more fully below, places it among this small group of larger almshouse charities. At the other end of the scale, 68.1 per cent include ten dwellings or less.[57]

One of the major initiatives affecting almshouses in the realm of social policy was the introduction of the HAG (now called the Social Housing Grant, SHG) through the 1974 Housing Act, before which the most important source of external funding for almshouse charities were the improvement grants offered by local authorities from 1949 onwards. From 1974 any housing association registered with the Housing Corporation could qualify for significant grants for expansion or improvement, and between 1974 and 1997 over 600 almshouse charities registered with the Corporation. In the period from 1976/7 to 1982/3 almshouses were allocated nearly £34 million, while from 1988/9 to 1994/5 funding totalled £46.4 million. While these are clearly valuable sums, the declining proportional contribution of the almshouse movement to social housing more generally is shown by the fact that these figures represent less than half of 1 per cent of

53   J. Pannell with C. Thomas, *Almshouses into the next millennium. Paternalism, partnership, progress?* (The Policy Press: Bristol, 1999), pp.11, 14. These figures for 1999 differ slightly from those presented by Bryson, McGuiness and Ford, cited above (Part IV, p. 111) for the same year.

54   The Almshouse Association, *Annual report 2008* (The Almshouse Association: Wokingham, 2009), p. 3.

55   www.almshouses.info, consulted 26 August 2009.

56   Almshouse Association, *Annual report 2008*, p. 3.

57   *Ibid.*

total HAG allocated in these years. We have also seen that after 1988 housing associations were required to raise a proportion of their funds in private finance markets, and in the latter half of the 1990s funding for almshouse charities fell by roughly half, to a little less than £2.5 million per annum, most of which was used for refurbishment rather than new build. In recent years HAG/SHG has met less than half the capital costs of works carried out.[58]

One disadvantage of registration with the Housing Corporation has been the increased bureaucracy that membership entails, which is particularly burdensome to small charities which often have to operate on an entirely voluntary basis. While having to submit annual reports to the Charity Commission, almshouse charities which have adopted RSL status also have to report to the Housing Corporation, which has operated 'an intense regulatory and financial regime'.[59] On top of annual reports and accounts, financial measures and indicators of tenant composition have also been required, as well as indicators of the scale and scope of any innovatory activities. All of these have been required to ensure that RSLs are conforming to the policy objectives of the Housing Corporation.[60] The consequence has been a marked trend of de-registration of almshouse charities from the Housing Corporation. Of the 604 almshouse charities registered with the Corporation in 1997, only 30 had joined between 1989 and 1997. The 1996 Housing Act allowed small housing associations which had received less than £1 million of funding to de-register, and by March 1997 97 almshouse charities had already done so.[61] In recognition of these difficulties, it was accepted in the late 1990s that almshouse charities managing 250 dwellings or less would be 'deemed to have complied with performance standards' if they adhere to *Standards of almshouse management*, a publication prepared by the Almshouse Association in discussion with other interested parties that is 'intended to be a document of good practice for all those who are involved in the administration and management of almshouses', now in its fifth edition.[62] The trend, however, continues: seven almshouse charities de-registered during 2008, bringing the total since 1997 to 241.[63] Further legislation set out in the 2004 Housing Act relaxed the rules still further, exempting some

58 Pannell and Thomas, *Almshouses*, p. 15. All of these figures are underestimates, as older figures are (under)estimates, allocations to almshouse charities working in partnership with housing associations are excluded, the substantial funding paid to the Durham Aged Mineworkers' Homes is treated separately, and monies paid via local authorities are also omitted.
59 Kendall, *Voluntary sector*, p. 154.
60 *Ibid.*, pp. 154–5.
61 Pannell and Thomas, *Almshouses*, p. 9.
62 *Ibid.*, p. 61; The Almshouse Association, *Standards of almshouse management. A guidance manual for almshouse charities* (5th edition, The Almshouse Association: Wokingham, 2008), p. iii.
63 Almshouse Association, *Annual report 2008*, p. 3.

RSLs from the need to submit their audited accounts to the Housing Corporation as long as they met certain exemption criteria, and as long as they provided an accountant's report instead.[64]

The report published in 1999 by Pannell and Thomas, *Almshouses into the next millennium*, was based upon a survey of 97 local almshouses situated in south-west England, with a particular focus on thirty almshouse projects that were deemed to be of special interest. Semi-structured interviews, often followed by site visits, were employed to elicit a range of information, which sheds a great deal of light upon the problems and possibilities of the almshouse movement at the turn of the century. Many of the difficulties identified will no doubt be familiar to almshouse trustees operating in other parts of the country. These include the intensified regulatory regime, particularly for those almshouse charities that chose to register with the Housing Corporation, but also experienced by non- or de-registered charities as a consequence of the adoption of voluntarism and pluralism by successive recent governments.[65] A 'plethora of changes in legislation and guidance affecting almshouse charities over recent years' has been identified, including the 1993 Charities Act, the 1996 Housing Act, as well as equal opportunities legislation on race, gender and disability, and a host of new regulations on health, safety and building standards.[66] To this list we might add the Data Protection Act of 1998, and the Working Time Directives issued in the same year by the European Economic Union, which necessitated significant changes to established practice at Doughty's.[67]

Some almshouse property is very old and unsuitable for elderly residents, particularly as it deteriorates, while it is also often expensive to upgrade. High ceilings, heavy oak doors and traditional window frames may be aesthetically attractive, but they are often impractical and have significant maintenance cost implications, while conservation requirements also have to be met when upgrading listed property. In this context the increasing frailty of many almshouse residents as the population ages and individuals attempt to stay in their own homes as long as possible, allied to rising expectations, presents particular difficulties.[68]

Redevelopment has often also posed problems. Courtyard almshouses may offer a greater sense of security than do terraces, but provide a layout that is difficult to develop. As modern expectations

---

64   Almshouse Association, *Standards of almshouse management*, p. 135.
65   See pp. 179–82.
66   Pannell and Thomas, *Almshouses*, p. 24.
67   See below, pp. 201–2.
68   Pannell and Thomas, *Almshouses*, pp. 18–20.

increasingly require one-bedroom flats rather than bedsits, this can often only be achieved by reducing the number of dwellings, as indeed has happened on successive occasions at Doughty's. On the strictly financial front further problems were also identified. Local authority improvement grants have rarely met the full costs of improvement, while until recently only almshouse charities registered with the Housing Corporation could claim HAGs or SHGs, and then they did so in competition with housing associations at large. Some smaller charities have struggled even to keep their properties in a reasonable state of repair, and have had to sell some of their assets, merge or lease their properties to housing associations, or have simply collapsed. While almshouse charities have been encouraged to work in harness with housing associations, many have remained aloof, unwilling to risk the loss of their identity and local control, and in consequence have not reaped the benefits of working closely with larger organisations, which are often in possession of wider contacts and able to employ more professional staff. While many almshouses in the survey were very well run indeed, others lack the necessary skills, or access to support and advice, to do their job to the highest standards. Finally, from the perspective of residents, almshouse tenants lack the legal security of tenure possessed by council and housing association tenants, have few opportunities for mobility and – unless the charity is registered with the Housing Corporation – depend upon the adoption of good practice by individual almshouse boards of trustees with regard to consultation, discipline and dismissal.[69]

Many of these difficulties have also been identified in recent Almshouse Association publications. Hence in his foreword to the fifth edition of *Standards of almshouse management*, Simon Pott, the Association's chairman, began by declaring that 'Everybody will be aware that new legislation, regulations and improvements are constantly being made and therefore all of us involved with almshouse charities need to be up to date with these changes', while because of 'changes and improvements to lifestyle, many of our residents now live to a remarkable age and it is very important that we maintain standards and make improvements where necessary'. Many charities, he noted, were managing admirably, while others were 'finding it difficult to keep up with the changes that are required'. Some were allowing the weekly maintenance contribution to remain static for too long, eventually leading to financial difficulties, while others were struggling to attract new trustees.[70] The *Annual report* for 2008 similarly notes

---

69   *Ibid.*, pp. 20–27, 32–9.
70   Almshouse Association, *Standards of almshouse management*, p. iii.

the ongoing need to convert bedsits into flats and while progress is being made in this direction still in 2008 fully 13 per cent of groups of almshouse accommodation took the form of bedsits, for which it is increasingly difficult to find tenants.[71] New legislation that almshouses had to come to terms with in the previous year includes a new Local Housing Allowance, changes in the delivery of the Supporting People programme and the introduction of Energy Performance Certificates.[72] The arrival of economic recession also had severe implications for the Association in 2008, and resulted in a fall in the value of its investments by approximately 25 per cent in a single year.[73] There can be no doubt that many local almshouse charities have been similarly affected.

While in recent years the almshouse movement has found itself subject to a wide range of stresses, due partly to ongoing demographic changes and rising expectations and partly to the enhanced regulatory framework that has resulted from central government's adoption of a policy of welfare pluralism, there is much to be positive about as we approach the end of the first decade of the twenty-first century. If almshouse charities now occupy only a small corner of the voluntary and social housing sector as a whole, that corner is now one that is positively promoted by central and local government, and whose role is respected as a valuable component of the mixed economy of welfare in housing, rather than being regarded – as it was in some circles in the post-Second World War period – as archaic, paternalistic, undemocratic and marginal. Second, it should be noted that some of the problems identified in *Almshouses into the next millennium* are more apparent than real. Very few examples could be identified of almshouse charities using their powers of eviction, and the report concluded that in practice 'The lack of legal security of tenure may not in fact make much difference to the lives of most almshouse residents'.[74] Furthermore, recent editions of *Standards of almshouse management* have provided clear, and increasingly extensive and diplomatic, guidelines on how to deal with those rare instances of difficulties with residents and the need for consultation, as well as providing model letters of appointment and complaints procedures.[75]

On the funding front, if the variety of funding opportunities that exist can be confusing, and possibly subject to onerous bureaucratic requirements and regulations, the existence of a wide range of possible

71   Almshouse Association, *Annual report 2008*, p. 3; The Almshouse Association, *Support and care for residents. A guidance manual for almshouses and smaller associations* (5th edition, The Almshouse Association: Wokingham, 2007), p. 2.

72   Almshouse Association, *Annual report 2008*, p. 1.

73   *Ibid.*, p. 11.

74   Pannell and Thomas, *Almshouses*, p. 34.

75   Almshouse Association, *Standards of almshouse management*, pp. 89–90, 97–105, 162–4.

funding sources is clearly as much a blessing as a burden. Some almshouse charities remain able to rely heavily upon their own accumulated resources, among which we can include Doughty's Hospital itself. Others can call upon local authority funding for improvement, support from English Heritage in the case of historic buildings, lottery funding, support from a wide range of other charities, as well as SHG mediated through the Housing Corporation.[76] Furthermore, while for so long HAG and SHG were available only to organisations registered with the Housing Corporation, the new Homes and Community Agency now enables non-registered almshouse charities to bid for statutory funds in consultation with the Housing Corporation's National Regulation of Small Associations team (RASA) based in Leicester, which has already attracted £2.5 million of funding.[77] Interest-free loans, repayable over a period of ten years, are also available from the Almshouse Association itself, and amounted to a total of £573,764 in 2008, while grants amounting to £6,500 were also made available by the Association to member charities.[78]

Finally we should note that the movement continues to receive support both internally and externally. A new fund-raising drive by the Almshouse Association has made a promising start by gathering £105,000 in 2008, besides £11,500 donated for specific projects.[79] The Association itself is clearly very active and amenable to approaches from its constituent charities for advice and guidance, while also keeping in touch via the quarterly *Almshouses gazette,* providing the financial assistance outlined above, as well as guidance through its publications *Standards of almshouse management* and *Support and care for residents.*[80] Increased collaboration between respective almshouse charities operating in particular regions has recently been advocated by its chairman, while the report *Almshouses into the next millennium* similarly advocates the need to work in partnership with local authorities and housing associations if almshouse charities are fully to meet the changing demands and expectations of the twenty-first century.[81] Finally, and most significantly of all, there is much evidence to suggest that almshouse residents themselves remain highly appreciative of the accommodation and care that almshouses continue to provide. From his recent visits to a number of almshouse charities, the Almshouse

76 Pannell and Thomas, *Almshouses,* pp. 14–15.
77 Almshouse Association, *Annual report 2008,* pp. 3, 8; Almshouse Association, *Standards of almshouse management,* p. 132.
78 *Ibid.,* pp. 7–8
79 *Ibid.,* p. 9.
80 *Support and care for residents* is partially funded by the Housing Corporation, and is endorsed by the Charity Commission for England and Wales, the Housing Corporation, Age Concern and the Centre for Sheltered Housing Studies.
81 Almshouse Association, *Annual report 2008,* p. 1; Pannell and Thomas, *Almshouses,* p. 62.

Association's chairman was able to report that 'most importantly, the residents themselves are invariably upbeat, and delighted with their homes'. 'That', he writes, 'must be the benchmark to which all of us as trustees should aspire'.[82]

---

82   Almshouse Association, *Annual report 2008*, p. 1.

CHAPTER 19
Twenty-first-century Norwich

According to the 2001 census the City of Norwich had a population of 121,550. Of this, 17.2 per cent was aged 60 or over, a figure slightly below the national proportion, which stood at 20.8 per cent. In Norwich, however, 4.9 per cent of the population was aged 80 or more, compared to the national figure of 4.2 per cent.[83] By 2008 the city had grown substantially to 135,829, and by that date 19.3 per cent of the population was aged 60 or above, 16.9 per cent was of pensionable age (65 for men, 60 for women), and 5 per cent was aged 80 or over. Comparison with the country as a whole shows that the percentages aged 60 or over still stood slightly below national levels, though closer than formerly, while the percentage aged 80 and over still exceeded the national total. These figures stand considerably below those for the county of Norfolk as a whole, however, where as much as 27.7 per cent of the population in 2008 was aged 60 or above, and 5.9 per cent aged 80 or over.[84] The high percentage of elderly within the population is, at the time of writing, proving to be a severe strain on the finances of the county council, a recent statement on the increasing cost of adult social care reporting that 'Norfolk's older than average population is placing an increasing strain on the county council's resources, with almost a third of the county aged 60 or above. This is set to increase by a further 58.1 per cent by 2031, with the number of people aged 85, or over, projected to increase by just over 100 per cent – much higher than the national average.' As at 27 October 2009, an exercise in cost-cutting, streamlining and the introduction of additional charges was under discussion.[85] If the stresses of an ageing population were being felt in Norwich, therefore, the situation across the county as a whole in the opening decade of the twenty-first century was considerably worse.

---

83 Calculated from figures presented in www.statistics.gov.uk/census2001/pyramids, consulted 30 October 2009.
84 www.norfolkinsight.org.uk, consulted 30 October 2009.
85 www.norfolk.gov.uk/consumption, consulted 30 October 2009.

The twenty-first century saw a city with a wider range of services available for elderly residents and a range of care homes managed by the National Health Service, the local authority and private contractors which were now in direct competition with voluntary organisations like Doughty's Hospital. Some 4,335 people, or 3.7 per cent of the total population of Norwich, were recorded as living in communal housing in 2001.[86] Despite the growth of this parallel provision, the two main almshouses in Norwich, Doughty's Hospital and the Great Hospital, continue to offer valuable services for elderly people in financial need.

In terms of employment, Norwich at the turn of the twenty-first century was similar to other UK cities, with the largest numbers of people being employed in the service industries, retail, education and health and social care. However, the largest single employer in the city was the banking and insurance sector: in 1998, 11.5 per cent of those working in Norwich were employed in the financial intermediation industries.[87] Several large insurance and banking companies are based in the city, including the Norwich Union Group (renamed Aviva in 2008) and the Norwich and Peterborough Building Society. Another large employer in Norwich is the media sector with regional television, radio and print media all based there. These include the offices of Anglia Television, BBC Television East, Radio Norfolk and the Archant Newspaper Group.[88]

Employment in the retail sector also accounts for a large proportion of overall employment. In 1998, 10.2 per cent of the workforce was employed in either food retail or other retail trades.[89] The Castle Mall shopping centre was opened in 1993 and at the time of writing houses fifty-eight separate stores, as well as four restaurants and take-away food outlets and an eight-screen cinema. The Riverside complex was completed shortly after at a site on the River Wensum close to the city railway station. The area boasts eight restaurants, four bars, a bowling alley, a cinema and a gym complex.[90] Further shopping and leisure facilities were built in 2005 at Chapelfield, on the site of the Caley's (later Rowntree Mackintosh and then Nestlé) chocolate factory, which closed on the site in 1999.[91]

Another growing employment sector in Norwich in the late twentieth and early twenty-first century is education, and in 1998 the

---

86 www.norfolk.gov.uk/norfolkoverview, consulted 8 July 2009.
87 Townroe, 'Norwich since 1945', Table 19.3, p. 476.
88 *Ibid.*, p. 475; www.norwich.gov.uk/intranet_docs/A-Z/Economic%20Strategy.pdf, consulted 8 July 2009.
89 Townroe, 'Norwich since 1945', p. 476.
90 www.riversidecentrenorwich.co.uk, consulted 8 July 2009.
91 Townroe, 'Norwich since 1945', p. 480.

education sector accounted for 8.2 per cent of the total workforce.[92] The growth of education as a major employer in the city is partly the result of the continuing expansion of the University of East Anglia. Founded in 1963 and designed by architect Denys Lasdun, the university soon gained an excellent reputation in subjects such as creative writing, British, European and American history, American literature, music, social work, and the chemical, environmental and biological sciences. The expertise in genetics at the School of Biological Sciences led to, and benefited from the arrival of, the John Innes Institute in 1967. Previously located at Bayfordbury near Hertford, the Institute is an independent research centre specialising in plant science and microbiology, and was first housed in temporary buildings at a site at Colney, just across the river from the university's main campus. The site, now known as the Norwich Research Park, was expanded first by the arrival of the British Sugar Research Institute (funded by British Sugar, and which has since closed) and then the Food Research Institute – part of the Low Temperature Research Station in Cambridge – moved to the site in 1968. Later still, in 1990, the non-privatised part of the Plant Breeding Institute joined the John Innes centre from Cambridge, while the Biotechnology and Biological Sciences Research Council's Unit of Nitrogen Fixation, previously at the University of Sussex, followed in 1995. The Research Park now has one of the largest concentrations of plant and microbial science expertise in Western Europe.[93] The Norfolk Sports Park opened on the site of the University of East Anglia in 2000, and the university is now one of the city's major employers and generators of local spending power.[94]

Employment in the health and social care sector also increased during the late twentieth and early twenty-first century. While in 1961 just 2,210 people were employed in health care, this number had risen to 11,140 by 1998.[95] In 1967 the East Anglian Regional Hospital Board proposed a new hospital for the city to replace the two main institutions in Norwich, the West Norwich Hospital on Bowthorpe Road and the Norfolk and Norwich Hospital. However, a site at Cambridge was chosen instead for a new teaching hospital and medical school after heavy lobbying and plans for a similar institution in Norwich were put on hold. Norwich consultants never forgot how close they had come to having their own medical school, however, and when the opportunity arose to develop a School of Health and Social Work they supported it wholeheartedly. This grew steadily in its scope

92   *Ibid.*, p. 476.
93   *Ibid.*, pp. 480–1.
94   *Ibid.*, p. 481.
95   *Ibid.*, p. 476.

and importance until health was able to stand on its own. The eventual
achievement of a new medical school was very important to the local,
especially hospital, medical community. After the resolution of issues
over the planned site for the new hospital, construction work began in
1998 on a site at Colney. The Norfolk and Norwich Hospital was soon
utilised by the new Medical School at the University of East Anglia
and renamed the Norfolk and Norwich University Hospital, and the
two institutions were linked through this partnership, which built upon
prior collaboration in medical research.[96] The new hospital was initially
planned to have 953 beds at a cost of £229 million, and in February
2003 a further 36 beds were created by the construction of a surgical
ward at the hospital.[97] The hospital was officially opened in February
2004 by Her Majesty the Queen and at the time of writing employs a
staff of over 5,700.[98]

In contrast, while the service, education and care sectors are
employing greater numbers of people in Norwich, more traditional
areas of employment have seen their businesses in the city contract, of
which the agricultural sector is a good example. In 1961 the agricultural
industries employed 2,130 people within the City of Norwich, whereas
by 1998 the sector had shrunk to a workforce of just 620. Non-metal
and non-chemical manufacture also declined from 20,100 employees
in 1961 to 5,320 in 1998, and metal manufacturing fell from 7,320 in
1961 to 3,640 in 1998.[99]

The economy of Norwich may have changed dramatically, but the
city's capacity for charity has not diminished with the passage of time.
At the time of writing in 2009 there are now 3,746 registered charities
in Norfolk, 332 of which operate within the City of Norwich.[100] For
example, the Great Hospital, which was originally built in 1249, still
functions as an almshouse, providing accommodation and support for
its inhabitants. Many of the original buildings (the Master's House and
Chaplains' House, along with St Helen's House) have been converted
into self-contained flats.[101] Cottages in the traditional almshouse
style, with modern interiors, have been built in the grounds, while a
Residential Care Home provides twenty beds for residents who need
a greater level of support. The hospital also provides sixty-seven flats/
cottages for use as sheltered housing, twenty-four flats which provide
housing with additional care facilities and twenty-one residential care

---

96   *Ibid.*, p. 481.
97   www.nnuh.nhs.uk/Page.asp?ID=95, consulted 8 July 2009.
98   *Ibid.*
99   Townroe, 'Norwich since 1945', p. 476. These figures are accurate for the City of Norwich
      but do not include the industrial estates on the outskirts of the city.
100   www.charitycommissioners.gov.uk/index.asp, consulted 1 July 2009.
101   www.thegreathospital.co.uk/history/middleyears, consulted 17 September 2009.

rooms. Like Doughty's Hospital, the Great Hospital has an admissions policy which requires that applicants must have lived in Norwich for a number of years before applying (in the case of the Great Hospital applicants must have lived or worked in Norwich for at least five years) and be unable to support themselves. While Doughty's Hospital now considers applicants over 60 years of age, the Great Hospital only accommodates those over 65 years.[102]

Other long-established charities continue to thrive in the city. For example, the Norfolk and Norwich Association for the Blind (NNAB) evolved from Thomas Tawell's Hospital, which was established in 1805. Today the charity consists of a residential care home, Thomas Tawell House, which provides accommodation and care for up to thirty-seven elderly blind and partially sighted residents, and Hammond Court – a complex of twenty sheltered flats with a warden, which provide independent living for blind and partially sighted people of all ages.[103]

While some charities, like the Great Hospital and the NNAB, are well established or have developed from historical organisations, other charities have been founded in response to new social problems or changing social attitudes. Norwich has a wide range of charities which cater to all manner of causes and campaigns, and which aim to support some of the most vulnerable groups in society. For example, the Magdalene Group is a Norwich-based charity, with 'a Christian ethos'. The charity, established in 1992, offers care and support for Norwich's sex workers and helps them to help themselves. It offers support and free hot meals at its drop-in centre in King Street, as well as referring clients to drug and alcohol rehabilitation programmes and providing help to get them off the streets.[104] Another Norwich-based charity, the Matthew Project, is a further example of the wide range of charities available in the city. It provides counselling and support for people living with drug addiction and their families and aims to provide education about the risks of drug and alcohol abuse.[105] The John Jarrold Trust, established in 1965, continues to provide charitable donations to a wide range of organisations, including health and medical charities, charities which support the arts, educational charities, welfare and community-based organisations, historic organisations and charitable activities in developing countries.[106]

Norwich Consolidated Charities, which incorporates Doughty's Hospital, is part of Norwich Charitable Trusts, along with the Town

---

102 www.greathospital.org.uk/hospital_today.shtml, consulted 4 September 2009.
103 www.nnab.org.uk/index.php, consulted 4 September 2009.
104 www.magdalenegroup.org, consulted 27 July 2009.
105 www.matthewproject.co.uk, consulted 27 July 2009.
106 www.jarrold.com/content/jjtrust.asp, consulted 30 July 2009.

Close Estate Charity and Anguish's Educational Foundation. The Town Close Estate uses funds raised from the rents of property owned by the charity as well as from investments to provide grants to needy freemen and their families. Grants are given to individual freemen for educational purposes, for 'the relief of need' and for pensions. The charity also uses its funds to make grants to other organisations that have a charitable and educational purpose, and whose intended beneficiaries live within a twenty-mile radius of the centre of Norwich.[107] Anguish's Educational Foundation was originally Anguish's Boys' Hospital, but became a scholarship fund in 1896.[108] The charity, which is administrated by the same chairman and trustees as Norwich Consolidated Charities, makes educational grants to individuals aged 24 and under who live in the City of Norwich and are in financial need. These grants are principally for school clothing, school trips, and higher and tertiary educational maintenance. Grants are also made to other registered charities for educational purposes.[109] The city can therefore be proud of the number and range of charitable foundations and activities that it continues to host.

---

107 www.charitycommissioners.gov.uk/index.asp, consulted 8 July 2009.
108 Hooper, *Norwich charities*, p. 74.
109 www.charitycommissioners.gov.uk/index.asp, consulted 8 July 2009.

CHAPTER 20
Rules and regulations

In common with the voluntary sector as a whole during this period, Doughty's Hospital experienced increasing government control and regulation. Speaking in interview, Lady Hopwood, at the time of writing chairman of the Almshouse Committee at Norwich Consolidated Charities, revealed that Doughty's Hospital had been run with virtually no paperwork, aside from the trustees' minute books, throughout most of its 300-year history. When the government and other regulatory bodies required information and reports on various aspects of the management of the almshouse, the trustees and the staff had to adapt quickly to the new systems in order to keep up to date with the increasing regulation of the hospital as a social care unit.[110] In 1975 Doughty's registered with the Housing Corporation as an RSL in order to take advantage of a Housing Association Grant, and this required the annual submission of accounts and ongoing monitoring. Although the accounting requirements for smaller organisations were relaxed from 1 April 1997, this still means that Doughty's is doubly accountable – to the Housing Corporation and to the Charity Commission.[111] While for the majority of the twentieth century the charity had been free to work to its own internal standards, the twenty-first century also saw the establishment of additional regulatory bodies, such as the Care Quality Commission, as well as new initiatives in social care such as the Supporting People programme. These new regulatory bodies were set up in order to maintain high standards of care within all adult social housing, a heading under which Doughty's Hospital fell.[112]

The first big change to affect Doughty's Hospital was the introduction of the European Union Working Time Directive in October 1998. Under these new rules, employees were unable to work over forty hours per week, and implementing these directives was to fundamentally change the role of the matron at the institution. When Doughty's Hospital had first been conceived, William Doughty had

---

110 DOHI 016.
111 NCC Minute Book 9, 1971–9, 15 January 1975; 2 April 1975; Pannell and Thomas, *Almshouses*, pp. 9, 21.
112 www.cqc.org.uk, consulted 1 July 2009.

specifically stated that the master of the hospital (who was later replaced by a matron) should 'dwell constantly' on the premises.[113] In 1961 the post of deputy matron was created and, after the two new staff cottages were built in 1966, the matron and the deputy matron had both lived on site.[114] Because they were always close by, the matron and deputy matron were often called upon while off duty, and as a consequence worked far more than forty hours per week.[115] In theory the new European Union Working Time Directive was designed to allow the matron, Mrs Freda Holland, and deputy matron, Mrs Christine Share, the opportunity to work fewer hours and to delegate more tasks to other members of staff.[116] However, because they still lived on the premises, it was very difficult to implement. Mrs Holland recalls that despite other nursing staff being on duty, residents would frequently ring her door bell if they needed assistance.[117] Full implementation of the Directive did not come into effect until Mrs Holland and Mrs Share moved into private accommodation, in 2006 and 2007 respectively.[118] At the time of writing, Mrs Karlene Parry, who took over as matron from Mrs Holland in 2008, and Mrs Share both live in private housing, and there are no care staff living on site at Doughty's Hospital.

The Care Standards Act of 2000 meant that Doughty's had to sign up as a domiciliary care agency with the Commission for Social Care Inspection, which the almshouse did in 2007 at a cost of £497.[119] Domiciliary care agencies provide care and support for people living in their own homes. Because the flats at Doughty's Hospital are regarded as separate properties, and hence the residents are regarded as living in their own private accommodation, it was necessary for the charity to register as a domiciliary care agency rather than as a care or nursing home.[120] The Commission for Social Care Inspection, renamed the Care Quality Commission in 2009, is the independent regulator of social care in England. The Commission regulates all health and social care services for adults in the country, including National Health Service run facilities as well as private institutions and voluntary and charitable organisations. The aim of the Care Quality Commission is to regulate care and ensure that facilities are kept to a high standard. All qualified facilities are registered, and the Care Quality Commission then has the right to impose monitoring and inspection upon them. If a care agency

---

113 NRO case 20f/14, William Doughty's Will, 25 April 1687.
114 *Eastern Daily Press*, 20 April 1966; NCC Minute Book 8, 14 December 1961.
115 DOHI 003.
116 NCC Minute Book 13, 1996–9, 2 December 1998; DOHI 003.
117 DOHI 003.
118 Correspondence with Mrs Holland, 13 July 2009.
119 NCC Minute Book 14, 2000–4, 4 December 2002.
120 www.ucarewecare.com/agencies, consulted 27 July 2009.

is under-performing, or fails to meet the national minimum standards, the Care Quality Commission has powers to act. These include the ability to impose fines or to issue public warnings and, in extreme cases, they are able to force the closure of a facility until it is able to meet those standards.[121]

The domiciliary care provision at Doughty's Hospital was last inspected by the Commission in January 2009 and the information that was obtained from this inspection, and undoubtedly in due course from future inspections, is, and will be, available online for those wishing to check the performance of the institution. These inspections compare a domiciliary care agency to the national minimum standards set out by the Health Department. Doughty's Hospital was inspected in two ways. First, a questionnaire was completed by the matron of the hospital, and second, the hospital was given a surprise inspection in order to check the day-to-day management of the services. The inspector, later described by Lady Hopwood as 'formidable', also spoke to residents at their weekly coffee morning, attended a residents' committee meeting and spoke to various almspeople privately in their flats.[122] The conclusions of the report were very positive, and the inspectors particularly praised the hospital for its individual response to residents, the staff's high level of training and the respect and kindness with which the residents felt they were treated.[123]

In April 2003 Supporting People was launched by the office of the deputy prime minister. The programme's aim is to provide housing-related support for vulnerable people, such as young people, disabled people, people with mental health problems and vulnerable elderly people. The scheme is administered locally by district and county councils and provides a working partnership between all the authorities with which vulnerable people might come into contact. So, for example, probation offices, health authorities, voluntary sector organisations, housing associations, support agencies and service users should all benefit from the higher standards of communication that the Supporting People programme provides. The deputy prime minister's office is responsible for allocating grants to local governments, who in turn allocate the money to local projects that support vulnerable people.[124] Many residents of Doughty's Hospital are eligible for these grants because of their age, and because they are classed as in financial need. The programme itself is concerned with maintaining

---

121 www.cqc.org.uk, consulted 1 July 2009.
122 Correspondence with Lady Hopwood, 22 September 2009.
123 www.cqc.org.uk/registeredservicesdirectory/RSSearchDetail.asp?ID=0000070520
   &Type=DCA, consulted 1 July 2009.
124 www.spkweb.org.uk, consulted 1 July 2009.

the independence of the individual and providing a high standard of support, two aspirations that Doughty's Hospital passionately advocates.[125]

When Supporting People was first established, the trustees encountered a problem. Although the hospital was functioning well, there was absolutely no documentation to prove that this was the case, which would leave the hospital at a distinct disadvantage if it were to apply for the grants from Supporting People.[126] In consequence the trustees agreed to implement a 'practical quality assurance systems for small organisations' (PQASSO) system as a tool for the introduction of systematic quality improvement and assurance in the management process at Doughty's Hospital.[127] PQASSO is a quality assurance system for small to medium-sized voluntary organisations which helps them to run more effectively and efficiently. The self-assessment system shows areas in which the organisation is working well, as well as highlighting areas which need to be improved, and then allows it to make improvements at its own pace.[128]

As Mr David Walker, at the time of writing clerk to the trustees of Norwich Consolidated Charities, explained in interview, there are several positive outcomes from the involvement with regulatory bodies such as the Care Quality Commission and Supporting People. First, the funds generated are always very welcome, especially for an institution like Doughty's Hospital, which is entirely voluntary and funded through investments, rents on properties and monetary gifts. The grants that organisations like Supporting People are able to give to Doughty's are vital for the general maintenance of the residents and the buildings at the hospital. Second, the reports issued by such independent regulatory bodies provide independent proof that the care and management at Doughty's Hospital is of a high standard. This, he notes, will benefit the hospital in the long run by attracting more potential residents, ensuring that standards can continue to improve and providing a basis upon which to rectify any areas where the hospital is perceived to be performing less well.[129]

However, Mr Walker also concedes that there are problems linked with the systematic assessment of quality that these services provide. In order to obtain grants, Doughty's has had to adhere to different sets of guidelines and regulations in order to meet the standards of the institutions which support the hospital, and hence they provide

---

125 *Ibid.*
126 NCC Minute Book 14, 2000–4, 9 July 2003.
127 *Ibid.*, 3 September 2003.
128 www.ces-vol.org.uk/index.cfm?pg=172, consulted 30 July 2009.
129 DOHI 007.

another example of the recent expansion of the regulatory framework in both housing and in social welfare more generally.[130] Although it is important to be able to demonstrate the high standards of care on which Doughty's prides itself, there is concern that the regulations 'threaten the informal and responsive nature' of Doughty's Hospital.[131] Lady Hopwood agrees that the amount of paperwork required is sometimes in danger of overshadowing the main aim of supporting residents, and many people involved with Doughty's feel acutely the precarious balancing act of ensuring that standards are met while at the same time enabling the compassion that draws people to the hospital to remain intact.[132]

In terms of finance, Doughty's Hospital is still funded largely by the charity's endowments, investments and property.[133] Norwich Consolidated Charities, the body of which Doughty's is part, owns total assets of between £20 million and £25 million, depending on economic circumstances. The annual return for the year to 31 December 2008 showed total assets of £23.2 million, against liabilities of £0.34 million. Its income in 2008 was £1.71 million, of which 64 per cent was earned through investments (made up in almost equal parts of rents and 'interest receivable and similar income') with the remaining 36 per cent earned from charitable activities such as fees and grants specifically for goods and services provided by the charity.[134] The first call upon the income of Norwich Consolidated Charities is Doughty's Hospital, which takes a responsible approach to its priority in that its trustees recognise that there are other calls upon these funds. Secondly, there is the Marion Road Day Care Centre, which receives a substantial yearly grant. This was formerly needed to run the centre, but since Norfolk Adult Social Services stepped in to provide funding this money is now used to fund pioneer outreach work in the community for elderly people. Thirdly, there is a system for awarding grants both to needy individuals and to other charities. Fourthly, there is a relatively small subsidy to the second almshouse belonging to Norwich Consolidated Charities, dedicated to those with mental health problems, located at Bakery Court.[135]

Total expenditure for the year ending 31 December 2008 stood at £1.81 million, of which £1.51 million was spent on charitable

130 *Ibid.*

131 *Ibid.*

132 DOHI 006; DOHI 016.

133 DOHI 007.

134 www.charity-commission.gov.uk/index.asp, charity number 1094602, consulted 2 November 2009.

135 DOHI 007; The Charity Commissioners for England and Wales, *Scheme for Norwich Consolidated Charities,* 3 September 2002: Commissioners' References, Sealing 120(s)02, Case No. 154283.

activities, the remaining £0.3 million covering the costs of maintenance and management of the trust's property and other investments, and governance.

Doughty's Hospital itself generated an income of £608,422 in this financial year against a total expenditure of £807,752 (including repairs and redecoration and overheads), to produce an operating deficit of £199,330. Staffing costs, at £464,685, dominate annual almshouse expenditure. Grants to other charitable organisations unconnected with Doughty's and to individuals (331 of whom benefited in this year) amounted to £401,008 (up from £274,856 in the previous year) while £104,634 was paid to Age Concern for management of the day centre on Marion Road.[136]

In terms of the day-to-day running of Doughty's Hospital, residents pay a small charge for heating and electricity as well as a care and support charge.[137] The scheme of Doughty's Hospital states that residents must be in financial need – meaning that they must have a below average annual income, or be unable to afford the basic goods and services needed to live comfortably – and a large proportion of the residents are eligible to receive state benefits.[138] The Charity Commission rules state that private charities must not utilise their funds in situations where the government can provide. This means that all residents must apply for available state benefits before the hospital can begin to pay for their accommodation and care. Even with this provision in place, Mr Walker explained, Doughty's Hospital still subsidises each resident by approximately £3,000 a year, and these surplus costs reflect the high standard of care that Doughty's Hospital aims to provide.[139]

At present, the object of Norwich Consolidated Charities is the provision of housing accommodation for beneficiaries, charitable purposes for the benefit of those beneficiaries, and the relief of persons in financial need or hardship and financial need complicated by medical problems.[140] The trustees can make grants to individuals or organisations as well as providing goods, services and facilities for those in need of financial help. There are now seven nominated trustees (six from Norwich City Council and one from Norfolk and Norwich University Hospital Trust) and seven co-opted trustees. The trustees are in close contact with the residents of Doughty's Hospital and the Almshouse Committee receives the minutes of the Residents'

---

136 www.charity-commission.gov.uk/index.asp, charity number 1094602, consulted 1 July and 2 November 2009.
137 DOHI 007.
138 *Ibid.*
139 *Ibid.*
140 The Charity Commissioners for England and Wales, *Scheme for Norwich Consolidated Charities*, 3 September 2002: Commissioners' References, Sealing 120(s)02, Case No. 154283.

Committee. The trustees act on all points raised both formally and informally and residents are consulted before any changes are made, including changes to rent charges.[141] Doughty's therefore conforms admirably in this respect to the guidelines laid down by the Almshouse Association in *Standards of almshouse management* and *Support and care for residents.*[142]

141 *Ibid.*
142 Almshouse Association, *Standards of almshouse management,* pp. 89–90; Almshouse Association, *Support and care for residents*, p. 8.

CHAPTER 21
From bedsits to bedrooms

In 1991 the trustees of Doughty's Hospital considered the need for further modernisation. Doughty's had grown substantially during the twentieth century, and after the building of Grace Jarrold Court, Cooke's Court and Hesketh Court, and the conversion of properties at Mottram House and 20 Golden Dog Lane, the institution now boasted fifty-four units of accommodation.[143] However, many of the units of accommodation, including the twenty-four rooms in the original courtyard block, were bedsits. The deputy chairman of the Almshouse Association visited the hospital in October 1991 and observed that while it provided bedsits comprising one large room and a small kitchen and bathroom, it was now the norm for residents of almshouses to live in larger one-bedroom flats, with a separate bedroom and sitting room.[144] The provision of mainly bedsit accommodation was becoming a problem, especially in attracting new residents to the almshouse, as indeed was proving to be the case for almshouses more generally. Mrs Claire Frostick, a former chairman of Norwich Consolidated Charities, remembered in interview how some potential residents, who were keen at first to come into the hospital, were put off by the small, cramped conditions of the rooms.[145]

It was proposed by the trustees that the bedsits in the square should once again be converted from three units into two, with each new flat comprising a bedroom, living room, bathroom and kitchen. The architect for the project, Mr Norton, produced plans for the redevelopment of the accommodation, which included extension of the old courtyard, with the twenty-four bedsits being converted into eighteen flats. He also produced plans for the conversion of seven houses in Calvert Street, recently acquired by Norwich Consolidated Charities, into eight more flats and the creation of two new flats on the land between the Calvert Street properties and Hesketh Court.[146] The

---

143 *Eastern Evening News*, 7 April 1975; *Eastern Evening News*, 22 April 1980; *Eastern Evening News*, 15 April 1985.
144 'Norwich Consolidated Charities Scheme revitalises Doughty's Hospital almshouses', in *The Almshouse Gazette*, issue 161, autumn/winter 1995, p. 4.
145 DOHI 009.
146 NCC Minute Book 12, 1989–95, 18 January 1993.

Figure 10.   The refurbishment of Doughty's courtyard, 1994–5

properties on Calvert Street were a row of two-up, two-down terraced houses which the architect planned to convert into one-up, one-down flats.[147] This would mean that the total number of tenements created would be twenty-eight, despite the loss of six bedsits in the square.

Hanover Housing Association was approached to provide temporary accommodation for residents while the work was completed. Fortunately, the Association had recently finished building a block of flats next to Doughty's Hospital in Golden Dog Lane and offered the use of fourteen flats at an annual rent of £67,980.[148] The elderly people were moved into the new housing association buildings for the duration of the refurbishments. Mrs Whitlam, the matron at the time of the redevelopment, remembers that she and Miss Muriel Smith, the deputy matron, had personally to help move each resident and their belongings from Doughty's to the housing association flats. Each removal required the assistance of two removal men with a removal trolley, an electrician, a plumber, a British Telecom technician and a member of Doughty's staff. The removals all went smoothly, which was

---

147 DOHI 017.
148 NCC Minute Book 12, 1989–95, 3 January 1991; 18 January 1993.

Figure 11. The refurbishment of 1994–5, showing internal courtyard walls removed

somewhat surprising to Mrs Whitlam as both she and Miss Smith were suffering with bad cases of 'flu' at the time.[149]

The courtyard complex is a grade II listed building and, in consequence, any redevelopment had to be carried out within the existing parameters of the main external walls. On beginning the construction work, the architects found to their dismay that the second storey of the courtyard, built in 1868, had been constructed directly over the original seventeenth-century single-storey structure, with no consideration for the suitability of the foundations of the building. Physical investigations revealed that the foundations needed considerable improvement and a system of piling and rafting was developed to render the structure more secure. It was also discovered that during the nineteenth-century rebuild many of the walls had not been tied together, and temporary shoring was used to prevent collapse while stitching and enhancement work was carried out.[150] These problems notwithstanding, the conversion of the courtyard flats was completed in March 1995 while the Calvert Court conversions

149 DOHI 001.
150 'Norwich Consolidated Charities Scheme revitalises Doughty's Hospital almshouses', pp. 4–5.

Figure 12.   Calvert Street, before the renovations of 1994

were finished in August of the same year.[151] Mrs Frostick recalled how some residents complained at the disruption the refurbishments caused, saying that the bedsits were fine and there was no need to spend money on converting them. However, when they saw the new one-bedroom flats, the same residents remarked how 'wonderful' they were![152] The newly refurbished flats were officially opened in September 1995 by the chairman of the Almshouse Association, Lady Benson, with a garden party for all the residents, trustees and staff of the hospital.[153]

To fund this huge project the trustees secured a grant from the Housing Corporation of £400,000, while the Town Close Estate Charity gave an additional £85,000 towards the redevelopment.[154] The construction work itself, including the improvements to the houses in the courtyard and the conversion of seven houses in Calvert Street into ten one-bedroom flats, cost in excess of £2 million. Mr Matthew Martin, clerk to the trustees at the time of the conversions, explained in interview that the remaining funding was taken from the accumulated

---

151 NCC Minute Book 12, 1989–95, 23 June 1995.
152 DOHI 017.
153 'Norwich Consolidated Charities Scheme revitalises Doughty's Hospital almshouses', p. 1.
154 NCC Minute Book 12, 1989–95, 10 March 1993; 1 September 1993.

Figure 13.   Calvert Street renovations, 1994

internal surpluses of Norwich Consolidated Charities. There was also money available in the Almshouse Improvement Fund, the account that had been started in the 1950s and that was used to fund any large-scale routine maintenance or refurbishment of the hospital and its accommodation.[155]

There was increasing urgency in the need to modernise and modify the remaining bedsits at Doughty's during the late 1990s. With new competition in housing for the elderly in the form of government-funded and private sheltered housing schemes, it was becoming ever more difficult to let accommodation that was not up to standard, as new and potential residents expected one-bedroom flats rather than bedsits.[156] After the refurbishment of the courtyard and the conversion of the houses in Calvert Street, however, the trustees decided that improvements to the staff accommodation should be prioritised.[157] Between 1996 and 1998 the staff block was refurbished at an estimated

155 DOHI 006; and see above Part IV, p. 131.
156 *Doughty's Hospital reordering 1995, initial design report September 1995.* Wearing, Hastings and Norton, chartered architects, 14 Princes Street; NCC Minute Book 15, 2004–5, 6 December 2005.
157 NCC Minute Book 12, 1989–95, 6 December 1995.

cost of £225,000 and in 1998 a new modern kitchen was built, which in turn gave rise to the employment of a cook.[158] Grace Jarrold Court was the next block to be converted, a project that was first mooted in 1995, and due to begin in April 2000, but by December 1999 planning permission for the improvements was still outstanding.[159] Work finally began in September 2000.[160] In 2003, the reading room was extended for a third time to accommodate the growing population of the hospital.[161]

By 1999 the trustees of Norwich Consolidated Charities owned two buildings which provided facilities for the elderly, Doughty's Hospital and the day care centre on Marion Road. The Charities also owned a piece of land just off the Dereham Road to the west of the city centre. Matthew Martin, clerk to the trustees of Norwich Consolidated Charities, explained in interview that the trustees were interested in building a second day centre on this site.[162] However, the costs of the Marion Road Day Care Centre had begun to increase during the late 1990s and the trustees were wary of becoming involved in another difficult project.[163] In need of advice about what to do with the site, the trustees consulted other bodies, including the local authority, Age Concern and Social Services. In interview Claire Frostick recalled that Tom Wilson, the chief executive officer of Julian Housing, suggested a framework for what was later to become known as Bakery Court. Julian Housing is an organisation in Norwich which provides housing and support services for people with mental health problems and Mr Wilson suggested that an almshouse for people with mental health issues would be greatly appreciated.[164]

The clerk examined the Scheme of Norwich Consolidated Charities and found that it made no specific provision for the elderly, only that the charity must help 'poor Norwich people', and it was the omission of the word 'elderly' that allowed the trustees to consider building an almshouse for the relief of other vulnerable groups in Norwich.[165] People with mental health problems, it was reported, often lived in a continuous cycle of being discharged from hospitals into unsuitable accommodation, only to relapse and have to return to medical care.[166] Norwich Consolidated Charities sought to provide high quality accommodation so as to lessen that chance of relapse. Bakery Court was completed in 1999, and at the time of writing provides quality

158 NCC Minute Book 13, 1996–9, 19 June 1996; DOHI 003; DOHI 004.
159 NCC Minute Book 13, 1996–9, 6 September 2000; 1 December 1999.
160 NCC Minute Book 14, 2000–4, 6 September 2000.
161 *Ibid.*, 5 March 2003.
162 DOHI 006.
163 DOHI 006; DOHI 016.
164 www.julianhousing.org/pages/about.html, consulted 10 July 2009.
165 DOHI 006.
166 *Ibid.*

accommodation and support for up to twelve residents. The services are managed by Julian Housing, although Norwich Consolidated Charities owns the building and is responsible for its maintenance. Bakery Court will celebrate its tenth anniversary in 2009 and the almshouse has served as a blueprint for similar projects in Norwich. Devonshire Place, for example – another housing scheme for people with mental health problems – was built in the mould of Bakery Court and opened in 2005.[167] There are also plans to develop similar projects in Great Yarmouth and King's Lynn in the county of Norfolk.[168]

Since 2005, Doughty's Hospital has continued to consider new ways of providing modern accommodation for the elderly in its care. In 2008–9 the rooms at Cooke's Court were converted from bedsits into one-bedroom flats.[169] The process of refurbishment is ongoing, and the need to adapt in line with changing legislation, as well as the needs of an ageing population, ensures that there will always be room for improvements to the hospital buildings. Doughty's now has fifty-eight tenements and Bakery Court has twelve flats, meaning that in total Norwich Consolidated Charities makes provision for seventy people. It has been suggested that Doughty's Hospital might thrive more easily if it were moved out of the city centre, as this would allow the residents to benefit from brand new facilities and allow the trustees room for further expansion. However, at present both the residents and trustees are happy to stay on William Doughty's original site – 'in some convenient place in Norwich'.[170]

167 www.julianhousing.org/pages/services/devonshire.html, consulted 10 July 2009.
168 DOHI 016.
169 Correspondence with Mr David Walker, 2 June 2009.
170 NRO Case 20f/14, William Doughty's Will, 25 April 1687.

CHAPTER 22
'Inside out and all change': evolving staffing structures

M rs Whitlam and Miss Smith both retired in 1997 and Mrs Freda Holland and Mrs Christine Share were appointed as matron and deputy matron respectively.[171] In interview Mrs Holland said that the main reason that she was attracted to the position was the ethos of the almshouse. She described the atmosphere as welcoming and communal, and liked the idea of giving the almspeople the independence to live as they wished while at the same time providing them with support if necessary.[172] However, Mrs Holland was a little concerned by the requirement of staff to live on the premises. This was because of the surrounding landscape rather than the property itself. During the course of the twentieth century large office blocks had been built in the area which overlooked Doughty's Hospital on three sides, while the inner link ring road, or the Magdalen flyover as it was now known, ran almost parallel to the northern border of the hospital.[173] But Mrs Holland explained that her worries about a lack of privacy were laid to rest when she and her husband moved into the matron's house. It quickly became apparent that the office blocks and the ring road did not pose as much of a problem as she had first anticipated, while the gardens at Doughty's Hospital were remarkably peaceful considering their proximity to the main road and the shopping precinct in Magdalen Road.[174]

In January 1998, about six months after Mrs Holland and her husband had moved into the matron's house, Mr Holland died suddenly. Understandably, his death came as a great shock to Mrs Holland, who threw herself into her work in order to cope with her loss. The staff of the hospital were an extremely close team and Mrs Holland remembers the 'tremendous support' she received from the trustees,

---

171 NCC Minute Book 13, 1996–9, 18 June 1997; 3 September 1997.
172 DOHI 003.
173 *Ibid*.
174 *Ibid*.

staff and residents alike during that difficult time.[175] In particular, Mrs Share supported Mrs Holland, and the former matron remembers that they were far more than mere work colleagues, but also neighbours and friends.[176] Looking back, Mrs Holland was most impressed by the high level of support she received, especially considering how new she was to the hospital, and which she regards as a perfect example of the caring, supportive atmosphere of Doughty's.[177]

The role of matron was particularly demanding and, because both the matron and the deputy matron lived on the site, they were effectively on call twenty-four hours a day. Mrs Holland recalled the experience as both exhausting and very rewarding.[178] When the European Union Working Time Directive was introduced in October 1998, the trustees restructured the staffing system at the hospital – as already discussed – increasing the number of hours worked in both the morning and evening shifts, bringing in more care staff and allowing the matron and the deputy matron to take on a more supervisory role in the care of residents.[179] However, because the two women still lived in the staff houses on site, they continued to be 'on-call', and so their free time was limited. In 2006 Mrs Holland remarried and became Mrs Freda Turner. She moved, with her husband, out of the hospital and into a property in Colegate. The house in Colegate was only a few minutes walk from Doughty's and hence allowed Mrs Turner to continue her on-call duties. However, when Mrs Share moved into private accommodation in 2007, it signalled the end of resident staff at the institution. This made it easier for the workload to be divided between a larger number of carers working on a shift basis, and allowed the matron and deputy matron to work fewer hours as a result.

This change has been greeted with mixed reactions by the residents of Doughty's Hospital, for when interviewed some of them were unhappy with the current lack of resident staff. This is especially true of those almspeople who have lived at the hospital for a number of years and remember when Mrs Whitlam and Mrs Bowen were matrons. Although there are always trained members of staff on duty and care and support is available twenty-four hours a day, a small number of residents have admitted to feeling less safe without the matron in residence.[180] One resident spoke of the family atmosphere being lost as a result of the matron and deputy matron moving off site. However, this feeling is by no means universal among the residents, and another

175 *Ibid.*
176 *Ibid.*
177 Correspondence with Mrs Holland, 13 July 2009.
178 DOHI 003.
179 NCC Minute Book 13, 1996–9, 2 December 1998; DOHI 003, and see above, pp. 201-2.
180 DOHI 012; DOHI 014.

almswoman expressed the view that, as long as everyone was well looked after, the proximity of the matron was not as important as some residents might have originally thought.[181]

The ageing population at Doughty's Hospital has meant that an increasing number of care staff have had to be employed, mostly to deal with the rise in instances of ill-health or infirmity. In December 2000, for example, the trustees discussed the need to increase the number of carers on duty at the hospital. Before this the hospital had managed with only one carer during the afternoon shift between 1.30pm and 6.30pm, and it was now agreed that because the need for the 'lifting, handling, feeding and toileting' of residents was increasing, two carers should operate on all shifts.[182] From this point on, former carer Mrs Sue Hills remembered, carers always worked in pairs.[183]

In 2001 Roger Pearson was elected chairman of Norwich Consolidated Charities, and was responsible for a total rethink of the organisation of the Charities. He insisted on going back to basics and questioning first principles, thereby ensuring that all that was done was totally in line with the new constitution and with currently accepted modern practice. For instance, to clarify the committee system Mr Pearson proposed that each committee within Norwich Consolidated Charities ought to elect a trustee to be chairman, and that no trustee should chair more than one committee. So, the chairman of Norwich Consolidated Charities would be chairman of Anguish's and Marion Road Trust, but all the other committees would elect their own chair.[184] Mr Pearson also thought that Doughty's Hospital ought to be run more independently of Norwich Consolidated Charities and have more autonomy over its own affairs, so, with this in mind, and the current chairman Harry Boreham having just retired, he set about acquiring a new chairman for the Almshouse Committee. Lady Hopwood was duly elected to the position in December 2001, despite her protestations that she did not have enough experience with the elderly to warrant being entrusted with that particular responsibility.[185] Mr Pearson was also responsible for bringing Doughty's Hospital and Bakery Court, the two almshouses run by Norwich Consolidated Charities, under one committee, the Almshouse Committee.[186]

The third major change that Mr Pearson sought to effect was a change in the visiting of residents by members of the trustees. The trustees had begun visiting the residents of Doughty's Hospital in 1896

---

181 DOHI 010; DOHI 012; DOHI 014.
182 NCC Minute Book 14, 2000–4, 6 December 2000.
183 DOHI 004.
184 DOHI 016.
185 *Ibid.*
186 *Ibid.*

and the practice continued as a way for residents to voice any grievances without having to refer to matron or another member of staff.[187] The practice of visiting was thus a long-established one, and comments following these visits were recorded in a designated book until this was formally discontinued in January 2002, the last entry in the book being dated 2 December 2001.[188] However, there were disadvantages to the practice, and Mr Pearson was aware that some residents were uncomfortable with the idea of trustees coming into their homes, particularly in the case of male trustees visiting female residents.[189] When Mr Pearson became chairman of Norwich Consolidated Charities, he began to inquire into the possibility of employing an independent group of people to check on the residents and ensure that their needs were being met. When Lady Hopwood was appointed chairman of the Almshouse Committee, she recalled how she tried to employ Age Concern in a visiting capacity. However, Age Concern in Norwich felt that the residents at Doughty's Hospital did not display the same level of need as more isolated old people elsewhere in the community, as they already received a high level of contact and support.[190] As a result, residents were consulted on whether they wanted to be visited or not, and members of the Almshouse Committee who have time available now visit the residents on a regular basis, to have a friendly discussion and in the process check on their living conditions and address any complaints and grievances.[191]

After Mrs Holland left the hospital, Mrs Karlene Parry was appointed as matron in March 2008 and is the first manager – matron or master – never to have lived at Doughty's Hospital. In interview Mrs Parry remembered being warmly welcomed into the hospital, but recalls also that there was an air of caution surrounding her arrival, as residents and staff were unsure of the changes she might make. Some of the residents, she felt, now find it hard to understand Mrs Parry's role, which is more managerial and less 'hands on' than that of previous matrons, and she conceded that it is sometimes difficult to explain the reasons for change (which are usually a consequence of current legislation or registration requirements) especially to residents who have been at the hospital for a number of years. Despite this, Mrs Parry has worked hard to build relationships and earn the trust of residents during her first eighteen months at the hospital, and has been very successful in so doing.[192]

187 NRO, N/CCH/115, 18 December 1895; NRO, N/CCH/115, 15 January 1896.
188 NCC Minute Book 14, 2000–4, 31 January 2002.
189 DOHI 016.
190 *Ibid.*
191 NCC Minute Book 14, 2000–4, 3 September 2003; DOHI 016.
192 Correspondence with Mrs Parry, 10 July 2009.

Mrs Parry was employed during a major staff restructuring programme implemented by the trustees of Norwich Consolidated Charities in 2007–8. Under this scheme a new tier of senior carers was introduced to the staffing structure. The hierarchy of carers now comprises four levels of staff – the matron and the deputy matron, followed by two assistant matrons, a tier of senior carers and finally the carers.[193] There are now thirty-two members of staff at Doughty's Hospital, twenty-two of whom are carers. All caring staff work on a part-time, shift basis, apart from the matron and the deputy matron who are the only full-time members of the caring staff at the hospital. Additionally, a gardener and a decorator/handyman are employed full-time, at the time of writing Mr Geoffrey Beck and Mr David Scott respectively.

In interview, one of the changes that Mrs Parry said she hoped to implement in the near future was a further change in the staff structure at Doughty's Hospital, fine-tuning the hierarchy of carers put in place upon her arrival. From September 2009 the senior carers would run all three shifts covering each twenty-four-hour period (early, late, and night shifts). As of this date the new system was indeed put into operation, the post of assistant matron disappeared, while that of deputy matron was retained.[194] The new system means the matron is the only member of staff to be a registered nurse. There are concerns that some residents might again find this change unsettling, particularly those long-established residents who have been used to a different regime and find change difficult to accept.[195] However, the night staff are well-trained to cope with minor problems, while emergencies under the new system are dealt with by fully trained paramedics and rapid hospitalisation.

While all staff are trained to a high standard, because the almshouse is a domiciliary care facility and not a nursing home the carers are not required to be qualified registered nurses.[196] National expectations, laid down by the Care Quality Commission, state that 50 per cent of carers in a domiciliary care environment should be trained to at least national vocational qualification (NVQ) level 2 standard in health and social care. At Doughty's Hospital, all carers have obtained the NVQ level 2 and all senior carers are trained to NVQ level 3 in health and social care. This means that the hospital exceeds the national expectations for staff training.[197] All staff are reassessed every six months so as to

193 *Ibid*.
194 Correspondence with Mr David Walker, 25 November 2009.
195 Correspondence with Mrs Parry, 10 July 2009.
196 *Ibid*.
197 www.charitycommissioners.gov.uk/index.asp, consulted 1 July 2009: Charity Commission summary information return 2007, submitted by David Walker on 28 October 2008.

keep a record of their progress and competencies. The deputy matron, Mrs Christine Share, is a trained nurse although the period of her registration has lapsed. Instead of renewing her registration she is now studying for an NVQ level 4 in health and social care.[198]

Mr David Walker, clerk to the trustees of Norwich Consolidated Charities, explained in interview that the present objective of Doughty's Hospital was to allow residents to live as independently as they are able to, with twenty-four-hour care and support available as necessary. As each flat has its own front door residents are able to come and go as they please.[199] Some residents are able to do their own cleaning, cooking and shopping, living similar lives to their contemporaries in private homes.[200] However, residents have varying degrees of dependency and the team of cleaners, cooks and carers step in to help once cleaning, cooking and general independence becomes difficult. Every resident is offered a daily visit by a carer to ensure they are happy, healthy and secure.[201] As Doughty's is obliged to cope with an ageing population, no doubt the number of carers it employs will continue to grow, in order to continue to provide the high level of care that residents have come to expect, and to which the trustees and staff aspire.[202] While the removal of both matrons off-site and the employment of a phalanx of shift-working carers has led one witty observer to characterise recent staffing changes at Doughty's as a case of 'inside out and all change', the one consistent aspiration of the hospital is to continue to achieve the highest possible standards of care, compassion and respect for its residents.

198 Correspondence with Mrs Christine Share, 10 July 2009.
199 DOHI 007.
200 DOHI 013; DOHI 015.
201 DOHI 004.
202 DOHI 004; DOHI 009.

CHAPTER 23
Modern-day residents

Celebration

In September 1995, after the completion of the refurbishment of the courtyard cottages, the then clerk to the trustees, Mr Mathew Martin, arranged for Lady Benson, chairman of the Almshouse Association, to be the guest of honour at the formal opening.[203] The day was celebrated by an afternoon tea for residents and staff, during which Lady Benson unveiled a plaque commemorating the refurbishment. Mr Martin remembers Lady Benson asking over the telephone if it was to be a formal occasion and whether or not she should wear a hat. Mr Martin suggested that she should and subsequently recalled how 'she really went to town on that hat!'[204] 'That hat' is featured in Plate 12, commemorating the formal reopening of the hospital in 1995.

A short time later, in April 1996, the Lord Lieutenant contacted the clerk to the trustees of Norwich Consolidated Charities, to say that the Queen and Prince Philip would be in Norwich on Maundy Thursday to hand out the Maundy Money. The Lord Lieutenant suggested that Doughty's Hospital should invite the Queen to visit after the Maundy service, which was duly arranged.[205] Security was tight before the visit and every room in the hospital was inspected beforehand by security officers with sniffer dogs. The reading room, which was to host the visit, had been completely searched by royal security with every sheet of music and every book on the book shelves being checked to make sure the room was safe for the Queen.[206] Mrs Whitlam remembered security men searching her house and one of the officers losing his dog in the cottage, only to find that it had ignored its duties and was eating from the cat's dish![207] Manhole covers in the surrounding streets were welded shut and security staff patrolled the roofs of the courtyard, but

---

203 DOHI 006; 'Norwich Consolidated Charities Scheme revitalises Doughty's Hospital almshouses', p.1.
204 DOHI 006.
205 DOHI 006.
206 DOHI 001.
207 *Ibid*.

fortunately the occasion passed off without incident.[208] A photograph of Her Majesty the Queen being shown around by Jean Whitlam, matron, is at Plate 13.

The gardener, Mr Geoffrey Beck, recalled that the lateness of the season forced him to bring in pots filled with daffodils to sink into the flowers beds in order to bring the gardens into full bloom.[209] The matron, Mrs Whitlam, walked the Queen around the first storey of the new courtyard, while the assistant matron, Miss Smith, took Prince Philip around the ground floor. The Queen signed a photograph of herself, with a pen from Philip's pocket, as the one the hospital had provided had run out of ink. 'They never do work,' Prince Philip said to Mrs Whitlam, on finding that the pen was broken, 'There's a jinx on them'.[210] The residents were gathered in the reading room and the Queen and Prince Philip made the time to speak to everyone, including all the staff as well as the surveyors, architects and builders who had been responsible for the conversion.[211] As they were leaving, Mrs Frostick remembers that Prince Philip had asked her what the staff and residents planned to do after they had gone. When Mrs Frostick said that they were planning a party, the Duke replied 'People always have parties when we leave!'[212] The visit was the highlight of many trustees' time at Doughty's Hospital, not least Mrs Claire Frostick who had organised the event.[213]

Rules and regulations

The rules at Doughty's Hospital are now very informal, as residents are expected to treat their flats exactly as their own homes, which stands in distinct contrast to the injunctions laid down by its founder.[214] Originally, it will be recalled, they were required to 'dwell constantly' in the hospital, wear their gown of purple cloth and to 'live peaceably and ... as becomes Christians, neither cursing, swearing, keeping bad hours nor being drunk'.[215] Although these rules are now completely redundant, a slab bearing them hangs on the wall of the north-west staircase in the courtyard as an historical curiosity for both residents and visitors. When asked if residents had to abide by any specific rules, former carer Mrs Sue Hills said that rather than a formal set of rules, the running of the hospital was based on 'common sense'.[216]

---

208 *Ibid.*
209 DOHI 005.
210 DOHI 001.
211 *The Almshouse Gazette*, issue 163, summer 1996, p. 8; DOHI 005; DOHI 006; DOHI 009.
212 DOHI 009.
213 DOHI 009.
214 See Part II, p. 31, above.
215 NRO Case 20f/14, William Doughty's Will, 25 April 1687.
216 DOHI 004.

Despite this lack of formal rules, guidelines for behaviour are still in place. In 1999 Mrs Holland, the matron, drafted a resident's handbook which was presented to each almsperson upon their arrival at the hospital.[217] This conforms to the guidelines established by the Almshouse Association, who advise that 'It is important for all almshouse charities, however small, to have a resident's handbook which can be provided to each new resident', and they now provide a specimen resident's handbook for their member charities to adopt or adapt.[218] The handbook drafted for Doughty's by Mrs Holland was approved by the trustees and distributed to residents in March 2000.[219] It contains advice on living at Doughty's Hospital, and describes the services that the hospital provides and how to receive them. It also advises that any cash should be banked to avoid risk of burglary and that trustees cannot be held responsible for loss of money or other property. The only rule in place which is similar to William Doughty's original regulations is that residents must not take prolonged absences from their flats, as this would mean denying the accommodation to someone else who might be better suited to the facilities.[220] Finally the booklet states that 'although we are sure this will never apply in your case, in the interests of other residents the trustees have the right to discharge any resident guilty of misbehaviour'.[221] The wording of this final statement is interesting, for if the trustees were really 'sure that this will never apply' in the case of the reader, the clause would be entirely redundant. Its inclusion was no doubt an attempt to avoid offending the sensibilities of incoming residents, and in this respect Doughty's resident's handbook exceeds the requirements of the model proposed by the Almshouse Association.[222]

It was, however, all too easy to offend the sensibilities of some residents, and a poorly worded letter was to cause a great deal of trouble for the trustees in the winter of 2001. Lady Hopwood had been elected chairman of the Almshouse Committee in December 2001 while she was away in the United States. When she returned she was not only greeted by the news that she had been elected to the position in her absence, but also that 'angry pensioners [were] in revolt' at Doughty's Hospital. It seemed that the hospital had sent a letter to all resident almspeople asking that they pay their winter fuel allowance over to the charity, to put towards the cost of heating during the winter months.[223]

217 DOHI 003.
218 Almshouse Association, *Standards of almshouse management*, pp. 85, 177–89.
219 NCC Minute Book 14, 2000–4, 8 March 2000.
220 Doughty's Hospital, resident's handbook.
221 *Ibid.*
222 Almshouse Association, *Standards of almshouse management*, pp. 185–6.
223 DOHI 016; NCC Minute Book 14, 2000–4, 31 January 2002.

The tone of the letter had created a chasm between some residents and staff. While many accepted that it was perfectly reasonable for Doughty's to ask for the money, as the grant from the government was for the purpose of heating which the charity provided, other residents thought it was an utter disgrace for the hospital to demand money in this way at such short notice. The tension between the two groups was palpable, and some of those residents who agreed with the charge paid immediately and gave the rebelling residents the cold shoulder. The negative press from the local media did not help matters. On 22 December a local newspaper, the *Eastern Evening News*, ran a front-page story on the disagreement between residents and trustees over the £200 winter fuel payments, which were granted by the government to every person over the age of 60. The article quoted one angry resident who said '[The letter] really upsets me, it is my money. I have no intention of paying the £200 unless I am legally bound'.[224] The newspaper had also spoken to representatives from the Benefits Agency, who administered the winter fuel payments, and the local branch of Age Concern, and both appeared to criticise Doughty's Hospital for its handling of the situation. However, it soon became apparent that the CEO of Age Concern, Brenda Arthur, had been misquoted in the article. Although the agency had received 'a small number' of what the newspaper referred to as 'complaints' regarding Doughty's, it transpired that not all of the correspondence received had been negative. Some of the correspondence took the form of queries from people wanting to know more about their rights with regard to the winter fuel payments. Lady Hopwood and Brenda Arthur were able to resolve this misunderstanding over the phone, and any concern felt by the agency was quickly dispersed.[225]

This negative press coverage further augmented the need to find a satisfactory solution to the disagreement. After careful consideration Lady Hopwood decided that the only course of action would be to visit every resident in turn in order to introduce herself, and to find out exactly what the residents thought, since feelings were clearly running high. This she did between Christmas and the New Year and identified six residents who formed the 'rebellion'.[226] These six maintained that it was appalling to ask pensioners, many of whom, they claimed, were in financial difficulty, to pay their winter fuel allowance straight to the almshouse. One man cited the specific case of another resident who lived a very parsimonious lifestyle, and who he assumed was very badly

---

224 *Eastern Evening News*, Saturday 22 December 2001, p. 1.
225 *Eastern Evening News*, Saturday 22 December 2001, p. 5; correspondence with Lady Hopwood, 17 September 2009.
226 DOHI 016.

off. However, Lady Hopwood was aware that this particular resident was living frugally out of choice, because she had personally told her so, and had given away substantial amounts of her money to charity. Unable to discuss the woman's personal details, she could only advise the disgruntled gentleman that things might not always be as they seem.[227] After several weeks of difficulty, Mr Pearson, the chairman of Norwich Consolidated Charities, reversed the decision, on the basis that it was unfair for some to pay but not others, and allowed every resident to keep their winter fuel allowance or to have the money refunded if it had already been paid. Some of them refused to accept the refund.[228]

At this date it was clear that the trustees had been subsidising the cost of services to the residents for some time, and when the Supporting People programme came into force in 2003, they decided that the weekly contributions must be further increased. This was because Supporting People required residents to be charged at rates which reflected the actual cost of the amenities, in order that grants could be made to help to fully cover the costs. As a result, the Weekly Maintenance Contribution almost doubled.[229] However, not all residents were in receipt of government benefits and those living off their own means found the rise in costs particularly difficult to manage. Because the trustees were unwilling to operate a two-tier system, they agreed to grant an annual subsidy of £80 per week to each resident or couple not in receipt of benefits, in order to help them defray the increased charges. This subsidy was to diminish by £10 per week each year and was thus designed to ease those people who did not receive benefits into paying for the increased costs.[230] Another consequence of this incident was for the trustees to vet correspondence before sending it to the residents, as the blunt tone of the letter regarding winter fuel payments had been the cause of much of the anger. Mr Martin, speaking with the benefit of hindsight, said that not only should the letter have been worded more clearly and carefully, but the trustees should have simply levied a charge or put up the Weekly Maintenance Contribution by the amount of the fuel allowance, rather than demand the money.[231]

Applicants and residents

Doughty's Hospital has also had to contend with social changes, the most pressing of which is the rise in the numbers of elderly people who

---

227 *Ibid.*
228 *Ibid.*
229 NCC Minute Book 14, 2000–4, 5 March 2003.
230 DOHI 016.
231 DOHI 006.

own their own homes, which creates difficulties for those homeowners who can no longer remain independent and thus seek a place at Doughty's. The majority of the residents at Doughty's Hospital are in receipt of government benefits, which go a long way towards paying for their care and maintenance. Homeowners, however, are unlikely to be able to claim benefits and so have to pay all charges themselves. Lady Hopwood, current chairman of the Almshouse Committee, explained that, because Doughty's Hospital does not operate a two-tier system of charges, the costs for someone who is not in receipt of benefits are relatively expensive, even if cheaper than equivalent private accommodation. Although only two or three residents currently pay for themselves, the situation is far from ideal, and in their attempts to resolve this problem the trustees consider each case on its merits.[232]

The waiting list of applicants to Doughty's Hospital has changed in recent years. In December 1996 the secretary to Doughty's suggested that people should only put their names on the list if they were prepared to take up residency within the next two years, because there had been several instances of candidates signing up to the waiting list before they were ready or able to come into the almshouse. This was agreed, and in December 1997 it was also agreed that candidates who refused two vacancies without good reason should be removed from the list in favour of potential residents who had greater need of the facilities.[233] In July 1997 the trustees noted in the minute books the difficulty of attracting potential residents, and particularly in attracting couples.[234] This is a difficulty which remains apparent at the time of writing.[235] By March 2000 the majority of residents were in their late eighties and early nineties, many of whom were very frail and in need of extra care. At one meeting of the trustees there were four birthdays of residents noted in the minutes, three of whom had reached the age of 90, while the other was 92.[236] In March 2000 only one candidate on the waiting list for Doughty's Hospital was under the age of 75.[237] In March 2003 two residents celebrated their 92nd birthday while a third resident reached the age of 94.[238] Lady Hopwood confirms that the most recent applicants to the hospital are usually over 80, with many over 85 and several over 90. She also reports that nowadays people are seldom interested in coming into a community like Doughty's while they are fit and healthy, and few are interested in moving to a domiciliary care

232 DOHI 017.
233 NCC Minute Book 13, 1996–9, 4 December 1996; 3 December 1997.
234 *Ibid.*, 2 July 1997.
235 DOHI 016.
236 NCC Minute Book 14, 2000–4, 6 September 2000.
237 *Ibid.*, 8 March 2000.
238 NCC Minute Book 14, 2000–4, 5 March 2003.

facility while they are able to live comfortably and independently in their own homes.[239] As a result, people tend to move into the hospital later in life than was once the case, and often only after they are already experiencing health problems. This in turn means that the residents at the hospital require different facilities, and helps to explain the recent rise in the number of staff to cope with the increasing frailty of residents, and the diminishing ability of the residents to organise their own social activities.[240]

Of course, Doughty's Hospital is not a care home, and as such is unable to deal with people suffering from serious physical and mental illnesses. Lady Hopwood reports, however, that residents with health problems are housed and cared for at Doughty's Hospital for as long as possible, until their quality of life is significantly reduced and other specialist care facilities might be better suited to their needs. If, for example, a resident has terminal cancer, but the district nurses are able to manage their pain to allow them to continue to live comfortably at Doughty's, then every effort is made to facilitate this. However, when a resident is in the later stages of dementia, for example, it is regarded as unfair to both the resident and to those around them to keep them at the hospital. Lady Hopwood notes that in the ten years in which she has been a trustee, instances of dementia have increased dramatically, a phenomenon she attributes to the increasing age of residents upon arrival at the hospital and the longer life-spans of residents generally. Indeed, statistics published by Age Concern in 2005 indicate that 5 per cent of people over the age of 65 in the UK suffer from dementia, while for those over the age of 80 the proportion is as high as 20 per cent.[241] At Doughty's there are procedures in place to deal with severe cases of dementia and the process is handled as sensitively as possible. Residents and their families are consulted at every stage, and the resident will often receive respite care at specialist facilities before being moved permanently. Although it is emotionally difficult to lose residents in this way, Lady Hopwood explained that the trustees must think in terms of what is best for the resident, as well as what is best for the community at Doughty's Hospital.[242] Again this approach conforms to the guidelines laid down by the Almshouse Association.[243]

---

239 *Ibid.*, 8 March 2000.
240 DOHI 016.
241 Almshouse Association, *Support and care for residents*, p. 2.
242 DOHI 017.
243 Almshouse Association, *Standards of almshouse management*, pp. 96–7.

Social life

Obviously, the physical fitness and health of residents has had a huge effect on the types of recreation which the hospital provides. In the 1990s, as we have seen, the residents enjoyed many clubs and facilities which were organised by the staff, trustees and residents together. In the reading room concerts, talks and musical evenings were laid on for the residents' entertainment. They also enjoyed the benefits of a book club, a drama club and the choir which we have already mentioned.[244] One resident fondly remembered the craft club, which was organised by a member of staff and during which residents would make gifts and craftwork that would then be sold at jumble sales held on the lawn in Doughty's courtyard, the proceeds going towards the amenities fund.[245]

However, the recreational clubs at Doughty's Hospital have fallen into decline in recent years. One resident suggested that this was because of a lack of enthusiasm from the almspeople in general, especially those who were particularly elderly and infirm.[246] 'People don't seem to want to participate anymore', said another.[247] One almswoman blamed the recent renovations in the courtyard, and at Grace Jarrold Court and Cooke's Court, for disrupting the clubs and leisure activities at Doughty's.[248] The hospital still has evenings when singers and dancing troops come to entertain the residents in the reading room, and these are very much appreciated. However, the Residents' Committee often finds it difficult to organise events and to book entertainers, as many companies now advertise exclusively online. One of the members of the Residents' Committee complained that this was frustrating, as none of the residents were particularly computer literate and so they felt that they were missing out on opportunities.[249] The trustees and staff have tried to rectify this problem and have employed former matron Mrs Freda Turner as an events coordinator. It is hoped that with her help at least some of the clubs and societies will be re-established in the near future.[250]

At present the hospital has a weekly coffee morning on a Wednesday during which the residents can come together to socialise, and which has continued in the same format for more than forty years after having been started by Mrs Bowen when she was matron. It also boasts (more surprisingly) a keep-fit class on Wednesday afternoons, a church service once a month and a 'happy hour' on Friday evenings during which the

---

244 DOHI 003; and see above, Part IV, pp. 166–70.
245 DOHI 014.
246 DOHI 010.
247 DOHI 011.
248 DOHI 013.
249 DOHI 015.
250 DOHI 014.

residents play cards, darts and board games.[251] The hospital holds two annual parties – a summer garden party and a Christmas party – the latter being held in January and usually attended by the Lord Mayor. There is also a residents' family evening, which has developed out of the former cheese and wine evening.

The hospital organises two yearly outings, one in spring and another in the autumn, when the residents are taken by coach for a day trip.[252] Christine Share, the current deputy matron and an employee at the hospital for the past twelve years, reports that the residents are always given several choices of venue but invariably they vote for the same old favourites. One is usually a seaside destination and the other Bury St Edmunds, which has the attraction of its cathedral and also the Abbey Gardens. Variations have included a boat trip on the Norfolk Broads or a visit to a stately home, such as Sandringham. The outing always incorporates a meal at a hotel, pub or restaurant, and the most popular meal is fish and chips. These outings require military planning, Mrs Share reports: 'We cannot go too early because so many of our residents are getting frail and cannot cope with a very long day or journey. We have to ensure that we have the required number of "pushers" to man the wheelchairs. We have to make sure that we have a "bag of tricks" for any emergencies.' There have been occasions when the weather has been unkind, on one outing delivering all of the staff and residents a good soaking on Lowestoft seafront. On a trip to Southwold in Suffolk, one 'rather eccentric' resident announced that she was going for a paddle in the sea, and was last seen heading off into the waves. When this was reported to the staff panic stations set in: all the staff were mobilised to check every shop, the beach was scoured and just as the decision to involve the police was made a member of the public came along to say that the lady concerned was sitting outside a shop on the outer edge of the town waiting for a ride home! 'Needless to say', Mrs Share reports, 'she was given a very stony reception from the other residents when she got on the bus'.[253]

The residents always used to go to the local pantomime every year but about five years ago they decided that they had "outgrown" it so they go to the Amateur Dramatics Society production at the Theatre Royal in Norwich during February instead. They are also always invited to the Drayton Players Productions, which are held twice yearly, while further outings are arranged to the Cromer Pier Show and also, on occasion, to Gorleston Old Time Music Hall. Shorter visits are made to local shopping venues or places of interest, while the gardener

---

251 DOHI 003; DOHI 013.
252 DOHI 005.
253 Correspondence with Mrs Christine Share, 16 December 2009.

and handyman, Geoff Beck, takes small groups to market towns, garden centres and museums. Some of the able-bodied residents take themselves off on holidays further afield, recent destinations including Bournemouth, Hemsby and Scotland.[254]

These outings are funded by the residents themselves by way of an amenities fund. Each almsperson pays 50 pence a week into the fund, and the money is used to pay for entertainments and trips, including outings to watch local theatre productions and pantomimes.[255] There is also a bingo evening once a month with a fish and chip supper, organised by the residents and supported by Mrs Christine Share, the current deputy matron.[256] Social life at Doughty's is thus anything but completely moribund.

Despite this continuing activity, some residents mourn the loss of entertainments at the hospital, blaming it on a loss of community spirit in the institution.[257] On the whole, however, the residents appear to be very satisfied with their lives at the hospital. One of those interviewed explained how she had been provided with walk-in shower facilities, which had been arranged by the trustees as soon as she was seen to be struggling.[258] This is typical of the responsive care system at Doughty's Hospital. Another resident said that she enjoyed living at the institution as she could be independent, but also safe in the knowledge that support was always available. 'We have our independence, but the minute you're queer, they come in to help', she said.[259] The carers are described by the residents as 'wonderful' and one resident felt that Doughty's Hospital was 'one of the best places in the country' to live.[260] This ringing commendation would no doubt leave William Doughty – merchant gentleman, citizen, philanthropist – glowing with pride.

The achievement of Doughty's Hospital

Doughty's Hospital's 320-year history represents a remarkable story of the durability of a philanthropic institution in the face of three centuries of profound economic, social and political change. Although its role within the mixed economy of welfare may have diminished over the course of these three centuries, it still performs a very similar function in twenty-first-century Britain to that envisaged by its founder in the late seventeenth century. Its ability to both modernise and develop its accommodation and facilities over the last fifty or

254 *Ibid.*
255 DOHI 011.
256 DOHI 015.
257 DOHI 014; DOHI 012.
258 DOHI 010.
259 *Ibid.*
260 DOHI 012.

so years exemplifies what can be achieved in the almshouse sector given sufficient enterprise, flexibility and responsiveness to changing demands and expectations. Above all Doughty's Hospital, and the selfless efforts of the trustees who sustain it, stand as testimony to the continuing power of the voluntary impulse, without which British society in the twenty-first century would undoubtedly be the poorer, both materially and spiritually.

Bibliography

Primary sources

The National Archives

1841 census: HO107/791, book 1, civil parish: St Saviour, County: Norfolk, Enumeration District: Doughty's Hospital, fo. 41, p. 2

1851 census: HO107/1813, fo. 92, pp. 15–17; HO107/1812, fo. 315, p. 42

1861 census: RG9/1212, fo. 90, pp. 27–8; RG9/1211, fo. 14, p. 23

1871 census: RG10/1809, fo. 86, pp. 23–5

1881 census: RG11/1939, fo. 83, pp. 27–9

1891 census: RG12/1520, fo. 116, pp. 18–19

1901 census: RG13/1836, fo. 51, p. 2

1911 census: RG78/613, RD225 SD1 ED5 SN28

PROB 11, Cann 50, PCC will of John Winnocke, baymaker, of St Peters, drawn 1684, proved 1685

PROB 11/214, PCC will of William Doughty, gentleman, of East Dereham, Norfolk, drawn 1650, proved 1650

Norfolk Record Office

Case 20f/14, William Doughty's Will, 25 April 1687

Case 20d/10, Great Hospital Rental Book

N/CCH/5, Accounts Lady Day 1731–Lady Day 1732

NRO N/CCH/10, Small Accounts Lady Day 1736–Lady Day 1737

N/CCH/15, Accounts 1741–9

NRO N/CCH/77, Small Accounts 1834–7

MF 629/2, NCR Case 16a/24, Mayors Court Books 1666–77

MF 629/3, NCR Case 16a/25, Mayors Court Books 1677–95

MF 630/1, NCR Case 16a/26, Mayors Court Books 1695–1709

MF 630/2, NCR Case 16a/27, Mayors Court Books 1709–19

MF 630/3, NCR Case 16a/28, Mayors Court Books 1719–28

MF 631, NCR Case 16a/31, Mayors Court Books 1746–58

MF 632, NCR Case 16a/34, Mayors Court Books 1776–82

MF 632, NCR Case 16a/35, Mayors Court Books 1782–9

MF 632, NCR Case 16a/36, Mayors Court Books 1789–96

N/MC 2/3, Hospital Committee Minutes, April 1708–20

N/MC 2/4, Hospital Committee Minutes, May 1720–December 1733

N/MC 2/5, Hospital Committee Minutes, January 1734–July 1773

N/MC 2/6, Hospital Committee Minutes, August 1773–July 1811

N/MC 2/7, Hospital Committee Minutes, August 1811–December 1826

N/MC 2/8, Hospital Committee Minutes, December 1826–December 1835

NNH 71/3, Jenny Lind Hospital for Sick Children annual reports 1879–1904

N/TC 63/2: Charity Commissioners Report for Norwich 1835

ACC 2008 52, Norwich Charity Trustees Minute Book, January 1836–April 1837

N/CCH 108, General List Minute Book 1837–84

N/CCH 109, General List Minute Book 1837–47

N/CCH 110, General List Minute Book 1847–70

N/CCH 111, General List Minute Book 1861–71

N/CCH 112, General List Minute Book 1871–9

N/CCH 113, General List Minute Book 1879–86

N/CCH 114, General List Minute Book 1886–95

N/CCH 115, General List Minute Book 1895–1903

N/CCH 116, General List Minute Book 1902–9

N/CCH 117, General List Minute Book 1909–10

N/CCH 118, General List Minute Book, minute book for Anguish's charity

N/CCH 119, Norwich Consolidated Charities Minute Book 1, 1911–13

N/CCH 120, Norwich Consolidated Charities Minute Book 2, 1914–18

N/CCH 121, Norwich Consolidated Charities Minute Book 3, 1918–24

N/CCH 122, Norwich Consolidated Charities Minute Book 4, 1924–32

N/CCH 123, Norwich Consolidated Charities Minute Book 5, 1932–8

N/CCH 124, Norwich Consolidated Charities Minute Book 6, 1938–47

N/CCH 125, Norwich Consolidated Charities Minute Book 7, 1948–57

N/CCH 188, Doughty's Hospital Residents' Book 1893–1973

Uncatalogued papers: Doughty's Hospital

H. Boreham, *Doughty's Hospital tercentenary celebrations: a record* (July 1987)

Norwich Consolidated Charities Minute Book 8, 1958–70

Norwich Consolidated Charities Minute Book 9, 1971–9

Norwich Consolidated Charities Minute Book 10, 1980–6

Norwich Consolidated Charities Minute Book 11, 1986–9

Norwich Consolidated Charities Minute Book 12, 1989–95

Norwich Consolidated Charities Minute Book 13, 1996–9

Norwich Consolidated Charities Minute Book 14, 2000–4

Norwich Consolidated Charities Minute Book 15, 2004–5

Two volumes of newspaper clippings:

Eastern Daily Press, 16 November 1912

Eastern Daily Press, 10 June 1914

Eastern Daily Press, 9 February 1916

Eastern Daily Press, 4 March 1929

Eastern Daily Press, 28 January 1935

Eastern Daily Press, 7 May 1935

Eastern Daily Press, 2 July 1939

Eastern Daily Press, 27 November 1941

Eastern Evening News, 8 February 1951

Eastern Daily Press, 30 November 1951

Eastern Evening News, 27 August 1954

Eastern Daily Press, 20 April 1966

Eastern Evening News, 12 December 1968

Eastern Daily Press, 12 May 1972

Eastern Daily Press, 13 May 1972

Eastern Evening News, 11 June 1974

Eastern Evening News, 7 April 1975

Eastern Evening News, 22 April 1980

Eastern Evening News, 15 April 1985

Eastern Evening News, 14 September 1987

The Almshouse Gazette, issue 161, Autumn/Winter 1995

The Almshouse Gazette, issue 163, Summer 1996

Norwich Advertiser, 15 November 1996

Norwich Advertiser, 15 February 2002

Doughty's Hospital reordering 1995, initial design report September 1995.
    Wearing, Hastings and Norton, chartered architects, 14 Princes Street

Doughty's Hospital, Residents' Handbook (Norwich, 2000)

Oral history interviews
Doughty's oral history interview, nos. 001–017 (anonymised)

Acts of Parliament
The Charitable Trusts Act, 1855 (18 & 19 Victoria cap. 124)

British Parliamentary Papers
Abstract of the returns of charitable donations for the benefit of poor persons 1786–8,
    BPP 1816, Vol. XVI, A.1 (c.511)

Inquiry into charities in England and Wales: twenty-seventh report, BPP 1834, Vol.
    XXI.1 (c.225)

Inquiry into charities in England and Wales: twenty-ninth report, BPP 1835, Vols.
    XXI pt.I.1, XXI pt.II.1 (216)

*First report of the Commissioners appointed to inquire into the Municipal
    Corporations in England and Wales*, BPP 1835, Vol. XXIII.1 (c.116)

*Inquiry into charities in England and Wales: thirty-second report, part VI (city of
    London; general charities, Essex)*, BPP 1840, Vol. XIX pt.I.1 (c.219)

*Return from charity trustees in England and Wales of gross annual amounts of
    receipts and expenditure, 1853–7*, BPP 1859, Session 1, Vol. XX (c.11)

*Royal Commission to inquire into education in schools in England and Wales:
    volume viii. General reports of assistant commissioners (Midland counties and
    Northumberland)*, BPP 1867–8, Vol. XXVIII pt. I (c.3966)

*Endowed charities. Copies of the general digest of endowed charities for the counties
    and cities mentioned in the fourteenth report of the charity commissioners*, BPP
    1867–8, Vol. LII pt.II (c.433), County of Norfolk

*Royal Commission to inquire into existence of corrupt practices at the last election for
    the City of Norwich report, minutes of evidence*, BPP 1870, Vol. XXXI.1, 25
    (c.13 and 14)

Explanatory memoranda and tabular summaries of the general digest, BPP 1877,
    Vol. LXVI (15)

*Report from the select committee on Charitable Trust Acts: together with the
    proceedings of the committee, minutes of evidence and appendix*, BPP 1884,Vol.
    IX.1 (c.306)

Report of the Royal Commission on the Poor Laws and relief of distress, BPP 1909,
    Vol. XXXVII, appendix ix, xv, part 2 (c.4499)

Norwich charities: bill to confirm schemes of the Charity Commissioners, BPP 1910,
    Vol. IV.35 (c.69)

*A digest of the evidence taken before two of His Majesty's Municipal Corporation
    Commissioners at the Guildhall in the City of Norwich on Monday 25th day
    of November 1833 and twenty-one following days with an appendix* (Matchett
    and Co: Norwich, 1834) pp.176–80

Trade directories

Peck, Thomas, *The Norwich directory* (J. Payne: Norwich, 1802)

White, William, *White's Norfolk directory* (reprinted by Redwood Press Ltd:
    Liverpool, 1969, 1st publ. 1845)

Kelly, *Kelly's Norfolk directory* (Kelly's Directories Ltd: London, 1900)

Kelly, *Kelly's Norfolk directory* (Kelly's Directories Ltd: London, 1924)

Kelly, *Kelly's Norfolk directory* (Kelly's Directories Ltd: London, 1925)

Kelly, *Kelly's Norfolk directory* (Kelly's Directories Ltd: London, 1926)

Kelly, *Kelly's Norfolk directory* (Kelly's Directories Ltd: London, 1935)

Kelly, *Kelly's Norfolk directory* (Kelly's Directories Ltd: London, 1952)

Kelly, *Kelly's Norfolk directory* (Kelly's Directories Ltd: London, 1964–5)

Newspapers

Almshouse Gazette
Eastern Daily Press
Eastern Evening News
Norwich Advertiser
Norwich Mercury
The Times

Correspondence

Correspondence with Mrs Freda Holland, July 2009
Correspondence with Lady Joyce Hopwood, July–November 2009
Correspondence with Mrs Karlene Parry, July 2009
Correspondence with Mrs Christine Share, July 2009
Correspondence with Mrs Freda Turner, July 2009
Correspondence with Mr David Walker, June–November 2009

Secondary sources

Books and articles

Alcock, P. and Scott, D., 'Voluntary and community sector welfare', in Powell, M. (ed.), *Understanding the mixed economy of welfare* (The Policy Press: Bristol, 2007)

Almshouse Association, *Annual report 2008* (The Almshouse Association: Wokingham, 2009)

— *Standards of almshouse management. A guidance manual for almshouse charities* (5th edition, The Almshouse Association: Wokingham, 2008)

— *Support and care for residents. A guidance manual for almshouses and smaller associations* (5th edition, The Almshouse Association: Wokingham, 2007)

Armstrong, A., *Farmworkers in England and Wales. A social and economic history 1770–1980* (Batsford: London, 1988)

— *The population of Victorian and Edwardian Norfolk* (University of East Anglia: Norwich, 2000)

— 'Population, 1700–1950', in Rawcliffe, C. and Wilson, R. (eds), *Norwich since 1550*

Armstrong, M.J., *History and antiquities of the county of Norfolk. Volume X, containing the city and county of Norfolk* (J. Crouse for M. Booth: Norwich, 1781)

Bailey, B., *Almshouses* (Robert Hale: London, 1988)

Barringer, C., *Norwich in the nineteenth century* (Gliddon Books: Norwich, 1984)

Best, G., *Mid-Victorian Britain 1851–75* (revised edition, Granada Publishing Ltd: St Albans, 1973)

Bittle, W.G. and Lane, R.T., 'Inflation and philanthropy in England: a reassessment of W.K. Jordan's data', *Economic History Review*, Vol. 29 (1976)

Blomefield, F., *Essay towards a topographical history of the county of Norfolk* (Norwich, 1745)

Bonfield, L., Smith, R. and Wrightson, K. (eds), *The world we have gained. Histories of population and social structure* (Oxford University Press: Oxford, 1986)

Boyer, G.R., 'Living standards, 1860–1939', in Floud, R. and Johnson, P. (eds), *The Cambridge economic history of modern Britain. Vol. II: economic maturity, 1860–1939*

Britnell, R.H. and Hatcher, J. (eds), *Progress and problems in medieval England: essays in honour of Edward Miller* (Cambridge University Press: Cambridge, 1996)

Brundage, A., *The English poor laws, 1700–1930* (Palgrave: Basingstoke, 2002)

Bryson, J.R., McGuiness, M. and Ford, R.G., 'Chasing a "loose and baggy monster": almshouses and the geography of charity', *Area*, Vol. 34 (2002)

Bythell, D., *The sweated trades. Outwork in nineteenth-century Britain* (Batsford: London, 1978)

Caffrey, H., *Almshouses in the West Riding of Yorkshire 1600–1900* (Heritage: King's Lynn, 2006)

Campbell, J., 'Norwich before 1300', in Rawcliffe, C. and Wilson, R. (eds), *Medieval Norwich*

Chambers, J.D., *The workshop of the world. British economic history 1820–80* (Oxford University Press: Oxford, 1961)

Cherry, S., 'Medical care since 1750', in Rawcliffe, C. and Wilson, R. (eds), *Norwich since 1550*

City of Norwich, *The City of Norwich Plan* (Norwich, 1945)

City of Norwich and Norfolk County Council, *A joint growth study* (Norwich, 1966)

Clark, C., 'Work and employment', in Rawcliffe, C. and Wilson, R. (eds), *Norwich since 1550*

Clark, P. (ed.), *The Cambridge urban history of Britain, vol. II 1540–1840* (Cambridge University Press: Cambridge, 2000)

Clark, P. and Slack, P. (eds), *Crisis and order in English towns 1500–1700* (Routledge and Kegan Paul: London, 1972)

Clay, R.M., *English medieval hospitals* (Methuen: London, 1909)

Corfield, P., 'A provincial capital in the late seventeenth century: the case of Norwich', in Clark, P. and Slack, P. (eds), *Crisis and order in English towns 1500–1700*

Corfield, P., 'Economic growth and change in seventeenth-century English towns', in Phythian-Adams, C. *et al.*, *The traditional community under stress* (Open University Press: Milton Keynes, 1977)

Corfield, P., 'From second city to regional capital', in Rawcliffe, C. and Wilson, R. (eds), *Norwich since 1550*

Crafts, N., 'Long-run growth', in Floud, R. and Johnson, P. (eds), *The Cambridge economic history of modern Britain. Vol. II: economic maturity, 1860–1939*

Crouzet, F., *The Victorian economy* (Methuen and Co: London, 1982)

Crowther, M.A., *The workhouse system 1834–1929. The history of an English social institution* (Methuen: London 1983, 1ˢᵗ published 1981)

Cullen, M.J., *The Victorian statistical movement in early Victorian Britain: the foundations of empirical social research* (Harvester Press: Hassocks, 1975)

Cunningham, H. and Innes, J. (eds), *Charity, philanthropy and reform from the 1690s to 1850* (Macmillan Press: Basingstoke, 1998)

Dain, A., 'An enlightened and polite society', in Rawcliffe, C. and Wilson, R. (eds), *Norwich since 1550*

Dunn, P., 'Trade', in Rawcliffe, C. and Wilson, R. (eds), *Medieval Norwich*

Dyer, A., *Decline and growth in English towns 1400–1600* (Macmillan: Basingstoke, 1991)

Eden, F.M., *The state of the poor*, 3 vols (Thoemmes Press edition: Bristol, 2001; first published J. Davis: London 1797)

Edwards, J.K., 'The industrial development of the city 1800–1900', in Barringer, C., *Norwich in the nineteenth century*

Englander, D., *Poverty and poor law reform in 19th century Britain, 1834–1914* (Longman: London, 1998)

Finch, J., 'The churches', in Rawcliffe, C. and Wilson, R. (eds), *Medieval Norwich*

Floud, R., *The people and the British economy 1830–1914* (Oxford University Press: Oxford, 1997)

Floud, R. and Johnson, P. (eds), *The Cambridge economic history of modern Britain. Vol. I: industrialisation, 1700–1860* (Cambridge University Press: Cambridge, 2004)

— *Vol. II: economic maturity, 1860–1939* (Cambridge University Press: Cambridge, 2004)

— *Vol. III: structural change and growth, 1939–2000* (Cambridge University Press: Cambridge, 2004)

Fraser, D., *The evolution of the British welfare state*, 4th edition (Palgrave Macmillan: Basingstoke, 2009)

Fried, A. and Elman, R.M. (eds), *Charles Booth's London* (Penguin edition: Harmondsworth, 1971)

Galbraith, J.K., *The affluent society* (Penguin edn: Harmondsworth, 1962, first published 1958)

Ginsburg, N., 'Housing', in Page, R.M. and Silburn, R. (eds), *British social welfare in the twentieth century*

Glennerster, H., *British social policy 1945 to the present* (3rd edition, Blackwell: Oxford, 2007)

Godfrey, W.H., *The English almshouse with some account of its predecessor the medieval hospital* (Faber and Faber: London, 1955)

Goose, N., 'Immigrants in Tudor and early Stuart England', in Goose, N. and Luu, L. (eds), *Immigrants in Tudor and early Stuart England*

— 'The rise and decline of philanthropy in early modern Colchester: the unacceptable face of mercantilism?', *Social History*, Vol. 31 (2006)

Goose, N. and Basten, S., 'Almshouse residency in nineteenth-century England: an interim report', *Family and Community History*, Vol. 12 (2009)

Goose, N. and Hinde, A., 'Estimating local population sizes at fixed points in time: part II – specific sources', *Local Population Studies*, No. 78 (2007)

Goose, N. and Luu, L. (eds), *Immigrants in Tudor and early Stuart England* (Sussex Academic Press: Brighton, 2005)

Gorsky, M., *Patterns of philanthropy. Charity and society in nineteenth-century Bristol* (The Boydell Press: Woodbridge, 1999)

Griffith, P., Fox, A. and Hindle, S. (eds), *The experience of authority in early modern England* (Macmillan: Basingstoke, 1996)

Griffiths, P., 'Inhabitants', in Rawcliffe, C. and Wilson, R. (eds), *Norwich since 1550*

— 'Masterless young people in Norwich 1560–1645', in Griffith, P., Fox A. and Hindle, S. (eds), *The experience of authority in early modern England*

Guy, J., *Tudor England* (Oxford University Press: Oxford, 1988)

Hadwin, J.F., 'Deflating philanthropy', *Economic History Review*, Vol. 31 (1978)

Hallett, A., *Almshouses* (Shire Publications: Princes Risborough, 2004)

Harper-Bill, C. and Rawcliffe, C., 'The religious houses', in Rawcliffe, C. and Wilson, R. (eds), *Medieval Norwich*

Harris, J., 'Society and the state in twentieth-century Britain', in Thompson, F.M.L. (ed.), *The Cambridge social history of modern Britain 1750–1950*

Harrison, J.F.C., *The early Victorians 1832–51* (Panther Books: St Albans, 1973, first published 1971)

— *Late Victorian Britain 1875–1901* (Fontana Press: London, 1990)

Hatcher, J., 'The great slump of the mid-fifteenth century', in Britnell, R.H. and Hatcher, J. (eds), *Progress and problems in medieval England: essays in honour of Edward Miller* (Cambridge University Press: Cambridge, 1996)

Hinde, A., *England's population. A history since the Domesday survey* (Hodder Arnold: London, 2003)

Hindle, S., *On the parish? The micro-politics of poor relief in rural England c.1550–1750* (Oxford University Press: Oxford, 2004)

Hooper, J., *Norwich charities, short sketches of their origin and history* (Norfolk News Company: Norwich, 1898)

Hopewell, P., *Saint Cross. England's oldest almshouse* (Phillimore: Chichester, 1995)

Hoppen, K.T., *The mid-Victorian generation 1846–86* (Oxford University Press: Oxford, 1998)

Howson, B., *Houses of noble poverty: a history of the English almshouse* (Bellevue Books: Sunbury-on-Thames, 1993)

— *Almshouses. A social and architectural history* (The History Press: Chalford, 2008)

Humphrey, R., *Sin, organised charity and the poor law in Victorian England* (St Martin's Press: London, 1995)

Jewson, C.B., *History of the Great Hospital Norwich* (The Great Hospital: Norwich, 1966)

— *Doughty's Hospital* (Norwich, 1979)

Jordan, W.K., *Philanthropy in England 1480–1660. A study of the changing pattern of English social aspirations* (Russell Sage Foundation: New York, 1959)

— *The charities of London 1480–1660. The aspirations and achievements of the urban society* (Russell Sage Foundation: New York, 1960)

— *The charities of rural England. The aspirations and achievements of the rural society* (George Allen and Unwin: London, 1961)

Kay, A.C. and Toynbee, H.V., *The endowed and voluntary charities of Norwich: extract from Appendix to Volume XV of the report to the Royal Commission* (Norwich Charity Organisation: Norwich, 1909)

Kendall, J., *The voluntary sector* (Routledge: Abingdon, 2003)

Kidd, A., *State, society and the poor in nineteenth-century England* (Macmillan: Basingstoke, 1999)

King, D., 'Glass-painting', in Rawcliffe, C. and Wilson, R. (eds), *Medieval Norwich*

Kitson Clark, G., *The making of Victorian England* (Methuen: London, 1962)

Knight, B., *Voluntary action* (Centris: London, 1993)

Knights, M., 'Politics, 1660–1835', in Rawcliffe, C. and Wilson, R. (eds), *Norwich Since 1550*

Knowles, D. and Hadcock, R.N., *Medieval religious houses. England and Wales* (Longman: London, 1971, first published 1953)

Landry, D., 'Bentley, Elizabeth (bapt. 1767, d. 1839)', *The Oxford dictionary of national biography* (Oxford University Press, Oxford, 2004)

Lewis, J., 'Voluntary and informal welfare', in Page, R.M. and Silburn, R. (eds), *British social welfare*

Lloyd Prichard, M.F., 'The decline of Norwich', *Economic History Review*, Vol. 3 (1950–1)

Longmate, N., *The workhouse. A social history* (Pimlico edn: London, 2003, first published 1974)

Lowe, R., *The welfare state in Britain since 1945* (Palgrave Macmillan: Basingstoke, 2005)

Lund, B., 'State welfare', in Powell, M. (ed.), *Understanding the mixed economy of welfare*

McIntosh, M., *Autonomy and community. The Royal Manor of Havering, 1200–1500* (Cambridge University Press: Cambridge, 1986)

— 'Local responses to the poor in late medieval and Tudor England', *Continuity and Change*, Vol. 3 (1988)

— *Controlling misbehaviour in England, 1370–1600* (Cambridge University Press: Cambridge, 1998)

Mackie, C., *Norfolk annals. A chronological record of remarkable events in the nineteenth century*, 2 vols (Norwich Chronicle Office: Norwich, 1901)

Maddison, A., *Phases of capitalist development* (Oxford University Press: Oxford, 1982)

Malpass, P., *Housing associations and housing policy. A historical perspective* (Macmillan: Basingstoke, 2000)

Marwick, A., *British society since 1945* (Penguin: Harmondsworth, 1982)

Meeres, F., *A history of Norwich* (Phillimore: Chichester, 1998)

Millward, R., 'The rise of the service economy', in Floud, R. and Johnson, P. (eds), *The Cambridge economic history of modern Britain. Vol. III: structural change and growth, 1939–2000*

Milward, A.S., *The economic effects of the two world wars on Britain* (Macmillan: London and Basingstoke, 1970)

Musson, A.E., 'Industrial motive power in the United Kingdom, 1800–70', *Economic History Review*, Vol. 29 (1976)

Orme, N. and Webster, M., *The English hospital 1070–1570* (Yale University Press: New Haven and London, 1995)

Owen, D., *English philanthropy 1660–1960* (Harvard University Press: Cambridge, MA, 1964)

Page, W. (ed.), *The Victorian history of the county of Norfolk, vol. II* (Archibald Constable and Co Ltd, 1906)

Page, R.M. and Silburn, R. (eds), *British social welfare in the twentieth century* (Palgrave Macmillan: Basingstoke, 1999)

Palliser, D.M. (ed.), *The Cambridge urban history of Britain, vol. I: 600–1540* (Cambridge University Press: Cambridge, 2000)

Pannell, J. with Thomas, C., *Almshouses into the next millennium. Paternalism, partnership, progress?* (The Policy Press: Bristol, 1999)

Phythian-Adams, C. *et al.*, *The traditional community under stress* (Open University Press: Milton Keynes, 1977)

Pollard, S., *The development of the British economy 1914–1967* (Edward Arnold: London, 1962)

Porter, S., 'Order and disorder in the early modern almshouse: the Charterhouse example', *London Journal*, Vol. 23 (1998)

Postan, M.M., *An economic history of western Europe 1945–64* (Methuen: London, 1967)

Pound, J., 'The social and trade structure of Norwich 1525–75', *Past and Present*, No. 34 (1966)

— *Tudor and Stuart Norwich* (Phillimore: Chichester, 1988)

— 'Government to 1660', in Rawcliffe, C. and Wilson, R. (eds), *Medieval Norwich*

Powell, M. (ed.), *Understanding the mixed economy of welfare* (The Policy Press: Bristol, 2007)

Prochaska, F.K., *The voluntary impulse. Philanthropy in modern Britain* (Faber and Faber: London, 1988)

— 'Philanthropy', in Thompson, F.M.L. (ed.), *The Cambridge social history of modern Britain 1750–1950*

— *Philanthropy and the hospitals of London: The King's Fund 1897–1990* (Clarendon Press: Oxford, 1992)

Rawcliffe, C., *The hospitals of medieval Norwich* (Centre of East Anglian Studies: Norwich, 1995)

— 'Introduction', in Rawcliffe, C. and Wilson, R. (eds), *Medieval Norwich*

— 'Sickness and health', in Rawcliffe, C. and Wilson, R. (eds), *Medieval Norwich*

— *Leprosy in medieval England* (Boydell Press: Woodbridge, 2006)

Rawcliffe, C. and Wilson, R. (eds), *Medieval Norwich* (Hambledon Press: London and New York, 2004)

Roberts, M.J.D., 'Head versus heart? Voluntary associations and charity organization in England, *c.*1700–1850', in Cunningham, H. and Innes, J. (eds), *Charity, philanthropy and reform*

Rose, S.O., *Limited livelihoods. Gender and class in nineteenth-century England* (University of California Press: Berkeley and Los Angeles, 2002)

Rushton, N.S., 'Monastic charitable provision in Tudor England: quantifying and qualifying poor relief in the early sixteenth century', *Continuity and Change*, Vol. 16 (2001)

Rushton, N.S. and Sigle-Rushton, W., 'Monastic poor relief in sixteenth-century England', *Journal of Interdisciplinary History*, Vol. 32 (2001)

Rutledge, E., 'Immigration and population growth in early fourteenth-century Norwich, *Urban History Yearbook 1988* (Leicester University Press: Leicester, 1988)

— 'Economic life', in Rawcliffe, C. and Wilson, R. (eds), *Medieval Norwich*

Schofield, R., 'The geographical distribution of wealth in England, 1334–1649', *Economic History Review*, Vol. 18 (1965)

Seaman, L.C.B., *Post-Victorian Britain 1902–51* (Methuen: London, 1966)

Sheail, J., 'The distribution of taxable population and wealth in England during the early sixteenth century', *Transactions of the Institute of British Geographers*, Vol. 5 (1972)

Slack, P., 'Great and good towns 1540–1700', in Clark, P. (ed.), *The Cambridge urban history of Britain, Vol. II: 1540–1840*

— *Poverty and policy in Tudor and Stuart England* (Longman: London, 1988)

— *The English poor law 1531–1782* (Macmillan: Basingstoke, 1990)

Stevenson, J., *British society 1914–45* (Penguin: Harmondsworth, 1984)

Stewart, J., 'The mixed economy of welfare in historical context', in Powell, M. (ed.), *Understanding the mixed economy of welfare*

Stuart, L.E., *In memoriam Caroline Colman* (Norwich, 1896)

Sweetinburgh, S., *The role of the hospital in medieval England. Gift-giving and the spiritual economy* (Four Courts Press: Dublin, 2004)

Taylor, A.J., Laissez-faire *and state intervention in nineteenth-century Britain* (Macmillan: London and Basingstoke, 1972)

Thane, P., *Foundations of the welfare state* (2nd edition, Longman: London, 1996)

— *Old age in English history. Past experiences, present issues* (Oxford University Press: Oxford, 2000)

Thompson, F.M.L. (ed.), *The Cambridge social history of modern Britain 1750–1950* (Cambridge University Press: Cambridge, 1990)

Townroe, P., 'Norwich since 1945', in Rawcliffe, C. and Wilson, R. (eds), *Norwich since 1550*

Trinder, B., *The market town lodging house in Victorian England* (Friends of the Centre for English Local History: Leicester, 2001)

Waller, P.J., *Town, city and nation, England 1850–1914* (Oxford University Press: Oxford, 1983)

White, W., *White's Norfolk directory* (reprinted by Redwood Press Limited, 1969, first published 1845)

Wilson, R., 'Introduction', in Rawcliffe, C. and Wilson, R. (eds), *Norwich since 1550*

— 'The textile industry', in Rawcliffe, C. and Wilson, R. (eds), *Norwich since 1550*

Winston, M., 'The Bethel at Norwich: an eighteenth-century hospital for lunatics', *Medical History*, Vol. 38 (1994)

Wrigley, E.A., 'Men on the land and men in the countryside: employment in agriculture in early nineteenth-century England', in Bonfield, L., Smith, R. and Wrightson, K. (eds), *The world we have gained. Histories of population and social structure*

— *Continuity, chance and change. The character of the industrial revolution in England* (Cambridge University Press: Cambridge, 1988)

Wrigley, E.A. and Schofield, R.S., *The population history of England 1541–1871: a reconstruction* (Edward Arnold: London, 1981)

Ziegler, P., *The Black Death* (Penguin edition: Harmondsworth, 1970, first published 1969)

Unpublished dissertations

McGrath, E., 'The bedesmen of Worcester Cathedral: post-reformation cathedral charity compared with St Oswald's Hospital almspeople *c.*660–1900', unpublished PhD thesis, University of Keele, 2009

Satchell, M., 'The emergence of leper-houses in medieval England, 1100–1250', unpublished D.Phil. thesis, Oxford University, 1998

Websites

Almshouse Association: www.almshouses.info

Anchor Trust (housing for elderly people: www.anchor.org.uk

The Big C (cancer charity): www.big-c.co.uk

Care Quality Commission: www.cqc.org.uk

Care Quality Commission Report on Doughty's Hospital, 14 January 2009: www.cqc.org.uk/registeredservicesdirectory/RSSearchDetail.asp?ID=0000070520&Type=DCA

Charity Commission: www.charity-commission.gov.uk

Charities Evaluation Services (PQASSO): www.ces-vol.org.uk

Citizen's Advice: www.citizensadvice.org.uk

The Great Hospital: www.greathospital.org.uk

Housing 21 (housing for the elderly): www.housing21.co.uk

John Jarrold Trust: www.jarrold.com

Julian Housing: www.julianhousing.org

Magdalen Group (sex workers): www.magdalenegroup.org

Matthew Project (drug dependency): www.matthewproject.co.uk

Norfolk Federation of Women's Institutes: www.norfolkwi.org.uk

Norfolk Insight (key facts and figures about Norfolk):
    www.norfolkinsight.org.uk

Norfolk and Norwich Association for the Blind: www.nnab.org.uk

Norfolk and Norwich Scope Association: www.nansa.org.uk

Norfolk and Norwich Statistical Data: www.norfolk.gov.uk/norfolkoverview

Norfolk and Norwich University Hospital: www.nnuh.nhs.uk

Norwich's economic strategy 2003–8:
    www.norwich.gov.uk/intranet_docs/A-Z/Economic%20Strategy.pdf

Norwich Housing Associations:
    www.norwich.gov.uk/webapps/atoz/service_page.asp?id=1321

Nursing Homes Directory: www.ucarewecare.com/agencies/

Riverside Centre: www.riversidecentrenorwich.co.uk

Office for National Statistics: www.statistics.gov.uk

Round Table: www.roundtable.org.uk

Supporting People: www.spkweb.org.uk

Index of Subjects

Separate indexes for names and places follow after this subject index.

Index of Names

Index of Places